# ARGUMENTS IN RHETORIC AGAINST QUINTILIAN

# ARGUMENTS IN RHETORIC AGAINST QUINTILIAN

## TRANSLATION AND TEXT OF PETER RAMUS'S

## *Rhetoricae Distinctiones in Quintilianum*

## (1549)

*Translated by Carole Newlands*

*Edited by James J. Murphy*

SOUTHERN ILLINOIS UNIVERSITY PRESS
Carbondale and Edwardsville

Printed in the United States of America
13 12 11 10 4 3 2 1

Library of Congress Cataloging-in-Publication Data
Ramus, Petrus, 1515–1572.
[Rhetoricae distinctiones in Quintilianum. English & Latin]
Arguments in rhetoric against Quintilian : translation and text of Peter Ramus's Rhetoricae distinctiones in Quintilianum (1549) / translation by Carole Newlands ; edited by James J. Murphy. — Pbk. ed. with updated bibliography
p. cm. — (Landmarks in rhetoric and public address)
Originally published: DeKalb, Ill. : Northern Illinois University Press, 1986.
Includes bibliographical references and index.
ISBN-13: 978-0-8093-3014-0 (pbk. : alk. paper)
ISBN-10: 0-8093-3014-8 (pbk. : alk. paper)
ISBN-13: 978-0-8093-8614-7 (ebook)
ISBN-10: 0-8093-8614-3 (ebook)
1. Quintilian. Institutiones oratoriae. 2. Rhetoric—Early works to 1800. 3. Oratory—Early works to 1800. I. Newlands, Carole Elizabeth. II. Murphy, James Jerome. III. Title.
PA6651.R3613 2010
808.5'1—dc22 2010013542

The paper used in this publication meets the minimum requirements of American National Standard for Information Sciences—Permanence of Paper for Printed Library Materials, ANSI Z39.48-1992. ♾

The Bibliothéque Nationale, Paris, generously granted permission for the use of its copy of the first edition of 1549 of *Rhetoric distinctiones in Quintilianum.* The copy has the Bibliothéque Nationale number Z19120.

Designed by Jo Aerne.

# CONTENTS

# INTRODUCTION

THIS VOLUME offers the text and translation of a pivotal book by one of the most influential (and controversial) writers of early modern times. The public career of its author began in clamor and ended in assassination.

In September of 1543 the Parisian printer Jacobus Bogardus issued together in one volume two short technical books on logic[1] written in Latin by an obscure young college instructor. Their author, Pierre de la Ramée, twenty-eight years old, was then teaching in the small Collège de l'Ave Maria within the University of Paris.[2] One book was called *Dialecticae institutiones* (*Training in Dialectic*) and the other *Aristotelicae animadversiones* (*Remarks on Aristotle*). They were but two books among many published that year,[3] but they began one of the most spectacular careers of that century.

What shocked his fellow teachers, setting him on a collision course with the educational and philosophical establishment of his day, was that in these two books la Ramée (or Ramus, as he styled himself)[4] issued a direct challenge to the authority of Aristotle. The magnitude of this step may be difficult for many to understand today, when virtually nothing is beyond public challenge. But both the writings of Aristotle and the dialectical methodology of Aristotle had been dominant at Paris since the days of Peter Abelard in the twelfth century, and had been officially cemented into the university structure in 1215 with the approval of the first "curriculum" by the papal legate Robert de Sorbon.[5] For more than four centuries, then, Aristotle was the foundational author for Paris, "Mother of Universities." The whole edifice of scholastic philosophy—and theology—had an Aristotelian base. Since newer educational institutions throughout Europe tended to follow the Parisian model, the Aristotelian cast of mind had been equally familiar for centuries at universities from Oxford to Vienna.[6]

To say then as Ramus did that Aristotle did not understand logic, and did not even know how to use the logical syllogism, was to threaten an intellectual earthquake. Moreover, to bypass the whole medieval scholastic tradition was to cast aside half a millennium of theological scholarship as well.[7]

Reaction was immediate. Ramus shortly found himself forced into a public debate with one Antonio de Gouveia after some of his fellow teachers appealed directly to King Francis I to intervene in the case. Ramus spoke well, but was unable to control the outcome of the debate;[8] on March 26, 1544, Francis I issued a "Sentence given by the King against master Pierre Ramus, and the books composed by him against Aristotle."[9] Significantly, the decree not only accuses Ramus of being "temerarious, arrogant, and impudent" but castigates him for attacking "the art of logic accepted by all nations."[10] In other words, Ramus is accused of undermining the whole discipline. His two books are named, their destruction ordered, and their further printing forbidden. The king forbids Ramus to teach or write about either dialectic or philosophy "in any manner without our express permission."

In the long history of the official suppression of ideas, this might have been merely one more forgotten episode, if it had not been for two factors. One was the indomitable energy of Ramus, who immediately set about to circumvent the decree. The other factor, far more important as it turned out, was that Ramus had powerful friends.

## THE CAREER OF RAMUS

Ramus's biography reveals the importance of both these factors. Born in 1515 at Cuts, in the district of Vermandois in Picardy of a poor farmer's family, Ramus came early to Paris (at the age of eight) and as an impoverished student had to work his way through school in a time-honored fashion as servant to richer fellows.[11] He complains that he was twice forced to leave Paris for lack of funds. At the age of twelve he entered the Collège de Navarre and supported himself as valet to fellow student Sieur de la Brosse. Among his classmates were Charles Bourbon, future cardinal and king, and Charles de Guise, later Cardinal of Lorraine and then Cardinal of Guise. (Charles de Guise was to become the patron ["Maecenas"] to whom Ramus later dedicated many of his books.)

In 1547 Henry II became king. Following the intercession of Ramus's old schoolfellow, now Charles Cardinal of Lorraine, in that same year Henry II lifted the ban against Ramus that had been imposed four years earlier by Francis I. It is interesting to note that Ramus's *Brutinae quaestiones* (*Questions of Brutus*) of 1547 is already dedicated to Henry as dauphin, even before he became king.[12]

For the rest of his life Ramus enjoyed royal favor and protection. In 1551 he was awarded the prestigious title of Regius Professor, and thereafter styled himself "Regius Professor of Philosophy and Eloquence." When the Wars of Religion began in 1562, he was able to withdraw under royal protection to Fontainebleu. And after his Catholic patrons realized his Protestant leanings, much later, they did not act against him.[13]

His reputation increased throughout his lifetime and beyond. One modern scholar declares that in the middle of the sixteenth century Ramus was "far and away the greatest figure among the faculties of Europe."[14] "Truly," Theophilus Banosius was to say in his *Life of Peter Ramus* (1576), "there is no nation in the Christian world that has not admired the wisdom of Ramus."[15]

By the time of his murder at Paris during the St. Bartholomew's Massacre in August 1572,[16] Ramus had published more than fifty works in Latin and French, ranging in scope from editions of his individual orations to massive compendia such as his *Scholae in liberales artes* (1569) in 1,166 columns. Even during his lifetime he was anthologized, translated, reedited, opposed, and defended to the extent that today it is virtually impossible to untangle the welter of publications by Ramus and about him.[17] There were more than two hundred editions of his *Dialectic* alone during the sixteenth century, in half a dozen languages and in a bewildering variety of versions.[18] He sought to reform the teaching of grammar—Greek, French, and Latin—as well as dialectic, and throughout his academic life called for new approaches to mathematics. Ramus did not hesitate to lecture and write about metaphysics, nor to publish literary commentaries on major ancient figures like Plato, Virgil, and Cicero.

A much-quoted modern summary is worth citing here again, since it points out succinctly the "tremendous vogue" enjoyed by Ramus in the sixteenth and seventeenth centuries:

> There are over 750 separately published editions (including some adaptations) of single or collected works by Ramus or his collaborator Omer Talon (Audomarus Talaeus, ca. 1510–1562)—close to 250 editions of the important *Dialectic* alone. Counting separately each of the works in these 750-odd volumes, some of which include more than one item, one gets a total of around 1100 printings of individual works. All but a few of these fall in the century roughly between 1550 and 1650.[19]

Perhaps even more important were the scores, or even hundreds, of authors who took to the pen either to support his views or to oppose them. In Father Ong's *Ramus and Talon Inventory* it takes twenty-four pages (pp. 510–33) to list the authors arrayed for or against Ramus. Ramus was obviously of a temperament that provoked controversy. He had major public confrontations at Paris with Jacques Charpentier, Adrien Turnèbe, and Pierre Galland, as well as some more remotely conducted written disputes like that with Jacob Schegk. These exchanges were not always temperate in tone. Galland once called one of Ramus's books "an offensive dish of warmed-over cabbage"; this particular controversy attracted the satires of both Joachim du Bellay (*Petromachia*) and Rabelais, who proposed "petrifaction" for the two men.[20]

Perhaps the fervor of support and the ferocity of opposition added to the spread of "Ramism," but in any case Ramist views swept not only through France, but across her borders to Germany, Switzerland, Denmark, Poland, the Low Countries, Scotland, and England. (It was from Cambridge University that the colonists on the Charles River in the New England imported teaching masters in the 1630s for the new school that soon afterward was named for benefactor John Harvard, and thus Ramism reached America.) Spain proved a less fertile ground for Ramism, though even there rhetoricians such as Francisco Sánchez de las Brozas applied his method despite the fact that Ramus's works earned a place on the *Index* of books forbidden to Catholics.

Peter Ramus and his career thus provide many reasons why we should study him today, more than four centuries after his death in 1572. His European and American fame over two centuries is perhaps warrant enough—his reputation and influence being a socio-intellectual phenomenon not often matched in modern times. His efforts at university reform play a part in the history of education, for institutions not only in Paris but throughout the Western world. He made a contribution to the French language as an intellectual tool. To many of his successors he was a Protestant martyr, killed not only for his religion but for his academic principles. To others of his contemporaries he was a violent enemy of Aristotle and the whole scholastic apparatus inherited from the medieval university system; to certain others he was the savior of the true "method" based on a newly explained dialectic. His ambitions, after all, were on a grand scale: he redistributed the functions of logic and rhetoric, stressed the value of mathematics, attempted innovations in grammar, strove to reconstruct the curriculum, and added physics and metaphysics to the roster of "liberal arts"—all in support of a lifelong plan to demonstrate the one and true "method."

One nineteenth-century scholar, Charles Waddington, looked to the career of Peter Abelard in the twelfth century for an analogue to Ramus. It is an interesting idea. Like Ramus, Abelard also came as a young man to a Paris of methodological orthodoxy.[21] Abelard confounded teachers such as Anselm of Laon with his own dialectical skill, and for his pains he too was forbidden to teach. Abelard too nevertheless continued to teach growing crowds of students, and ultimately returned to Paris in triumph. He wrote a book, *Sic et Non*, whose methodological impact spread far beyond the Latin Quarter, just as Ramus's books on dialectic did. Perhaps, too, like Ramus he had earned a fame far greater than his real contribution to the history of logic.[22] The parallel is naturally not a perfect one, but it does raise some intriguing possibilities.

Naturally a good deal has been written about Peter Ramus. The monumental survey and bibliography of Walter Ong will probably never be surpassed. The excellent summaries of Wilbur S. Howell and Perry Miller, together with the works of Peter Sharratt, Norman Nelson, Pierre Duhamel, Wilhelm Risse, Frances Yates, Cesare Vasoli, Neal Gilbert, Franco Simone, as well as a host of others, provide ample opportunity for a reader to grasp either the whole of Ramism or (as with Yates on Memory)[23] a special aspect of it.

Ramistic influences in England and America have been probed in depth. A number of Ramus's works have been issued in facsimile editions within the past two decades; two of these include sixteenth-century biographies (by Freige and Banosius), while Sharratt has edited and translated the important 1599 Latin biography by Ramus's colleague Nicolaus Nancel. Even Charles Waddington's useful if sometimes worshipful biography of 1855 has recently been reprinted, as has the shorter French one by Charles Desmaze (1864), though the English-language biography by Frank Graves is now seventy years old. Details of these publications may be found in the Bibliography.

There is, in short, a wealth of modern scholarly analysis and some few Latin or French texts on which a reader might base a judgment about the worth of this man and his works. Moreover, there is a rough conceptual homogeneity among Ramus's main works, despite his constant verbal tinkering and rewriting, which makes it possible to enter his mind satisfactorily by a study of any one of a dozen or so of his books: Howell, for instance, bases his own extensive summary on the 1555 French-language *Dialectique*, while Miller and others often re-create Ramus through his follower's views as well as through the original sources.[24]

Nevertheless a major problem remains—that is, that there is no major text of Ramus available in modern English for direct study.

This volume is offered to provide that opportunity. The following sections explain how the *Rhetoricae distinctiones in Quintilianum* came to be written and why that particular book of Ramus is important as a key to his whole set of ideas about language.

## THE DOUBLE CAMPAIGN OF THE 1540S: ARGUMENTS FOR RAMUS AND AGAINST THE ANCIENTS

While the language of Ramus's texts continued to change throughout his lifetime—his biographer Nancel in fact says he complained to his mentor that he "revised his works remarkably often"[25]—Ramus seldom altered his main ideas even if he sometimes changed their wording.

One constant is an attitude toward what Ramus viewed as the inherent faults of the three great ancient *auctoritates*—Aristotle and his followers Cicero and Quintilian. It is clear that from the very outset Ramus viewed this group as related. In his *Dialecticae institutiones* (1543) he promises in the preface to simplify dialectic and thus purify it from the entanglements caused by Aristotle, but when he comes to the first page of the text itself it is Cicero and Quintilian who are named as sources for the Roman nomenclature of dialectic.[26] On the second page of the text he criticizes Quintilian twice.[27] In the companion book, *Aristotelicae animadversiones* (1543), he blames Aristotle for confusing the principles of invention, but quickly adds that "Cicero and Quintilian on the authority of Aristotle lapse into the same confusion."[28]

It is evident that at an early age Ramus laid out a program to bring down all three of these ancient giants. Modern observers sometimes conjecture that the two books of 1543 simply came out of his disgust at what he saw as overlapping and disorder among the arts relating to languages—grammar, rhetoric, dialectic—as he tried to explain them in his teaching at the Collège du Mans after taking his M.A. in 1536.[29] But if in the early 1540s he did already have a systematic plan to attack all three authors, of course, it could not be systematically pursued for a while because of Francis I's prohibition; after the events of 1543 his next major publications were in fact on Euclid (1545) and Cicero's *Dream of Scipio* (1546) plus three short academic orations.[30] It might be supposed, then, that because of the royal ban Ramus would have been obliged to steer clear of dialectic and philosophy.

Yet by October 1546 Ramus is found arguing in print for the joining of philosophy and eloquence. The occasion was his formal address at the beginning of his second year[31] as principal of the Collège de Presles. The *Oratio de studiis philosophiae et eloquentiae coniungendis* bears a dedication to Charles of Lorraine, by now an archbishop.[32] The oration outlines an ambitious plan of reading and exercises for the boys of the college; Ramus's colleague Audomarus Talaeus (Omer Talon) is to teach in the mornings, Ramus in the afternoons. Among the readings are Crassus and Cicero for oratory, Theophrastus and Plato (not Aristotle) for philosophy. It is proposed to teach both Greek and Latin, a practice not then common in Paris. Ramus does not mention Quintilian by name. Nevertheless he sketches out a series of progymnasmatic student exercises—including imitation, rewriting, interpretation, listening, and even declamation—which seem to echo the first two books of Quintilian's *Institutio oratoria*.[33] He argues that alternate sessions on eloquence and on philosophy will enable students to retain better what they have learned.[34]

Meanwhile Ramus was already working on rhetoric with his colleague and disciple, Omer Talon. Talon was a bit older than Ramus, but from the time (1544) he joined him in teaching at the Collège de l'Ave Maria until his death in 1562 he was, to use Ong's term, "Ramus' man."[35] Nancel calls Talon "Ramus's colleague and fellow-countryman, and his adopted or rather co-opted brother."[36]

Apparently Ramus worked for most of his career with what we would call today a "team" of disciple-colleagues who served as transcribers, collators, copyists, and proofreaders.[37] Among them were the brilliant Greek scholar Bartholomew Alexandre, the young Jean Péna from Provence (who died at age twenty-eight), a Jean Bagier who came in mornings to teach Ramus Greek grammar and check his Greek texts, and of course Talon and Nancel himself. Nancel also notes that for a period Ramus supported a number of mathematicians in the Collège de Presles so he could work out his ideas with them, "as fellow students." Talon was not the only helper of Ramus, even if he was the chief one. The kind of planning required to maintain such a team over a long period of time is some evidence of Ramus's calculating approach. His carefully orchestrated campaign of the 1540s is further proof of his ability to plot a course and to pursue it resolutely. For the modern observer seeking to understand the Ramistic viewpoint, then, the publications up to 1549 can provide a unique opportunity.

The attack on Quintilian is the most inclusive of all the works of the 1540s. It restates Ramus's concepts of dialectic and of "method," reiterates his views on the relation of grammar to other arts, re-explains his notion of rhetoric, recapitulates his objections to Aristotelian logic, applies to Quintilian the same objections Ramus had raised earlier to Cicero's concepts of inventional "topics," and—above all—attacks through Quintilian the basic contemporary organization of the teaching of the arts. It is clearly a book deserving careful attention.

What has seemed to escape the attention of many modern Ramus students is a quite basic function of argumentation—that is, that if Ramus did wish to establish a new set of ideas he not only had to express those ideas clearly, but he also had to defeat those who held opposite views. In other words he had to overthrow Aristotle, Cicero, and Quintilian. So avid a Ciceronian scholar as Ramus was clearly aware of the fundamental doctrine on that score. The double task of the rhetor was first of all *confirmatio* (proof of one's own case) and then *refutatio* (disproof of the opponent's case).[38]

The whole history of the Ramus team's activities in the 1540s shows how well Ramus understood this basic principle. By 1543 Ramus is already referring to Talon as "my dearest colleague and companion in studies," noting that Talon has already begun to explain rhetoric;[39] the earliest published product of that work, the rather generalized *Institutiones oratoriae* of 1545, is however soon supplanted by the more sharply defined *Rhetorica* of 1548. In his 1546 oration on joining philosophy to eloquence, Ramus announces a plan to have boys study the practice (*not* the theory) of Cicero and of Quintilian.[40] Then in 1547 comes an attack on Cicero, the *Brutinae Quaestiones*, followed two years later by the attack on Quintilian. Putting this sequence in rhetorical terms makes it seem a sensible program:

Confirmation of his own views:

- 1543 *Dialecticae institutiones*
- 1545 *Institutiones oratoriae* (of Talon)
- 1546 *Dialectici commentarii tres authore Audomaro Taleo editi*
- 1547 *Oratio de studiis philosophiae et eloquentiae coniungendis*
- 1548 *Audomari Talaei Rhetorica*

Refutation of the ancient opponents:

- 1543 *Aristotelicae animadversiones*
- 1547 *Brutinae quaestiones*
- 1549 *Rhetoricae distinctiones in Quintilianum*

By 1549, in other words, the basic Ramistic principles have been published. The system is in place. What comes after is refinement, internal commentary, and application.[41]

It is difficult to escape the conclusion that this was a purposeful program, especially in light of Ramus's declaration of intent at the outset of 1543, and in light of Talon's (Ramus's?) statements in the preface to the 1548 *Rhetorica.*

Indeed, it is interesting to find that after 1549 all of Ramus's public opponents are living contemporaries—not ancient giants of authority. The *refutatio* is completed.

This strategy places the *Rhetoricae distinctiones in Quintilianum* in a special position as the culmination (in Ramus's eyes) of a careful campaign begun in the early 1540s and carried out on two levels for most of the decade.[42] Items published after 1549 are far more diverse. A glance over the works published in the next five years shows a spate of commentaries on various ancient works—Plato's letters, Cicero's *De fato,* a number of Ciceronian orations, and the first book of Cicero's *Laws.* Then in 1555 come the *Dialectique,* Ramus's dialectic rendered into French, and also the *Arithmetica* in what Father Ong calls his dialectical or methodical phase (including the application of dialectic to mathematics).[43] Except for the spurt of grammatical publications beginning in the late 1560s there are few other observable patterns of publication during the rest of Ramus's career; his analysis of Ciceronian Style (not rhetoric) in the *Ciceronianus* in 1557 is coupled in that same year with his commentary on Cicero's treatment of Demosthenes' oration *On the Crown.*[44] Mathematics concerned him all his life, and of course, as Nancel reminds us, he continued his interest in the orations of Cicero. In 1569 his first major anthology of lectures appears: *Scholae in liberales artes,* a massive tome in 1,166 columns published in Basle by Nicholas Haredes; the subjects are grammar, rhetoric (the attacks on Cicero and Quintilian), dialectic (the attack on Aristotle), physics, metaphysics, and mathematics.[45] There is an index provided for each work, and each treatise is now divided into "books"; for instance the *Scholae rhetoricae,* in twenty books, devotes eight books to the attack on Cicero, twelve to the attack on Quintilian.[46] All of the contents had been previously published elsewhere. The comparative heterogeneity of publications after 1549, in other words, makes even more striking the systematic pattern of proof and refutation of the 1540s that culminates in the *Rhetoricae distinctiones in Quintilianum* of 1549.[47]

Before turning to that text, however, it would be useful to examine the congeries of ideas that came to be known as "Ramism." This analysis in turn can help us identify the arguments Ramus felt he could bring against Quintilian.

## THE FOUNDATIONS OF RAMISM

The young man who raised a storm at Paris in 1543 with his new dialectic and his attack on Aristotle was operating on two levels. At one timeless level Ramus was casting back over two thousand years of human thought to establish a sort of Socratic superiority that would invalidate Aristotle and Aristotelianism (including the whole of medieval scholasticism) in favor of a new simplicity of method.

At another simultaneous level Ramus was inescapably imbedded in the institutions, conflicts, and issues of his day—the kinetic inertia of the six-hundred-year-old university, the redefinitional urges of French humanism, the hazards of religious revolt, the virtues and vices of his own considerable compositional powers. At the timeless level Zeno, Socrates, Plato, Aristotle, and Aquinas are all equally worthy of treatment in his books. What may be less evident to us modern readers of these books, inevitably divorced as we must be from the everyday environment in which they were published, is the array of other men responsible for shaping that environment—Desiderius Erasmus, Lorenzo Valla, Rudolph Agricola, Martin Luther, Philip Melancthon, Johann Sturm, Jean Calvin, Pierre de Ronsard, Joachim du Bellay, Etienne Dolet, François Rabelais, Guillaume Budé, and innumerable others within and without France.

While it is clear from his biographers and from his own statements that both the timeless and the timebound interacted to shape his career, it also seems fair to conclude that Ramus viewed himself as making a contribution to thought that would be not only valuable but permanent. In this light he could view the petty carpings of contemporaries as mere annoyances.[48]

This was especially true of the period up to 1549, when Ramus was engaged in the publication of his basic views and in the demolition of the ancient triad of Aristotle, Cicero, and Quintilian. The royal prohibition of 1544 had of course prevented Ramus from systematic public reply to the local opponents who had surfaced in that year; he did not respond, for instance, to the 1543 *Pro Aristotele in Petrum Ramum orationes II* of Joachim de Perion.

The major printed controversies of his career all come later—

with Pierre Galland on curriculum in 1551, with Jacques Charpentier on dialectic during the period 1554–1567, with Adrien Turnèbe on dialectic and fate from 1550 to 1554, with Charpentier again on mathematics from 1566 to 1568, and finally with Jacob Schlegk on Aristotle in 1571.[49]

Consequently the utterances of the 1540s reflect a more basic Ramus than many of the later works complicated by his own tinkerings or by his adjustments to criticism.[50] (There is of course a bewildering prolixity inherent in Ramus's constant efforts to resay in newer words what he has already said many times before; he did not always play well the role of author-as-his-own-commentator.)

The two books of 1543—the Dialectic and the Aristotle—do not yet contain some of the specific terms (e.g. "Method" or "Axiom")[51] soon to be familiar to Ramists, but the concepts if not the *vocabula* are already there, at the outset of Ramus's public career. The reader taking up his attack on Quintilian published only six years later will find these key concepts recurring throughout that book. For this reason it will be useful here to provide a brief summary of Ramus's basic position as already outlined in his various works of the 1540s, to see how the implicit became explicit. Otherwise we may not be able to understand how Ramus reached the point at which he could attack Quintilian in the way he does.

## THE *DIALECTICAE INSTITUTIONES* (1543)

Ramus begins the *Dialecticae institutiones* with the statement that "Dialectic is the power of precise discoursing" (*Dialectica virtus est disserendi*).[52] The noun *virtus* carries a connotation of an excellent, strong, worthy capacity; the verb *dissero* denotes an examinative or probative use of language. Ramus goes on at once to point out that Cicero and Quintilian view dialectic as a judging or arbitrating activity.[53] Dialectic is described as having three parts: nature, theory (*doctrina*), and practice.[54]

Dialectic for Ramus has the two functions of Invention (*inventio argumenti*) and Disposition (*iudicium*).[55] Invention provides avenues for locating the species of arguments. An argument is developed to answer a *quaestio*, that is, an inquiry into a doubtful or doubted statement.[56] Ramus identifies fourteen "modes of invention," divided into two sets of five and nine respectively: the first set includes causes, effects, subjects, adjuncts, and contraries; the second set has genus, species, name, notation, conjugation, testimony, comparatives, diversion, and definition.[57]

Once discovered, arguments need to be arrayed according to Judgment or Disposition (*iudicium*), the second function of dialectic. The mode of arrangement is the Syllogism, which Ramus defines as a collocation (*collocatio*) of arguments that respond to a question (*quaestio*) in such a way as to reach a conclusion about a doubtful matter; he notes that Cicero calls the Syllogism a *ratiocinatio*. It has three parts: Proposition, or major question; Assumption, or minor question; and Complexion, or concluding jointure of the parts.

This "single" dialectic is to apply to all arts. Ramus declares that even orators agree that it applies to public speeches, for instance, since the four traditional parts of an oration (Exordium, Narration, Confirmation, and Peroration) are nothing else but another way to use the "second judgment" of dialectic in the three parts of a syllogism. An oration is but a syllogism "amplified by figures,"[58] and a public oration, after all, is simply a reply to a *quaestio* or doubtful matter. Thus the first part of second judgment comes from the "members" or parts of a thing; the second comes from the adjuncts of persons and things.

Memory is not a separate art, because Judgment or Disposition obviates the need for it. "Order" naturally leads to recall. Since there are three levels of Judgment—the true, the varied, and the multiplex—a knowledge of how to use those levels will make accessible to memory whatever is known. The reason why the rules of rhetoric are hard to master, Ramus says, is that they are not properly ordered—hence, they are easily forgotten. For the same reason, Aristotle's confusions make his doctrine hard to grasp. (A verse example from Ovid for memorization, offered a bit later in the book [54:50–55:30] as an example of Interpretation, also shows how knowing Order can assist Memory.)[59]

Above all, this dialectic is to be "used": *Summa igitur, ac prope disserendi virtus est in exercitatione* (44:8–10). Why else, Ramus implies throughout, would God have given men this "illumination" that enables them to reason?[60] Mathematics—that is, arithmetic, geometry, astronomy, music—is a case in which dialectic can dispel the shadows surrounding the true causes of quantification in the universe.[61]

It is in Interpretation, though, that dialectic works best to explicate the writings and speeches of orators, poets, and philosophers. Interpretation (which Ramus also calls "explication") seeks out the nature of an art; its types; the "architectonic" order of a work; the way this order is found; its "topics"; the rules followed; and all its parts. An epigram, for example, can be treated as a Proposition. Cicero's oration in defense of Milo is an instance of the joining of Argument to Question in order to remove doubt. On the other hand Plato is at fault in *Phaedrus* for providing only an incomplete Interpretation of Lysias's speech.[62]

Ramus then points out that his colleague Omer Talon is already at work on developing the art of rhetoric in light of dialectic.[63] Grammar is said to consist of the four elements of orthography, etymology, syntax, and prosody.

Writing and speaking are one activity, Ramus declares, so that the process of Interpretation can be applied to both.[64] The best way to writing and speaking is Imitation, as Cicero shows in his orations and letters; he adds that even Quintilian—"muddled as that ancient authority is"—realizes the same thing.[65] Yet precepts ought to be delivered briefly so that their exposition will not be arid and onerous to young schoolboys; practice must always be joined to theory at every level from basic grammar to rhetoric and then to dialectic.

Ramus then provides an extensive verse example—Ovid's complaint of Penelope about the absence of Ulysses—to show how a good teacher can make Interpretation work on a given text. The text is to be memorized by schoolboys. "From these twenty-eight verses," he points out, "flow four Propositions, sixteen Assumptions, and eight Conclusions."[66]

Near the end of the book Ramus provides a full-page chart (p. 57 recto) that he introduces as the "*summa* and universal outline of the art of dialectic" laid out for viewing by the reader's eye.[67] The book ends with a brief call once more for the joining of doctrine and practice: "This requires instruction in the art; it demands exercise from you."[68]

## THE *ARISTOTELICAE ANIMADVERSIONES* (1543)

The attack on Aristotle that was printed along with the *Dialecticae institutiones* is much more difficult to summarize, not only because it is much longer (161 pages compared to 116) but because it ranges over a number of Aristotle's logical works.[69] Such commentaries are necessarily unsystematic.

But it is Ramus's attitude toward Aristotle that is most important. He castigates what he calls the "stultifying errors," "wretched confusions," and "stubborn fallacies" not only of Aristotle himself (*vivus Aristoteles*) but of "The race of Aristotelians" (*Aristoteleorum natio*) who have distorted his books over many centuries. For example he says that Aristotle creates a "chaos of the categories of invention,"[70] produces sophistry by bringing grammar into dialectic,[71] fails to clarify the use of *quaestio* in the syllogism,[72] and above all complicates many things which should be made simple. At one place he notes that Boethius, in trying to clarify Aristotle, compounds his confusions by describing thirty-two modes of conclusions under two headings.[73] These examples could be multiplied, but it is Ramus's critical attitude that stands out even more than his specific statements.

His language is a telling sign, often verging on the sarcastic. There are more "vanities and errors" than clearly defined topics; there are "fantastic distortions" and "madnesses"; and Ramus says that when it comes to the discussion of disputation in the eighth book of the *Topics*, Aristotle is "stubborn, captious, sophistic, and demanding";[74] moreover, by fastening on the changeable instead of the certain, Aristotle changes dialectic from a noble and potent art to one that is "wretched and ridiculous." One favorite term for Ramus is *tenebras* (obscurity, gloom, shadow); another is *miser* (wretched, worthless).[75]

His frequent use of the rhetorical question is often ironic or sarcastic. How do we know what knowledge is, or virtue, or utility? "Because Aristotle says so" (*quia Aristoteles dixit*). Aristotle defines "sophistry" for us: "But what use is that?" (*sed quid habet utilitas*?). Or, on the same point, a little later, "So what?" (*quid ita*?). But some of Ramus's contemporaries must surely have been shocked by the irreverent, almost antagonistic manner in which he used apostrophe (direct address). Ramus says Aristotle unduly extends the parts of invention: "What is this, O Aristotle?" (*quid istud est o Aristotelei*?). Why "prattle on" about it?

In another place Ramus declares that Aristotle's infinite and indefinite categories of vices would produce a hydra-headed monster where only the true and the useful was needed: "But your glory is to confound, to entangle, and to render the clear-eyed blind" (*at tua gloria est perturbare, miscere, bene oculatos caecos reddere*). Given the tone of such apostrophes, it is easy to mistrust Ramus's motives when he refers to Aristotle as "public master" (*magister publica*) or the "distinguished legislator" (*o praeclarum legislatorem*), so famous that many faults are allowed him.

Of course, the conceptual quarrels with Aristotle are actually about his logic. Ramus devotes perhaps half of the book to criticisms of Aristotle's syllogistic doctrines, with lesser but continuing attention to Topics and to the relation of dialectic to grammar and rhetoric. There are numerous discussions of specific ideas from the *Categories*, *Prior* and *Posterior Analytics*, and *Topics*. One example may illustrate his approach. When Aristotle asks whether Socrates is a man—a famous example of syllogistic reasoning—Ramus answers that Socrates is a rational animal and therefore a man; but, Ramus says, this is a Definition and not a Syllogism; thus it belongs in the first or Inventional part of dialectic rather than the second or Judgmental part, where syllogisms are treated; Ramus declares this to be a quicker, easier, and clearer way to handle the matter.[76]

This example also points to another constant strain: Ramus's demand for simplicity that enhances utility.[77] In many places he refers to the ultimate testing ground for all such expositions—the minds of schoolboys. What good does it do if the lore cannot help in the interpretation of poets, orators, and philosophers? What if it cannot help boys to write better poems, letters, or orations? How are they going to use the dialectic of Aristotle?[78]

Thus Ramus repeatedly complains that Aristotle has too many predicates, too laborious a set of categories, too many unlimitable topics—and that his followers over the centuries have compounded these miseries. Aristotle himself does not understand the proper use of the "enthymeme" (which Ramus calls a truncated syllogism), nor does he know how to use the extended string of syllogisms called the "sorites." Above all, Ramus insists, Aristotle confuses Invention, even describing three different types (*triplex inventio*) in his *Rhetorica*: one from the kinds of causes, one from kinds of arguments, and one from the parts of an oration.[79]

The whole impression Ramus gives is that Aristotle left us an over-elaborate but muddled account of logic. Ramus does praise Aristotle for much, but damns him for more.

There was for a long time a legend that Ramus had taken for his M.A. thesis the proposition that "Whatever is affirmed from Aristotle is a fabrication."[80] The fact of the story has long since been discounted—it appears only in his biography by Joannus Freigius—

but the very fact that it could be believed for more than three centuries is surely indicative of Ramus's reputation as a controversialist.[81] Both the contents and the tone of the *Aristotelicae animadversiones* of 1543 would seem to reinforce that reputation.

## THE ANNOUNCEMENT OF "METHOD" (1546)

Ramus constantly strove to find better terms to describe his basic ideas. He began this practice very early in his public career. While some Ramistic extrapolations or amplified reexplanations were to appear in his works only after 1549—terms like "Axiom" and rationalizations like the "Three Laws of Method"[82]—Ramus took the opportunity in 1546 to develop a bit further some ideas only implicit in the 1543 books. In 1546 he was still under the royal prohibition of Francis I's decree of 1544, but Ramus simply "smuggled into print" (to use Ong's term) a revision of his *Dialecticae institutiones* by pretending it was the work of his colleague Omer Talon: *Dialectici commentarii tres authore Audomare Taleo editi.*[83]

The 1543 version is in unbroken prose, with some examples indented or marked off by italic type. The 1546 revision is divided into three parts, dealing with Invention (53 pages), Disposition (36 pages), and Practice (30 pages); it has centered headings for sections (which Ong sees as a further development of "spatial organization" in Ramism).

Here for the first time are explicit definitions of three terms fundamental to the later history of Ramism and important above all in his attack on Quintilian: Method, Genesis, and Analysis. Ong provides translations of all three definitions:

> Method is the arrangement of many good arguments. It is twofold, method of teaching and method of prudence. Not that both kinds do not make use of prudence, but rather that the latter has almost no training or art in it, depending merely on man's natural judgment and prudence. The method of teaching, therefore, is the arrangement of various things brought down from universal and general principles to the underlying singular parts, by which arrangement the whole matter can be more easily taught and comprehended. In such method, this alone has to be prescribed: that in teaching the general and universal explanations precede, such as the definition and a kind of general summary; after which follows the special explanation by distribution of the parts; last of all comes the definition

> of the singular parts and clarification by means of suitable examples. . . . We must go on to the method of prudence, which advises about disposition according to the condition of persons, things, times, and places. For, although the way of disposition mentioned above is most true and apt, nevertheless one must be cautioned that there is not always place for what is best, and that such clarity of disposition cannot always be maintained, since frequently enough the audience is sluggish, the matter to be explained disagreeable, the time not suitable, the place strange. Hence it is advisable to employ prudence in invention and syllogism when dealing with this difficulty, so as to see what is expedient.[84]

These remarks occur at the end of the second part, the one on disposition. Ramus adds a "Peroration on Method" in which he notes that Plato praised dialectical method. There were to be many more statements about Method over the years, the last one coming in the year of Ramus's death, 1572, but by 1546 he had flung down the term as a gauntlet before his Parisian colleagues, and the concept of Method was thereafter to be an embattled one. Neal Gilbert points out quite rightly that the *methodus* of 1546 is simply the *collocatio* of 1543 writ large.[85] But the implicit is now the explicit.

Pedagogical preoccupations color much of Ramus's writing—one of his critics said he should write about dialectic itself and not about the teaching of it—and this predilection shows up here again in his discussions of Analysis and Genesis:

> [Analysis is] the examination of our own or others' examples in which invention and composition are to be looked into. . . . In logic, analysis is the marshalling (*examen*) of the argument, enunciation, syllogism, method, in short the whole art of logic, as is prescribed in the first Book of the *Analytics* [of Aristotle].[86]
>
> Genesis is not the study of given examples as analysis is, but is rather the making of a new work. This exercise follows the one and the same way of writing and teaching. Now in writing, the first and easiest way is imitation. Hence we must look carefully to whom we imitate. . . . But next we must strike out for ourselves, and take our independent arguments from popular daily affairs, close to ordinary life; then draw the causes, effects, and other genera of the available arguments from the sources of invention, and finally, make use of all the

> ways of disposition with equal care, concluding now this way, now that way. . . .[87]

Ramus's discussions of these two opposing processes mean much, and they also mean little. On one level they actually describe Ramus's own processes of exposition, and can thus be illuminating for modern readers. Yet they do merely redescribe teaching methods standard at least as far back as Quintilian, common in the middle ages, and prevalent all over Europe in Ramus's lifetime.[88]

What did make all three of these terms significant in a historical sense was that Ramus imbedded them in the ponderous apparatus of a dialectical system enhanced by the authority of Socrates and Plato. Thus the followers of Ramus were to "analyze" Ramus himself and "synthesize" from his writings other terms like "dichotomy" (which he himself did not use) to describe his habit of pairing ideas.[89] The history of formal logic is of course extremely complex, and in the court of that history Ramus does not rank very high: terms like "nonsense" and "incompetence" are typical of what modern critics say.[90] Nevertheless, as we have seen earlier, the enormous proliferation of Ramistic publications over such a long time must attract our attention. The "system" tried to account for the entire range of language study (broadly conceived as the three arts of grammar, dialectic, and rhetoric), and to provide for the teaching of those arts for their use (*exercitatio*).

Even so, the system could not prosper until Ramus disposed of two other ancient giants.

## THE ATTACK ON CICERO'S RHETORIC (1547)

Ramus's two different attitudes toward Cicero's work mark one of the interesting paradoxes of his career. All his life he praised the oratory of Cicero, yet all his life he damned the Roman's rhetorical theory. The biographer Nancel reports that Ramus had a grand ambition to publish commentaries on all of the orations of Cicero.[91] The rhetoric of Cicero comes under fire as early as 1543, when Ramus links him pejoratively with Aristotle and Quintilian. It was evident thereafter that Cicero's rhetoric had to be a target in Ramus's campaign against the ancients. Ramus is not at all ambivalent about Cicero—rather he simply makes a clear distinction between his theory and his oratorical practice.

In 1547 Jacobus Bogardus published at Paris a quarto volume of fifty-six folios titled *Petri Rami Veromandui Brutinae quaestiones in Oratorem Ciceronis* (*The Questions of Brutus about Cicero's "Orator"*).[92] This is a work curiously neglected in studies of Ramus's career. Ong lists it in his *Inventory* but does not discuss it in his *Method and the Decay of Dialogue* that accompanies the *Inventory*, while Howell does not even list it in his index. Nevertheless it must have been fairly well known: it went through three separate editions by 1552, and then, beginning in 1569, it was routinely included in the frequently anthologized *Scholae rhetoricae* (*Lectures on Rhetoric*)—consisting of this work and the attack on Quintilian—which appeared another thirteen times by the end of the century.

The book is a direct attack on the rhetorical theory of Cicero, using the form of a commentary on Cicero's *Orator* (46 B.C.).[93] The *Orator* is written in the form of a letter to Cicero's friend Brutus, so Ramus puts his own work in the form of a reply from Brutus raising a number of questions or problems about what Cicero has said.

In the *Orator* Cicero presents his view of the ideal orator, one capable of instructing, pleasing, and moving his audience with adept use of the three levels of style appropriate to those three ends. Style is thus the unifying principle of oral discourse. No ideal orator has yet appeared, Cicero notes, but he wishes to describe his qualities anyway. The perfect orator must know all the means of discovering arguments, but that is an easier task than the eloquent presentation that sways an audience. Cicero discusses the sound patterns useful in an oration—rhythms, periodic structures, cadences, figures. He discusses the so-called "Asiatic" or florid style. Yet he emphasizes throughout that the oration must be a unified, almost organic whole as it reaches the consciousness of the audience member, so that no one part alone can be made the most important one.

In the preface to his work on the *Orator*, Ramus thanks King Henry for freeing him from the bonds of "our native Aristotelians" and restoring him to liberty of thought and expression. Now in gratitude he will dedicate to the king his book on the "regal" rhetorical art; the subject will be "the argument between the great republican leaders, Cicero and Brutus, concerning the important theory of ruling the republic."[94] For eloquence joined to wisdom made the ancient republic great. Cicero greatly mixed up the arts, and "in his rhetorical precepts he particularly followed Aristotle, who very greatly confused the arts of rhetoric and dialectic." So, Ramus says, he will have Brutus ask not only about Asiatic verbosity but also about the precepts proper to rhetoric and about Cicero's reasoning, consistency, and truthfulness.

The result is a wide-ranging polemic characterized by rhetorical questions, apostrophes, exclamations, syllogistic analysis, and a great many digressions. It is a vigorous (Ong uses the term "violent") assault in the form of an "interpretation" as described in Ramus's Dialectic. As in the attack on Aristotle the language is often highly colored or even sarcastic. Ramus uses terms like "absolutely stupid falsehood" and "amazing darkness covering the art of rhetoric." As in the *Aristotelicae animadversiones* he uses direct address in an insulting fashion: "But my Cicero, doesn't this reasoning lead you nowhere?" (*At mi Cicero, quam nihil ista procedet ratio*?)

One example of his syllogistic analysis may indicate his method:

> If a house is defined, the causes in its building and arrangement are listed: foundation, cellar, wall, dining room, bedroom, roof, and the other parts usually involved in the setting up of a whole house: but then, should you however build one wall and leave the other parts I named, you will be laughed at, you will not seem to have set up a house.
>
> Let this therefore be agreed, and in conclusion state: All causes by which we achieve a definition of the art of rhetoric must be explained in the art itself. Philosophy, logic, ethics, science, likewise laws and history, and finally rhetoric are causes by which we achieve a definition of the oratorical art, well described to be sure as teaching, pleasing, and moving: And you consider all these causes in this order, after the orator has been defined.
>
> And so if you wish to explain the art of the orator whom you have defined, you must explain all those arts. But you [Cicero] are like that architect: you describe a magnificent house of eloquence: you mark its parts as philosophy, laws, history, and rhetoric; when the house is to be begun, you put up, so to speak, the rhetorical wall and instead of so many arts you set up the least of all.[95]

Ramus also deplores Cicero's idea that a perfect orator is possible, citing "that poetic madness of yours which forcibly drives you into this line of reasoning rather than leading you by unwavering reason" (p. 27). He acknowledges that Cicero has many merits as a practicing orator, but repeatedly attacks his theory of oratory because "these many digressions, these many repetitions, these many false things mixed in everywhere, have not a grain of true rhetoric" (p. 33).

The book surely deserves more attention than it has received so far, especially since it has a direct bearing on the "Ciceronianism" controversies of the sixteenth century and is of course a counterbalance to Ramus's own later *Ciceronianus* (1557) in which he praises the oratory (not the rhetoric) of the Roman.[96] In the context of the attacks on Aristotle and Quintilian, though, the work on Cicero demonstrates once again the nature of the campaign that Ramus apparently felt obliged to wage against the triad of ancient authorities.

The next step in the Ramist program, however, was a positive rather than a negative one. It was in fact one of the most highly successful ones.

## THE RHETORIC OF RAMUS (1548)

By 1543 Talon and Ramus had been teaching colleagues at the Collège du Mans for half a dozen years. Their collaboration on rhetoric was already in evidence by 1545 when a rhetorical treatise was published titled *Training in Oratory* (*Institutiones oratoriae*).[97] Talon is listed as author. There are echoes both of traditional rhetoric and of the Ramist ideas of 1543. Ong is apparently the only modern writer who has studied in any detail what he calls "the extremely rare" *Institutiones oratoriae* of 1545.[98] He terms it the "first edition in any form" of the Ramist rhetoric. He also points out that the Ramist rhetoric "echoes Quintilian from the start" despite the consistently disparaging remarks elsewhere about the Roman rhetorician.

Significantly, it is "eloquence" rather than rhetoric that is defined here: "Eloquence is the power (*vis*) of expressing oneself well." "Expressing," as we have seen, includes both speaking and writing. There are three steps (*gradus*), Nature, Art, and Use or Exercise; these are parallel to the three "parts" of dialectic named in Ramus's *Institutiones* of 1543. Nature deals with the origins of eloquence in an individual man, which prove to be the God-instilled "motions" of thought, discretion, and embellishment. (Ong notes the resemblance to Ramus's previously enunciated concepts of Invention and Judgment as the two parts of Dialectic that precede the embellishments of Rhetoric.)

Art, or teaching, is rhetoric proper: "the artificial teaching of good expression in any matter." Rhetoric like dialectic applies to all subjects. Both figures of diction and figures of thought are discussed. (Ong notes again a parallel to Ramus's dialectic, imposing on rhetoric a division paralleling the unit-cluster partition of dialectic: invention [single arguments] and judgment [conjoined arguments].) Practice or exercise consists of interpretation, and of writing and speaking based on imitation of classical models.

Talon's *Institutiones oratoriae* of 1545, then, shows the strong influence of Ramistic views even if the theories are still expressed in somewhat generalized terms. But there is no mention of this book in the following year, 1546, when Ramus delivered at the Collège de Presles his oration on the conjoined teaching of philosophy and eloquence, despite the numerous times the oration mentions Talon by name. The peculiar circumstances of the royal prohibition may have led Ramus into an uncharacteristic caution—he is careful to point out in the oration that after all it is he who teaches *eloquentia* in the afternoons while Talon teaches *philosophia* in the mornings—but it is nevertheless a noteworthy omission. In any case the final version of the formal Ramist rhetoric was to be not long in coming. This rhetoric became more specific when *Audomari Talaei Rhetorica* (*Rhetoric of Omer Talon*) was published at Paris in December of 1548. Matthew David was again the printer.[99] There was another edition—the "third edition"—the following year, and then a surge of editions, reissues, and translations that brought the total number of new appearances for the next half century to more than one hundred. After Talon died in 1562 Ramus revised the text, dividing it into two books and publishing it in 1567 under the title *Rhetorica, Petri Rami praelectionibus illustrata*—that is, "Rhetoric, Elucidated with Explanations by Peter Ramus"—and still later (1569) calling it *Rhetoricae libri duo.* None of these title changes reflected major alterations in the subject matter, even though Ramus changed his mind over time in respect to the exact role of certain figures of speech discussed in the book.

The rapid diffusion of the book may be seen by the places outside Paris in which other editions appeared during the rest of the century: Lyons, Rheims, Dortmund, Basle, Cologne, Dusseldorf, Frankfurt, Antwerp, London, Cambridge, Wittenburg, Speyer, Bremen, Sieger, and Oxford. In fact only two of the nineteen Paris editions during that period appeared in the last quarter of the century (1581 and 1599) while the book was becoming available in Germany, Switzerland, the Netherlands, and England.[100]

Who was the author of the *Rhetorica*? The question is a difficult but important one. The fact that the 1549 issue is called a "third edition," as Ong points out, could be taken to mean that Talon's *Institutiones oratoriae* of 1547 was the first edition, and the *Rhetorica* of 1548 the second. This reasoning would tie the authorship more closely to Talon. Moreover, as we have seen, Ramus as early as 1543 said in his *Dialecticae institutiones* that Talon was already working on the subject of rhetoric, which he himself had not pursued in detail. Yet we also know that in both his 1543 works Ramus evinced detailed knowledge of Cicero and Quintilian (as well as Aristotle's *Rhetoric*), and that he lectured on "eloquence" at the Collège des Presles. We also know that he "smuggled" the 1546 revision of his Dialectic into print under Talon's name, and that later he was to use the same subterfuge in responding to Adrien Turnèbe. The "team" concept within the Ramus household further complicates the matter.

There are, however, several important pieces of evidence that bear close scrutiny. They come from Nicolaus Nancel, colleague and biographer of Ramus who spent twenty years with him:

> After Talon's death, when Ramus was engaged in the building up of his edifice of the arts, he appropriated to himself, with what right I do not know, the *Rhetoric* which had been published in Talon's name; he published it in an altered form as though it had been first invented and described by himself, and merely adorned with Talon's commentaries, as was in fact originally the case with the *Dialectic*, of which Ramus is the true author and Talon the commentator. I once wanted to find out the reason for this by asking Ramus, but I was afraid of annoying such a serious and irascible man, and preferred to judge for myself as follows: at one time Ramus and Talon worked together closely on the same subjects, and Ramus showed him the way and indicated the method of reducing rhetoric to an art. Because Talon seemed to have contributed more to the art, and to have enhanced it with his own style (which is much more familiar, more easy-going and more popular than Ramus's, yet without sacrificing elegance), he allowed him during his life-time the full credit for inventing it, and reclaimed it from him like usury once he was dead, so that he himself would then be accepted as the true primary author of a work which he merely originated and inspired. If this surmise of mine is not correct, I do not know what one is to think, since I know for certain that Ramus earned enough glory by his own exertions and never appropriated to himself by theft the original work of someone else. . . . I often wonder

> therefore why Ramus should have snatched away the credit of this distinguished work from such a deserving colleague, which everyone rightly gave to him anyway.[101]

As Ong points out, Ramus treated no other work of Talon's this way; this circumstance too could be taken as further indication of his proprietary authorship.

After all, the naming of the public author of a work produced by the Ramus team seems to have depended in part on the academic politics of the moment. According to Nancel, Ramus would lecture from brief notes, often with Nancel present in the room as prompter or holder of books from which quotations were to be read. Nancel gives several examples of Ramus's mode of composition. For instance Ramus was long engaged in an ambitious project to prepare a commentary on every one of Cicero's speeches. Each commentary was to derive from a classroom lecture. The next step is revealing:

> When he returned home he used to jot down in shorthand what he had lectured and commented on; after we had copied out these notes in our own hand in a beautiful script, he kept them at home together with other far more numerous manuscripts, with the intention of publishing them, not indeed that they should be edited by the author himself, but rather by one of his school, as though without his knowledge and without consulting him. At first he gave this job to me, in order that they should appear in my name. But because of some hesitation and delay, I am not sure what, the brief and penetrating commentaries on the ten speeches of Cicero dealing especially with the logical and rhetorical technique, transcribed by my hand as I have said, were held back, and never saw the light of day, though they had long since been prepared for this.[102]

In another case, when Ramus decided to reply to an attack by Adrien Turnèbe, Ramus drafted, Nancel edited—and Talon was given the credit:

> He wrote his reply to Turnèbe in the space of two or three days, writing day and night; he composed and wrote out himself an original, penetrating, subtle, and witty reply in this short space of time. With equal speed I read it over, punctuated

> it, copied it out, and delivered it to the printer, spending the night at Wechel's, in order to speed on the work by day and by night. It came out more quickly than anyone could have hoped or expected, at a time when everyone imagined it could not have been started, or if it had been started that it could not have made such progress. Now Ramus published this rapidly produced work under Talon's name, so as not to appear to be departing from his steadfast forbearance, and allowed him all the credit for this penetrating piece of writing, even though he did not write one single page of it (except to insert a few witticisms and jokes, for his was a truly ironic temperament); I am aware as I declare this that I am the only survivor, for there were only three of us who were party to this matter.[103]

Tracing the Talon-Ramus connection is complicated even further by the succession of textual changes and title changes that took place over the years.[104] Despite the heroic work of Father Ong—and after a quarter century he is still pursuing the goal of completing the *Inventory* begun in 1958—it is still true, as Sharratt reminds us, that "it is never certain exactly how much is the personal contribution of Ramus and how much is the work of his collaborators."[105]

While it may not be possible now to determine the precise details of the composition of the 1548 *Rhetorica* (Ong sometimes uses the term "Ramus and/or Talon"), one thing is quite clear—that is, that the *Rhetorica* fits within Ramus's scheme of things. Even its timing is important relevant to the campaign of the 1540s, staking out a positive claim for the true rhetoric in the midst of the Cicero-Quintilian refutations of 1547–1549. Even assuming some sort of collaboration, though, Ramus was, at the very least, proposer and outliner and probably editor as well. It is inconceivable that the *Rhetorica* could have reached print without his supervision.

For these reasons it seems best to identify Ramus as "author" of the *Rhetorica* of 1548. This identification is important in respect to the attack on Quintilian because of Ramus's frequent indictments of the Roman author for not following the principles of a true dialectic and a true rhetoric. The careful reader of *Rhetoricae distinctiones in Quintilianum* (and the *Brutinae questiones* as well) will find there many specific parallels to the 1548 *Rhetorica*.[106] With this in mind, it is worth looking carefully at the book.

The *Rhetorica* begins with a dedication to Cardinal Charles of Lorraine, the "Maecenas" to whom Ramus and Talon devote so many of their books. This short preface makes no mention of any earlier book on rhetoric by its supposed author, Talon, saying instead that Ramus had published books on Dialectic and on Aristotle and that the author would now take up rhetoric after having published the *Academia* "shortly before" (*paulo ante Academia*). The *Academia* was a short lecture by Talon published in 1547 as a defense of Ramistic philosophy. If the *Rhetorica* is indeed a second version of the 1545 *Institutiones oratoriae* of Talon, it seems strange that the supposed author, Talon, would neglect to mention his own earlier work on rhetoric when he is so specific about Ramus's works.

Having said that he studied rhetoric and dialectic for many years in the works of Aristotle, Cicero, and Quintilian (and found many confusions there), the author declares his intention to treat style and delivery ("the only proper parts of rhetoric"). Peter Ramus has already restored invention, disposition, and memory to dialectic, where they belong. Now, he says, the author will treat rhetoric by genus and species, illustrating his text with examples from poets and orators.

The style of this preface is periodic and almost florid, but the style of the treatise itself is concise often to the point of bluntness. Definitions are given, parts are named, examples provided. Reasons for definitions are seldom included—manifestly, the reader is expected to know the Ramist position before picking up the book. The language of the key sections may show the characteristics of the text:

### *Rhetorica*

> Rhetoric is the theory of expressing oneself well, as is evident from the origin of the name; for *heirēkenai*, from which derive *rhētor* and *rhētorikē*, means to speak and be eloquent.[107]
>
> PARTS OF RHETORIC
>
> There are two parts of rhetoric: Style (*elocutio*) and Delivery (*pronuntiatio*); these are of course the only parts, the ones proper to the art, and so for the sake of clear and easy teaching you should distinguish the general and common principles of Grammar, Rhetoric, and Dialectic, and not mix in matters foreign to each discipline. Each is marked off by its own proper ends: Grammar, through its four parts of etymology, syntax, prosody and orthography, will safeguard clear and correct speech; Dialectic will furnish the invention and disposition of matters, and through its disposition will provide the concomitant of memory; Rhetoric therefore will keep this particular task, that it takes the matter found and related by Dialectic,

and laid out in clear and correct speech by Grammar, and then embellishes it with the splendor of the ornaments of style, and renders it acceptable with the grace of vocal tone and gesture.[108]

### STYLE AND ITS SPECIES

Style therefore is the adornment of speech. Its two species are Trope and Figure.

### TROPE

A Trope is a locution (*elocutio*) in which the proper signification is changed into another, from the verb *tropus* (Greek), that is, "to alter."

### THE KINDS OF TROPES

There are four kinds of tropes: Metonymy, Irony, Metaphor, and Synecdoche.[109] [Each is then discussed briefly with examples, pp. 3–22: Metonymy in four modes according to the *loci* of Causes, Effects, Subjects, and Adjuncts; Irony, based on opposites; Metaphor, from-like-to-like, "not in one word but in connected speech"; and Synecdoche, part to whole or whole to parts, thus based on Cause and Effect. These four are the total: "no more are possible."]

### FIGURE

Having explained the trope as the first kind of Style in rhetoric, let us now turn to the second topic for expression, the Figure. A Figure is a locution in speech that departs from ordinary usage; not that ordinary people never use these rhetorical ornaments, but that these brilliant flashes of language shine out more rarely in the common speech of uneducated men.[110] [Figures are divided into figures of thought and figures of diction, then each of these categories is further divided by function; some nineteen figures of thought and nine categories of figures of diction are discussed, pp. 23–82, with examples mainly from Cicero and Virgil; the final figure, *numerus*, includes a five-page treatment of rhythms.]

### CONCERNING DELIVERY

Style, which is the first part of the art of rhetoric, has been explained through the precepts of the tropes and figures. Let us come now to Delivery (*pronuntiatio*), the other part of the principles of the art and theory.

### DELIVERY

Delivery is the apt expression of the language devised, nor is the theory of Delivery any different from that of Style. But

> Style emerges from thought as the form of expression suitable to the subject matter, whose Delivery stands in the same relationship to Style as Thought.
>
> PARTS OF DELIVERY
>
> There are two parts: Utterance, also called pronunciation, and Gesture, also known as action. And thus one part pertains to the ears, the other to the eyes—the two senses through which nearly all knowledge comes to the soul. [The subsequent discussion, pp. 83–104, is more general than schematic, despite the two-part division that is promised.][111]

One striking feature of the 1548 *Rhetorica* is the relative space granted to Style (pp. 3–82) as compared to Delivery (pp. 83–104). Another feature is the adamant simplicity of the method: for each subject it is a procedure of definition, division, and example.[112] There is little effort to provide a rationale for the definitions or divisions; rather, as in the opening section on the parts of rhetoric, there is simply a statement of fact (i.e., that grammar is thus and dialectic is thus and that therefore rhetoric is thus). Sometimes the author will argue whether this or that figure is properly named or properly assigned to a category, but except for limiting tropes to four, these are seldom substantive differences from tradition. The book's clear-cut statements no doubt made it eminently suitable for the classroom; shortly (by 1553), in fact, it began to accumulate an even more significant sign of accommodation to young boys' minds—a set of *tabula* or schematic charts that digested even further the stark contents of the book.[113]

With the publication of the 1548 *Rhetorica*, then, Ramus and his team had made the basic Ramistic statement and had (at least in their eyes) demolished both Aristotle and Cicero. Only Quintilian remained. The nature of that target is therefore important.

## THE *INSTITUTIO ORATORIA* OF QUINTILIAN

Quintilian was one of the best-known teachers of ancient Rome, and the author of one of the most influential books on education ever produced in the Western world.[114]

Marcus Fabius Quintilianus was born about A.D. 35 in Calagurris (modern Calahorra) in Spain. Coming to Rome as a young man, he apprenticed himself, as was the custom with ambitious young men, to a practicing lawyer, Domitius Afer. Quintilian returned to Spain when he was about twenty-five, but later was among the group that came to Rome in A.D. 68 with the provincial governor, Galba, who became emperor in that year. He was a successful pleader and teacher for many years thereafter, numbering Pliny the Younger among his pupils, and perhaps Tacitus and Suetonius as well. In A.D. 72 and again in A.D. 88 he was awarded an imperial subsidy for his teaching; after Quintilian's retirement about A.D. 90 Emperor Domitian accorded him the signal honor of consular rank. Quintilian died at some time after A.D. 95.

A well-known epigram by Martial, written in A.D. 84, gives some idea of Quintilian's reputation at that time:

> O Quintilian, supreme guide of unsettled youth,
> Glory of the Roman toga, O Quintilian.

Even the satirist Juvenal remarks several times on Quintilian's good influence on the young.

Quintilian himself tells us that upon retirement he spent two years in research before beginning a book to sum up the lessons of his career—or, as he more modestly puts it in the preface to Marcellus Victorius, "to write something on the art of speaking." The result was a work in twelve books titled *Institutio oratoria* (*Education in Oratory*).[115]

The *Institutio oratoria* deals with the lifelong education of the orator. Unlike earlier books that merely provide sets of rules for the mature speaker to follow, Quintilian declares, his book will describe the entire learning process by which the ideal orator can be shaped. For Quintilian that process begins in the cradle with the earliest acquisition of language skills by the child listening to the sounds of his nurse's voice; at the other end of a life span there is a discussion of tasks to follow retirement from public life. In between there is a detailed explanation of the early education of the citizen-orator (from about age six to seventeen or eighteen), a complete textbook on the five-part Roman system of rhetoric, a discussion of literature and literary criticism, and finally a description of the ideal orator himself. It is nevertheless a unified, well-integrated book. Charles E. Little has described the *Institutio* as four major works blended into one: a treatise on education, a manual of rhetoric, a reader's guide to the best authors, and a handbook on the moral duties of the orator.[116] Here is Quintilian's own statement of his plan:

> My first book will contain those subjects which are preliminary to the task of the teacher of rhetoric. In my second I shall deal with the rudiments of the schools of rhetoric and with problems concerned with the essence of rhetoric itself. The next five books will deal with Invention, and also Arrangement. Four will be given over to Style, under which head come Memory and Delivery. There will be one final book in which the orator himself is delineated so that, as far as I am able, I can discuss his character, the rules which guide him in undertaking, studying, and pleading cases, the type of style, the time at which he should cease to plead cases, and the pursuits he should follow afterward.[117]

Quintilian does indeed follow this plan, but in a flowing, sensible manner that defies easy summary. Each point is discussed fairly, with contrary views noted; he uses experience and precedent to support his own views based, as he points out several times, on his own twenty years of teaching. The personality of the author shines through in many ways, whether it is in connection with the necessity of allowing young boys some freedom—"it is easier to prune a tree than to grow one"—or in praising Marcus Cato the Censor for taking up the study of Greek at the age of sixty. He notes his own sadness in losing his young wife and their five-year-old son in the same year, then later his remaining son. The *Institutio*, in other words, is not only a technically efficient book but a very human one as well.[118]

Quintilian's attitude toward "rules" is typical of his humane approach to the education of the citizen-orator:

> But let no man require from me such a system of precepts as is laid down by most authors of books of rules, a system in which I should have to make certain laws, fixed by immutable necessity, for all students of eloquence, . . . for rhetoric would be a very easy and small matter, if it could be included in a short body of rules; but rules must generally be altered to suit the nature of each individual case, the time, the occasion, and necessity itself. Consequently, one great quality in an orator is

> discretion, because he must turn his thoughts in various directions, according to the various bearings of his subject.[119]

Quintilian's thrust is therefore toward the formation of the whole personality of the potential orator of discretion. The ultimate aim, as he explains in detail in Book Ten, is "facility" (*facilitas*)—the quality that will enable a person to cope well with any subject in any situation.[120] This then requires not just technique but character.

Indeed one element that runs through the entire book is an emphasis on morality. Quintilian defines the ideal orator as "A good man speaking well" (*vir bonus dicendi peritus*). So pervasive is the concept that it occurs no less than twenty-three times in the book. (It is also the first idea attacked by Ramus.) Quintilian's argument is that neither mere wisdom nor mere eloquence will suffice, but that the general welfare depends on the existence of men able to exercise "not only consummate ability in speaking, but also every excellence of mind." This means that matters of justice or temperance or other virtues cannot be left merely to philosophers. Active participation in public life based on moral standards is the hallmark of the good Roman citizen. The aim, then, is to educate a "man of discretion," able to apply in various practical ways what he has learned of the good.

What Quintilian proposes is that morality is to be imbibed rather than studied. That is, the student of rhetoric or even of grammar is to hear, read, and say things with high moral value in school so that unconsciously over time the virtues absorbed in this way will become second nature to him even as he learns the techniques of oratory for applying the virtues in real life. He will not have to study them in textbooks of philosophy.

Consequently the highly detailed curriculum laid out in the first two books of the *Institutio oratoria* has two related purposes: first, to bring the boy carefully from the simplest elements of language (i.e., letters of the alphabet) up to the capability of delivering the most complex orations on technical subjects in law or politics years later in the debating exercise known as *declamatio*; and second, while taking the boy through this graded set of exercises (*progymnasmata*), to provide models for imitation (*imitatio*) that demonstrate moral lessons as well as rhetorical and literary values. This "imitation" includes a number of well-crafted assignments calculated to increase technical skill while forcing attention to the content or thought as well as the form; the assignment to paraphrase Homer's description of the character of Achilles, for instance, would require the student to ponder moral qualities as well as word choices. (The exercise called *ethologia* asked the student to write or speak on the character of a given person; the *chria* assigned the task of preparing a moral analysis of an act or person.)

It is within this context that Quintilian next moves to a consideration of the art of rhetoric itself. As might be predicted, he has high expectations for the usefulness of rhetoric in public life. He is thoroughly Roman in his presentation over the next nine books, following a basic tradition shared by Cicero and so many other Romans of the time that the terms "Roman rhetoric" and "Ciceronian rhetoric" are for many people interchangeable. For that reason it is probably better here to provide a basic summary of Roman rhetorical doctrine than to follow Quintilian step by step through Books Three to Eleven.[121]

Cicero and others followed the fifth-century Greek writer Isocrates in stating that oratory derives from Nature, Doctrine (Precept), and Practice. Nature gives every man some talent, though some more than others. Precept or Doctrine provides theoretical rules for success. Practice enables the orator to develop applications of theory to actual situations. Rhetoric—literally, "the lore of the rhetor"—lays out the theory to follow.

Roman theory said that the operation of speaking consists in the five steps of finding ideas, then putting them in order, then putting words to the ideas, then remembering them for the final outward step of oral and physical presentation to an audience. Each step in this sequence is a separate operation, but each after the first one depends on the ones prior to it.

A famous Roman statement of these steps (or "canons" or "parts" of rhetoric) may be found in the anonymous *Rhetorica ad Herennium* (circa 86 B.C.), which is so similar to Ciceronian rhetorical texts that for fifteen hundred years it was actually thought to have been written by Cicero himself. After noting that it is the duty of the public speaker to speak as though to secure the agreement of his hearers, the author (often called "Pseudo-Cicero") declares that the orator must deal with three types of "causes": Deliberative, or political; Forensic, or legal; and Epideictic, or concerned with praise or censure of a person. To speak capably the orator must possess the following faculties:

1. Invention (*inventio*) is the devising of matter, true or plausible, that would make the case convincing.
2. Arrangement (*dispositio*) is the ordering and distribution of the matter, making clear the place to which each thing is to be assigned.
3. Style (*elocutio*) is the adaptation of suitable words and sentences to the matter invented.
4. Memory (*memoria*) is the firm retention in the mind of the matter, words, and arrangement.
5. Delivery (*pronuntiatio*) is the graceful regulation of voice, countenance, and gesture.[122]

Roman theory offered two different modes for the finding of ideas (Invention). One was to derive ideas from a "place" or "topic" (Greek *topos*)—what Cicero calls "the region of an argument." The Latin word is *locus*. Roughly, a topic is a category of thought process that when pursued can lead to ideas about a given subject. Cicero, for instance, names such topics as definition, division, circumstances, antecedents, causes, effects, and testimony.[123] The orator in a forensic case might seek ideas for a defense of his client by looking to the definition of "murder," and might also ponder the circumstances of the crime in seeking ideas for his speech. Thus each "topic" is like a "place" to look for ideas. Quintilian discusses a number of these in Books Five and Seven. Another mode of discovering ideas was through "status" (*constitutio* or *status*) of the question at hand. While there were some differences between authors (Cicero himself having changed his own mind on this subject during his career), the basic approach was to ask a series of questions about the "state" or status of the issue(s) involved in a case.[124] Quintilian (*Institutio III.* 6) says that every cause rests on a status (basis) that brings the opposing sides into conflict and thus points to the issue to be decided; he notes that Cicero identified four bases: the Conjectural (fact—is it?); the Definitive (name—what is it?); the Qualitative (kind—what kind is it?); and the Translative or Legal (jurisdiction—who should decide the case?). The defense in a murder case might for instance admit that a man's death has occurred, but elect to argue from the Qualitative issue that the death was accidental and therefore not of a kind that deserves punishment.

As for Arrangement, Roman manuals specify four to six parts for an oration. Cicero's youthful *De inventione* (written when he was but twenty years old) names six parts: Exordium or introduction;

Narration, or statement of background; Partition, or preliminary outline for the audience; Confirmation, or proof of the case; Refutation, or disproof of the opponent's case; and Peroration, or concluding section including recapitulation and arousal of emotions. The *Rhetorica ad Herennium* also lists these six parts of an oration. Cicero also admits of an optional Digression just before the end of the speech to provide emotional relief. In his later *De partitione oratoria* (a summary written in 46 B.C. for his son Cicero) he reduces these six parts to four—omitting Partition and Refutation—while noting that circumstances may require more or fewer parts to any speech. Quintilian is of course aware of these standard "parts of a speech" but his concluding statement on Arrangement in Book Seven is typical of his broader approach to such rule-bound matters:

> This gift of arrangement is to oratory what generalship is to war. The skilled commander will know how to distribute his forces for battle, what troops he should keep back to garrison forts or guard cities, to secure supplies, or guard communications, and what disposition to make by land and sea. But to possess this gift, our orator will require all the resources of nature, learning, and industrious study. Therefore let no man hope that he can acquire eloquence merely by the labour of others. He must burn the midnight oil, persevere to the end, and grow pale with study; he must form his own powers, his own experience, his own methods; he must not require to hunt for his weapons, but must have them ready for immediate use, as though they were born with him and not derived from the instruction of others. The road must be pointed out, but our speed must be our own. Art has done enough in publishing the resources of argument; it is for us to know how to use them. And it is not enough merely to arrange the various parts: each several part has its own internal economy, according to which one thought will come first, another second, another third, while we must struggle not merely to place these thoughts in their proper order, but to link them together and give them such cohesion that there will be no trace of any suture; they must form a body, not a congeries of limbs. This end will be attained if we note what best suits each position, and take care that the words which we place together will not clash, but will mutually harmonize. Thus different facts will not seem like perfect strangers thrust into uncongenial company from distant places, but will be united with what precedes and follows

> by an intimate bond of union, with the result that our speech will give the impression not merely of having been put together, but of natural continuity.[125]

Style, the management of verbal language, comes after Arrangement in the Roman scheme of things. The most influential single Roman statement in this area was that provided in the fourth book of the *Rhetorica ad Herennium*—a statement so striking that for much of the Middle Ages and early Renaissance the fourth book was circulated separately as a self-contained treatise. By about 86 B.C., the time of the composition of the *Rhetorica ad Herennium*, Roman teachings about style had resulted in a highly codified system of "tropes" and "figures" that could be used to achieve "distinction" (*dignitas*) of language. Each of the three "levels" of style—Grand, Middle, and Plain—could be enhanced through the use of tropes and figures. The *Rhetorica ad Herennium* divides all the figures into two classes: Figures of Diction (also known as Figures of Speech) occur if the adornment is comprised in the fine polish of the language itself, while Figures of Thought derive a certain distinction from the idea rather than the word.[126] Although the *Rhetorica ad Herennium* does not itself use the term, it identifies ten special figures of speech that involve the transference of meaning; these later came to be called "tropes." A total of sixty-four figures are defined and exemplified.

Despite the fact that Cicero, Quintilian, and most other Roman authors argue forcefully that Clarity should be the first quality of Style, and that other stylistic elements besides the figures (e.g. Propriety, Taste) should be considered, historically the vast amount of attention paid to the figures as ornaments has sometimes tended to overshadow the importance of other matters in the rhetorical tradition.[127] Quintilian himself devotes two of his twelve books to the subject; Book Eight discusses style in general, then the tropes, while Book Nine is a measured consideration of various viewpoints, continually asking whether this or that verbal operation (e.g. Questioning) is really a figure or just a natural part of speaking. Quintilian concludes with a discussion of vocal rhythm. Nevertheless it must be noted that his two books on style are very detailed; this too is a particular feature of discussions of style, since the necessity for numerous examples makes them inherently lengthy.

A special feature of Quintilian's *Institutio oratoria* is that it devotes a book and a half (Book Ten and part of Eleven) to further, more general aspects of language use. Book Ten emphasizes the interrelation between reading, writing, and speaking in the preparation of the orator. "Speaking," Quintilian says, "makes writing easy; writing makes speaking precise." A lifetime of adaptation prepares the orator for the ultimate everyday tests of improvising his responses in rapidly changing speaking situations.

As for the two last parts or five canons of rhetoric—Memory and Delivery—Quintilian allows them only half of book Eleven. He agrees that memory can be developed, though it is basically a natural gift. Delivery is treated very generally, again with the acknowledgment that it is an important element in the speaker's success.

Finally, in Book Twelve, Quintilian offers his description of the ideal orator: a man able to speak well on all subjects in all times and places, possessed of great presence of mind, judicious in his choice of cases, able to improve himself through self-analysis, careful of honor and justice, and above all studious of morality. He must know when to retire from public life, and what activities to pursue after retirement.

During the Middle Ages the *Institutio oratoria* was not generally available as a complete text.[128] A *textus mutilatus*, or partial version, was known to have been used at various times; it was influential during the so-called "Renaissance of the Twelfth Century," however, with writers like John of Salisbury making enthusiastic reference to Quintilian in his *Metalogicon* (A.D. 1159).[129] The poet Petrarch so admired Quintilian that he included a letter to him among his literary letters to dead authors. The humanist Gasparino de Barzizza (1370–1431) tried to re-create the sections he knew must be missing from the incomplete text of the *Institutio*.

Then in September of 1416 two Italian travelers taking a tour of Switzerland while the Council of Constance was in temporary recess came across a complete text of the *Institutio oratoria* in a monastery at St. Gall. One of the pair, Poggio Bracciolini, was so excited by the discovery that he sat down and with his own hand copied out the entire manuscript, a task that required thirty-six days.[130] The reaction of Leonardo Aretino was typical of many:

> We have now the entire treatise, of which, before this happy discovery, we had only one half, and that in a very mutilated

> state. O what a valuable acquisition! What an unexpected pleasure! Shall I then behold Quintilian whole and entire, who, even in his imperfect state, was so rich a source of delight? I entreat you, my dear Poggio, send me the manuscript as soon as possible, that I may see it before I die.[131]

The impact of the discovery on humanism was widespread and long lasting. Lorenzo Valla wrote a commentary on the book. Vittorino da Feltre was so imbued with principles of the book that he became known as *Quintilianus redivivus*—"Quintilian living again." In addition to the excitement in Italy there was interest among scholars in many other parts of Europe: in Spain, Juan Vives; in the Low Countries, Desiderius Erasmus; in Germany, Martin Luther and Philip Melancthon; in England, Sir Thomas Elyot and Richard Mulcaster.

The publication history of the book is itself some proof of its influence. The *Institutio oratoria* was among the first books printed. The earliest datable edition is from Rome in 1470, where it was published twice in that year.[132] There were eleven separate editions of the text itself by the end of the fifteenth century, and another twenty-six by the time Ramus published his *Rhetoricae distinctiones in Quintilianum* in 1549. There were no Paris editions before 1500, but of those published after that date a total of thirteen came from Paris. Three separate editions appeared in Paris in one year (1541) even while Ramus was preparing his own first works.

When one looks to other editions of the *Institutio* that were accompanied by the *Declamationes* then usually attributed to Quintilian, one finds twenty-four more issues up to 1549, including thirteen published in Paris. If one then adds the commentaries (usually with text) and the epitomes published up to 1549, there are thirteen published in Paris alone and another twenty-six in various other centers from Basle to Venice to Hagenau and Cologne. All these are in Latin. (The first vernacular rendering of the *Institutio* was in Italian, by Oratio Toscanella at Venice in 1566. An anonymous *La declamations du fameux orateur Quintilien* came out in Paris in 1569, but the first French version of the *Institutio* itself was to be a century later in the translation by Michel de Pure published in Paris in 1663.)

Taken altogether, then, the evidence indicates that up to the time Ramus published his attack there had been an even one hundred separate editions of the *Institutio* in some form. Of these, a rather large proportion—thirty-nine out of the hundred—had been published in Paris itself. Clearly, Quintilian was a popular author, and one especially popular in Paris. In the very year of the Ramus attack, for example, five separate editions appeared. One was in Basle, one in Lyons, but three were in Paris.

Quite apart from the numerical evidence, it must also be noted that even a partial listing of the array of commentators, editors, and explicators of Quintilian shows us a good deal about his reception in the late fifteenth and early sixteenth centuries: Omnibonus Leonicensus, Raphael Regio, Pierre Galland, Guillielmus Philandrus, Jodocus Mosellanus, Antonio Pini, and Joannus Philologus. This list of course does not include those other authors who simply assimilated Quintilian's ideas into their own works without publishing direct commentaries on the text itself. The total influence of Quintilian in this period has never been assessed completely, and perhaps never can be.

There is one name in this list of commentators and redactors that may be particularly significant in relation to Ramus's attack on Quintilian. In 1538 Franciscus Gryphius published at Paris an edition of the *Institutio* with the *argumenta* or summaries of Pierre Galland added at the beginning of each book (and in a number of other places) to explain the contents of the text.[133] This edition was reprinted by itself in 1543; and then in 1543, 1546, and again in 1549 it was joined in a volume with Quintilian commentaries by Mosellanus, Camerarius, and Pini; the 1549 version also included the *Declamationes* of L. Annaeus Seneca with the commentary of Rudolph Agricola. All these editions were published in Paris.

Pierre Galland, of course, came to be one of Ramus's bitter opponents after the events of 1543. It would be tempting to conjecture some personal element on Ramus's part in his attack on an ancient author so clearly approved by one of his opponents, but of course as we have seen earlier Quintilian may have been targeted much earlier in the 1540s—long before Galland came to be an enemy. It is nevertheless an interesting sidelight—if nothing else demonstrating once more the central position that Quintilian occupied in the minds of so many in Paris. (And it might be noted as well that another adversary, Adrien Turnèbe, later published his own commentary on the *Institutio*.)[134]

What all this means, then, is that in attacking Quintilian Peter Ramus was tilting at a major authority in the field of education, and especially in those areas of education dealing with the language arts.

Such an attack was for Ramus a natural, final step in the systematic demolition of the ancient triad of Aristotle, Cicero, and Quintilian. As such, it surely deserves our attention.

## COMMENTS ON THE TEXT AND TRANSLATION OF THE *RHETORICAE DISTINCTIONES IN QUINTILIANUM*

As was so often the case with Ramus, he published the *Rhetoricae distinctiones* twice in the same year with different publishers. The text provided here is that of the Matthew David edition, and the translation is of course based on that. However, the Grandolinus edition of the same year is identical. David's is chosen here as being from the Parisian printer most often used by Ramus during that period. It is number 183 in the Ong *Inventory*.[135]

The book is a small octavo with 4 unpaginated leaves following the title page and then 104 numbered pages. Pages 42 and 43 are mistakenly paginated as 26 and 27. The small italic type is eminently readable in the Paris Bibliothèque Nationale copy. There are no markings or underlinings in the book. Syllogisms and most verse examples are indented from the left margin, with inverted quotation marks used to mark direct quotations included within the text; as is common in items produced at that stage of printing development, the quotation marks appear opposite every quoted line, and are outside the left-hand margins of the text blocks rather than within the paragraph sets.

There are no internal divisions marked in the book, nor are there centered headings of the type found in the *Rhetorica* of the preceding year. Occasionally an indented line will indicate a transition to a new subject or a new book of Quintilian's *Institutio*; however, this is not done consistently. The outside margins (either left or right) often contain key-word indicators that do provide some guidance to the reader, as in the section where names of individual tropes and figures are listed in this fashion. It is not clear whether Ramus or the printer has supplied these indicators. Since their meaning is usually clear from the translated text, they have not been translated separately.

The translation uses modern rather than Renaissance punctuation. As a perusal of the Latin text will show, Ramus uses a highly periodic style—with some sentences ranging over eight or ten lines—and his constant use of parallel structures makes modernization difficult at times. Moreover, the colon mark (:) is frequently used in situations that today would call for a comma, a semicolon, or even a period. The translation attempts to preserve Ramus's meaning rather than his punctuation. Neal Gilbert has a pertinent statement on this subject: "Part of the difficulty in translating Renaissance Latin is due to the punctuation of the printed text, which is usually chaotic and sometimes absolutely perverse."[136] We have found nothing in the Ramus text to make us doubt Gilbert's judgment in the matter.

Paragraph breaks have been introduced where desirable to enhance the clarity of the translation. In all cases the primary objective has been to preserve Ramus's intended meaning as it would best be understood with modern paragraphing practices. This has produced an English text of 34,142 words divided into 279 paragraphs. As can be seen from an examination of the Latin text, the typical prose block in the original is far longer than the 122-word average for paragraphs in the translation.

The Latin text provided here is a transcription of the Matthew David text of 1549. Since the original pages were not suitable for photographic reproduction, it has seemed best to provide the text in transcribed rather than facsimile form. The original punctuation is preserved with the one exception that the placement of quotation marks follows modern practice. Greek words within the text are transliterated. For the convenience of modern readers some commonly used printers' abbreviations have been expanded routinely without notice; these typographic conventions were inherited from medieval practice. Medieval scribes, to speed up their laborious hand-copying of texts, had developed a number of abbreviating conventions that were carried over into the early days of printing. One of the most common is the use of a short bar over a vowel to indicate that an "m" or "n" has been omitted; for example, the Latin *cuipiā* is to be expanded to *cuipiam*. Another example is that the letter "q" followed by a subscript "3" is an abbreviation for *que*.

We are grateful to Isabella d'Este for her transcription of the Latin text. Translation of the book's title is a particular problem. It is noteworthy that all three of Ramus's attacks on the ancients have titles that are rather bland or even neutral by Renaissance standards. For Aristotle it is "Remarks" (*animadversiones*) and for Cicero it is "Questions" (*quaestiones*). The term *distinctio* in the university context has a long but consistent history stretching back to twelfth-century Paris, where it first began to be used to designate the analysis of specific scriptural passages to uncover their true "significations."[137] The use of any of these three terms in a title would not by itself indicate to a reader in advance that the publication would be an attack on the author named. By contrast many Renaissance titles used violent, even virulent, language about their subjects, and it must be remembered that one of Ramus's own critics (Jacques Charpentier) was jailed briefly because of the language he used in print.[138]

The term *distinctio* as used in the university had another useful methodological nuance; that is, it implied the selection only of particular passages for comment rather than promising a detailed explication of every point in a book. Ramus's title, then, enables him to pick and choose—as indeed he does when he starts off by attacking a key idea from Quintilian's twelfth book (the definition of the ideal orator) before even dealing with the first book.

Because the nuances of the Latin term *distinctio* have long since been lost in modern English, we have translated the title as *Arguments in Rhetoric against Quintilian.* This wording also in effect clarifies the subject matter of the book, which is a direct attack on Quintilian. Its purpose is announced in the opening paragraph of its dedication to Charles of Lorraine: "I have a single argument, a single subject matter, that the arts of dialectic and rhetoric have been confused by Aristotle, Cicero, and Quintilian. I have previously argued against Aristotle and Cicero. What objection then is there against calling Quintilian to the same account?" As if this statement were not clear enough, three paragraphs later Ramus adds:

> Yet now Quintilian follows Aristotle's and Cicero's confusion of dialectic and rhetoric. Indeed he makes it worse by fabrications of his own, and by including in his teachings all the disputes concerning all the arts he has read or heard something about—grammar, mathematics, philosophy, drama, wrestling, rhetoric. We shall distinguish the art of rhetoric from the other arts, and make it a single one of the liberal arts, not a confused mixture of all the arts; we shall separate the true

> properties, remove weak and useless subtleties, and point out the things that are missing. Thus, just as I previously attacked the Aristotelian obscurity of Cicero, so now in almost the same way I shall attack it in Quintilian.

Ramus then proceeds to question Quintilian's definition of the orator as "a good man speaking well," using a syllogism of his own to ridicule the definition, before turning to a more systematic analysis of the *Institutio oratoria.*

All the elements of the Ramistic position appear in this one book. "Method" is of course one of his favorite terms, appearing forty-three times. If the arts were taught with "the true method" instead of confusedly, he laments halfway through the dedication, he would not have "known the wretchedness of wasting so much of my youth in this way." He accuses Quintilian of lacking method, since he and Cicero are both misled by Aristotle. To clarify the matter he later outlines the correct procedure:

> The dialectical method (as I have stated in my teachings) gives the following instruction: that in a great debate which we wish to conduct along straight and orderly lines, the matter in its entirety should be put in the first position and then divided into genera and species; and we should follow to the limit each separate part and its lesser divisions (by proof and explanation), so that the universals go first and the particulars follow.

Quintilian errs, Ramus often declares, because by being unable to see how different things are separate he is correspondingly unable to sort out their universals from their particulars; thus the confused Quintilian cannot tell the difference between the "topics" of Invention and the "methods" of Style.

True to his opening pledge to "apply dialectic, the mentor of speaking with truth and constancy," Ramus uses the term "syllogism" a total of fifty-one times in the book. Usually this is done in connection with an actual syllogism he has constructed to test an idea of Quintilian's, as in his several discussions of "trope" in Book Nine. Sometimes the term occurs in a blanket judgment: "Quintilian lacked one instrument, but an absolutely essential one for the teaching of his art—the syllogism, I repeat, the syllogism; and in actual fact he was also radically deficient in method." One recurrent theme, reflecting his view that an oration is simply an embellished syllogism, is that Quintilian does not properly understand Cicero's oratory:

> If Quintilian had recognized that the arts of invention and arrangement are distinct, and if he had evaluated Cicero's speeches according to their standard, he would have found more frequent syllogisms in Cicero's speeches than could be observed in any philosophical writings.

Ramus also takes Quintilian to task for misunderstanding the nature and use of the "topics." Ramus of course reiterates that the ten topics he names are the only ones—"nothing better can be shown for teaching and helping youth"—and when it comes to Invention he declares flatly that "our ten topics explain all these things thoroughly." The second page of the dedication points out that the error of Quintilian was originally the fault of Aristotle: "He left out many definitions and partitions of argument; instead of one art of invention embracing the ten general topics—causes, effects, subjects, adjuncts, opposites, comparisons, names, divisions, definitions, witnesses—he created unfathomable darkness in his two books of *Posterior Analytics* and eight books of *Topics* with their confused account of predicables, predicaments, enunciations, abundance of propositions, and the invention of the middle term." Altogether Ramus discusses "Topic" some forty-nine times in the course of the book.

These few examples may indicate the extent to which the *Rhetoricae distinctiones in Quintilianum* can provide us with a clear insight into the mind of Peter Ramus. As the culmination of his efforts to explain himself and to crush the ancient authorities, the book is both a defense and an attack. It is thus an index of Ramism.

# MAJOR EVENTS IN THE LIFE OF PETER RAMUS

1515 Born at Cuts in Picardy, in district of Vermandois

1527 Enters Collège de Navarre in Paris

1529 Attends lectures of Johann Sturm on Agricola's *De inventione dialecticae*

1536 Takes M.A., begins teaching at Collège du Mans, then later moves to Collège de l'Ave Maria

1543 Publishes *Dialecticae partitiones* (Structure of Dialectic) and *Aristotelicae animadversiones* (Remarks on Aristotle)

1544 Engages in public debate with Antonio de Gouveia

Charles I issues royal decree forbidding Ramus to teach or write on "Philosophy" without the king's permission

1545 *Audomari Talaei Institutiones oratoriae* (Institutes of Oratory by Omer Talon) appears

Moves to Collège de Presles as acting principal

1547 Publishes *Brutinae quaestiones* (Questions of Brutus to Cicero)

Henry II succeeds Charles I as king

Charles of Lorraine intercedes with Henry II to rescind the ban against Ramus's teaching philosophy

1548 Publishes *Audomari Talaei Rhetorica* (Rhetoric of Omer Talon), written jointly with Talon or by Ramus alone

1549 Publishes *Rhetoricae distinctiones in Quintilianum* (Arguments in Rhetoric against Quintilian)

1551 Appointed Regius Professor (University of Paris); styles himself "Regius Professor of Eloquence and Philosophy"

1555 Publishes *Dialectique* (French version of his Dialectic)

1556 Publishes *Dialectica libri duo* (revised edition of his Dialectic)

| | |
|---|---|
| 1557 | Royal writ is issued granting copyright for all past and future works |
| | Publishes *Ciceronianus* (The Ciceronian) |
| 1559 | Publishes *Grammatica Latina* (Latin Grammar) |
| 1560 | Publishes *Grammatica Graeca* (Greek Grammar) |
| 1561 | Becomes Protestant |
| 1562–63 | Withdraws under royal protection to Fontainebleu |
| 1562 | Publishes *Gramere* (French Grammar) |
| 1565 | Becomes dean of group of Regius Professors eventually styled the Collège de France |
| 1568–70 | Resides in Switzerland and Germany |
| 1572 | Condemned by Synod of Nîmes for favoring lay government in the church |
| | August 26: Killed in his rooms at Collège des Presles, on third day of St. Bartholomew's Day Massacre of Protestants |

# NOTES

1. For bibliographic details see below, notes 26 and 28.

2. For a description of this college and its curricular history, see Astrik L. Gabriel, *Student Life in Ave Maria College, Mediaeval Paris,* Notre Dame Publications in Mediaeval Studies, No. 14 (Notre Dame, Ind., 1956).

3. For example, the *De revolutionibus* of Nicolaus Copernicus also appeared in 1543.

4. According to his long-time colleague and biographer Nicolaus Nancel, Pierre de la Ramée chose to use the surname "Ramus" rather than the more accurate Latin "A Rama" or "Ramaeus" because it "appealed more to someone who was particularly keen on praise, and by means of such an omen he dared to covet and hope for a flourishing reputation from the beginning, and even to promise it to himself." While Nancel does not explain further, the Latin term *ramus* ("branch") was at times used in antiquity to indicate a branch or arm of the Greek letter *mu,* used by Pythagoras as a symbol of the two paths of life leading to virtue or vice. See Peter Sharratt, "Nicolaus Nancelius, *Petri Rami vita.* Edited with an English translation," *Humanistica Lovaniensia: Journal of Neo-Latin Studies* 24 (1975): 161–277; the quoted remark is on p. 177. This work is hereafter referred to as Nancel.

5. Teaching masters at Paris literally invented the concept of "curriculum" in the late twelfth century as a statute-ordered plan of study to control student progress. The origins and development of the concept are admirably treated in Gordon Leff, *Paris and Oxford Universities in the Thirteenth and Fourteenth Centuries: An Institutional and Intellectual History* (New York, 1968). See also the excellent study by A. B. Cobban, *The Medieval Universities: Their Development and Organization* (London, 1975). The texts of the major Parisian statutes, especially those of 1215, 1255, and 1367, appear in Hastings Rashdall, *The Universities of Europe in the Middle Ages,* ed. F. M. Powicke and A. B. Emden, 3 vols. (Oxford, 1936).

6. Later foundations of an academic corporation (*universitas*) such as Vienna and Prague often copied Parisian statutes verbatim. See Rashdall, passim.

7. Another biographer of Ramus, Theophilus Banosius, said in 1576 that his critics really believed "that in opposing Aristotle he weakened theology" ("Hoc unum dicam, novum & inauditum crimen suisse Ramo obiectum, Quod Aristoteli repugnando, Theologiam enervaret"). Text in *Petri Rami Veromandui, philosophiae et eloquentiae Regii professoris, celeberrimi, commentariorum de religione Christiana, libri quatuor. nunquam antea editi. Eiusdem vita a Theophilo Banosio descripta.* Francofurti apud Andream Wechelem. M.D. LXXVI. Facsimile repr. (Frankfurt, 1969), Sig. Blv. (Ong, *Inventory,* no. 637; see note 17.) The reader is cautioned that a number of pages in the Banosius *vita* are misbound and out of order; there is no pagination. This work is hereafter referred to as *Petri Rami vita.*

8. That is, Ramus held his own in the debate but he lost out when two of his supporters ceased to back him. The best single treatment of Ramus and his career is that of Walter J. Ong, S.J., *Ramus, Method, and the*

*Decay of Dialogue: From the Art of Discourse to the Art of Reason* (Cambridge, Mass., 1958; repr. New York, 1972); a capsule summary of his life, including this debate, is on pp. 17–35. This absolutely indispensable book is cited hereafter as Ong, *Method.* (See also Ong's *Inventory*, below, note 17).

9. "Sentence donnée par le Roy contre maistre Pierre Ramus, et les livres composez par icelluy contre Aristote." Text in Charles Waddington, *Ramus (Pierre de la Ramée), sa vie, ses écrits et ses opinions* (Paris, 1855; repr. Dubuque, Iowa, n.d.), pp. 49–52. This sympathetic and often entertaining biography is useful today even after a century and a quarter and even after some factual statements have been corrected by later research.

10. ". . . temeraire, arrogant et impudent d'avoir reprouue et condamne le train et art de logicque receu de toutes nations" (Waddington, p. 51). Ironically, it is the provost of Paris who is directed to execute the order—the very provost against whose office the twelfth- and thirteenth-century masters of Paris had organized themselves into faculties. As Ong points out, by the time of Ramus the University of Paris had long since ceased any pretense of independence from the Crown. For other university issues of that day, some mundane and some exalted, see Sharratt, "Peter Ramus and the Reform of the University: The divorce of Philosophy and Eloquence," in *French Renaissance Studies, 1540–70*, ed. Peter Sharratt (Edinburgh, 1976), pp. 4–20.

11. Nancel (pp. 176–78) says that as a student Ramus worked so hard that he seldom slept more than three hours a night. Later, when Ramus became head of a college himself, he personally supported twelve boys in school as part of his customary duties in that post.

12. Judiciously, though, the title pages of later editions refer to the dedicatee as king.

13. Nancel (p. 276) says that the murder of Ramus in 1572 "was shamefully and ignominiously perpetrated by villainous paid assassins, against the expressed will and order of the King and Queen." And Nancel adds (p. 255) that his great friend Cardinal Charles of Lorraine once advised Ramus to accept an offer to go to Bologna rather than stay in France. Ramus also sometimes used the title "Lecteur du Roy en université de Paris," as in the 1572 edition of *Grammaire.*

14. Perry Miller, *The New England Mind: The Seventeenth Century* (Cambridge, Mass., 1956), p. 116. Miller also suggests that the logic of Ramus had as great an effect on New England Puritans as did the theology of Augustine or Calvin.

15. "Nulla siquidem est Christiani orbis natio quae Rami sapientam non amaverit." *Petri Rami vita*, Sig. B2$^{r}$.

16. Nancel (pp. 267–71) has a horrifying account of the episode, which for some of Ramus's supporters made him a Protestant martyr. Ramus was shot, stabbed, and then thrown five stories to the ground before his headless body was thrown into the Seine.

17. Far and away the best treatment of these complex textual relations is that of Father Ong, *Ramus and Talon Inventory: A Short-Title Inventory of the Published Works of Peter Ramus (1515–1572) and of Omer Talon (ca. 1510–*

*1562) in Their Original and Variously Altered Forms with Related Material: 1. The Ramist Controversies: A Descriptive Catalogue. 2. Agricola Check-list: A Short-Title Inventory of Some Printed Compendia of Rudolph Agricola's "Dialectical Invention" (De inventione dialectica).* (Cambridge, Mass., 1958; repr. Folcroft, Pa., 1970). Hereafter referred to as Ong, *Inventory*.

18. This problem is further complicated by the involvement of Ramus's colleague Omer Talon with a number of key works. As Sharratt reminds us, "Nobody has ever had the courage to try to separate the works of Ramus from those of Talon in their joint works, or works published by Ramus under Talon's name." "The Present State of Studies on Ramus," *Studi francesci* 47–48 (1972): 205.

19. Ong, *Method*, p. 5.

20. Ong, *Inventory*, pp. 492–532, lists the works published in these various controversies.

21. Ong, *Method*, pp. 61–62, notes that the dialectic of Abelard, Aquinas, Peter of Spain, and other "scholastics" presumed a balance between probabilities even though actual practice for schoolboys made one of the disputed sides a favored or more certain one. See J. Jolivet, *Arts du langage et Theologie chez Abelard* (Paris, 1969).

22. In fact, the *Sentences* of Peter Lombard rather than Abelard's *Sic et Non* became a dominant text in the medieval university. Yet the *Sentences* probably would not have been worked out the way they were if it had not been for Abelard's methodological impetus. Like Ramus, Abelard may have started arguments whose outcomes he could not have foreseen.

23. Frances A. Yates, *The Art of Memory* (London, 1966). Yates devotes two chapters to Ramism, pp. 231–42 and 266–86.

24. David L. Parker, for instance, has shown that in America some features of Ramism as found in Thomas Hooker and Thomas Shepard were of greater importance than even Perry Miller had suggested: see "Petrus Ramus and the Puritans: The 'Logic' of Preparationist Conversion Doctrine," *Early American Literature* 8 (1973): 140–62.

25. "He had a hankering for novelty; his was a versatile, restless and utterly changeable character: at one moment he would approve of something, at the next reject it; he revised his works remarkably often, inserting passages and altering others almost every year." Nancel, p. 249.

26. ". . . quanquam duo latinae orationis principes Cicero, Fabiusque velut agentes latine videntur dialecticam alter disceptatricem, alter disputatricem nominasse." *Petri Rami Veromandui Dialecticae institutiones, ad celeberrimam, et illustrissimam Parisiorum Academiam.* Parisiis, Excudebat Iacobus Bogardus mense Septembri. 1543. Facsimile repr. (Stuttgart, 1964), folio 5, lines 22–26. (Ong, *Inventory*, no. 1.) This text, like the accompanying *Aristotelicae animadversiones* (Ong, no. 18) published at the same time by Bogardus, has numbered folio sheets with continuous line numbers that begin on the recto side and end at line 52 on the verso side. Citations to these two works hereafter will therefore include both folio and line numbers (e.g., for the above citation, 5:22–26). Ramus had published the book on dialectic earlier in 1543 under the title *Dialecticae Partitiones* (*Struc-*

*ture of Dialectic*) (Ong, no. 1), and Ong reports that an even earlier version apparently survives in manuscript form: Paris Bibliotheque Nationale Ms. fonds latin 6659, dedicated to King Francis I.

27. *Dialecticae institutiones*, 5:27–34.

28. ". . . quam in confusionem Cicero, Fabiusque autoritatem Aristotelis secuti lapsi sunt." *Petri Rami Veromandui Aristotelicae animadversiones*. Parisiis, Excudebat Iacobus Bogardus mense Septembri. 1543. Facsimile repr. (Stuttgart, 1964), 27:11–13. (Ong, *Inventory*, no. 18.) This constant grouping of Cicero and Quintilian with Aristotle into a triad of mistaken ancients is already by 1543 a significant indicator of Ramus's long-range plans.

29. The influence of outside sources has not yet been fully explored. The German humanist Johann Sturm lectured at Paris while Ramus was a student, bringing to the university the ideas of Rudolf Agricola (Rudolf Huesmann) (1443–1485); Agricola's *De inventione dialectica libri tres* (1480) had already gone through some fifteen editions by the time Ramus took his M.A. in 1536. Sturm himself was the author or editor of thirteen rhetorical works. For the possible influence of Agricola on Ramus, see Ong, *Method*, esp. pp. 42–43, and *Inventory*, pp. 534–36. For printed editions of Agricola and Sturm, see James J. Murphy, *Renaissance Rhetoric: A Short-Title Catalogue of Works on Rhetorical Theory from the Beginnings of Printing to A.D. 1700 . . . with a Select Basic Bibliography of Secondary Works* (New York, 1981), pp. 2–4 and 276–79. For the title of Ramus's purported M.A. thesis against Aristotle, see below, note 80.

30. A complete list of Ramus's works, with English translations of their titles, may be found in Ong, *Inventory*, pp. 37–43.

31. Ramus came to the Collège des Presles to find that the principal, Nicolas Lesage, was too feeble to carry on his duties but at the same time was unwilling to give up his post. After some rancorous dealings that included an appeal to the Parlement, it was settled that Ramus would in effect take on the job while Lesage retained the title temporarily. Thus the *oratio* of October 1546, delivered at the beginning of Ramus's second year, is properly an "inaugural address" to open his official administration. It is important therefore as an announcement of intentions. See Nancel, p. 187.

32. *Petri Rami Oratio de studiis philosophiae et eloquentiae coniugendis Lutetiae habita anno 1546*. Parisiis Iacobus Bogardus, 1546. (Ong, *Inventory*, no. 53.) A reprint of the text, with an introduction by Walter J. Ong, is available in *Petrus Ramus, Audomarus Talaeus Collectaneae: Praefationes, Epistolae, Orationes* (Hildesheim, 1969), pp. 244–254. This facsimile of the 1599 Marburg edition was published by Georg Olms; it is an extremely useful resource, not only because it reproduces the original work's index but because it includes Ramus's will and the biography of Freigius.

33. For Quintilian's educational program, see the discussion under the heading "The *Institutio oratoria* of Quintilian."

34. Otherwise, he claims, teaching different subjects in long and separated blocks will lead to a loss of memory ("ut tandem grammaticae & rhetoricae studiis longa oblivione deletis"). *Oratio*, p. 247.

35. Ong, *Method*, p. 271.

36. Nancel, p. 217.

37. Nancel frequently describes Ramus's working methods; see especially pp. 179–81, 191–93, 195, 205, 215, 219. At one point (p. 188) Nancel uses the term "workshop" (*officina*) to describe the enterprise at the Collège des Presles.

38. For instance Cicero, *De inventione* I.xxiv.34: "Confirmation or proof is the part of the oration which by marshalling arguments lends credit, authority and support to our case." And I, XLII.78: "The Refutation is that part of an oration in which arguments are used to impair, disprove, or weaken the confirmation or proof of our opponents' speech." See Cicero, *De inventione. De optimo genere oratorum. Topica*, trans. H. M. Hubbell, Loeb Classical Library, 386. (Cambridge, Mass., and London, 1948).

39. ". . . sed eam partem amicissimus studiorum socius, consorsque, laborum meorum, Audomarus Talaeus illustrabit. *Dialecticae institutiones*, 51:26–28.

40. Orators are to be heard and imitated, but to teach mere rules of rhetoric as Aristotle did would be stultifying for the boys; Cicero did not become a great orator by following rules: "Hinc gloriatus est Cicero se oratorem non ex rhetorum officina, sed ex Academiae spaciis extitisse." *Oratio*, p. 246.

41. Ong describes this period as the first or "rhetorical" phase of four phases in Ramus's career. See Ong, *Method*, pp. 30–33.

42. See Ong, *Inventory*, p. 39.

43. Ramus of course dealt with mathematics all his life; see Nancel, pp. 221–23. There is a good account of Ramus's mathematics in R. Hooykaas, *Humanisme, Science et Reforme, Pierre de la Ramée, 1515–1572* (Leiden, 1952). Also see Ong, "Christianus Ursitius and Ramus' New Mathematics," *Bibliothéque d'Humanisme et Renaissance* 36 (1974): 603–10, dealing with an unpublished manuscript that consists of Ramus's revisions of three mathematical works.

44. That is, Ramus published a commentary on the *De optimo genere oratorum* of Cicero, written in 46 B.C., as an introduction to a translation of Demosthenes' speech "On the Crown." No record of the translation itself remains. With his fierce interest in Cicero's orations, Ramus took pains all his life to separate his praise of Cicero's oratory from his disdain for the rhetorical theory of Cicero. In the case of Quintilian, on the other hand, Ramus has censure for both his theory and his style.

45. *P. Rami Scholae in liberales artes. . . .* Basileae, per Eusebium Episcopium & Nicolai F. haeredes. Anno Salutis humanae M.D. LXIX. Mense Augusto. (Ong, *Inventory*, no. 695.) A reprint of the text is available with an introduction by Walter J. Ong (Hildesheim, 1970). It is interesting to note that this 1569 reissue is a product of Ramus's semivoluntary exile during the religious wars; no doubt the exigencies of lecturing and traveling slowed down any original work during this period. It was also the time of the correspondence with Jacob Schecgk. Theophilus Banosius accompanied Ramus on the trip to Germany, where he was apparently lionized; see Nancel, p. 265.

46. Columns 997 through 1,166 of the anthology reprint a number of Ramus's orations connected with university affairs.

47. This pattern has not been generally recognized. The excellent study by Cesare Vasoli, for example, which devotes an entire chapter (pp. 405–511) to the period 1544–1551, marks instead the inaugural address as Regius Professor in 1551 as the final point in Ramus's early development. Vasoli barely mentions the *Rhetoricae distinctiones in Quintilianum*, lumping it in with the Cicero commentaries (p. 436). He does, however, note "La polemica condotta da Pietro Ramo contro 'tutta' la tradizione peripatetica e contro lo stresso Aristotele" (p. 409). See Vasoli, *La dialettica e la retorica dell'Umanismo: "Invenzione" e "Metodo" nella cultura del XV e XVI secolo* (Milan, 1968). The best treatment of Ramus in English, after Ong, is that of Wilbur S. Howell, *Logic and Rhetoric in England, 1500–1700* (Princeton, N.J., 1956; repr. New York, 1967); however, Howell's basic text for analyzing the Ramist position (pp. 150–56) is the *La dialectique* of 1555, and he never mentions the attack on Quintilian. Ong himself (*Method*, p. 34) dismisses Ramus's attacks on Cicero and Quintilian as lectures "which he delivered simply as a master of arts, to how public an audience, it is difficult to say," though elsewhere he lists the Quintilian book as a part of the Ramus-Galland curriculum dispute.

48. "He had great courage, enough to rival Socrates," says Nancel (p. 247), "especially in putting up with insults, and in taking no notice of the calumnies and rivalries of his enemies and opponents. He never persisted in replying to any of them (except in the end to Charpentier, when he made a speech against him in parliament), overcoming their outrageous insolence by his patient silence." Yet see below (note 101) for his private, as opposed to his public, behavior.

49. A detailed account of the publications to and fro may be found in Ong, *Inventory*, pp. 492–506, and in various places in Ong's *Method*. Ong also notes (*Inventory*, p. 493) that "countless individual attacks on Ramus or defenses of his stands, such as Jean Dorat's or William Ames's, invite no special listing in series with other works and are so numerous that they cannot possibly be attended to here."

50. By 1554, for example, Jacques Charpentier was able to go over seven different editions of Ramus's *Dialectic* to point out inconsistencies.

51. The term "Method" was to be defined later, in 1546, after Antonio de Gouveia had pointed out that what Ramus called "second judgment" was what the Greeks called *methodos*. See Neal W. Gilbert, *Renaissance Concepts of Method* (New York, 1960), p. 133.

52. For bibliographic details of this text, see note 25 above.

53. ". . . disputatricem nominasse" (5:23–25).

54. "Comparatur igitur dialectica, sicuti vis artium reliquarum, natura, doctrina, exercitatione: Nature namque disserendi principium instituit, institutum doctrina propriis, et congruentibus consiliis instruit, instructum ab exercitatio in opus educit, atque absolvit" (5:39–46). This division may be compared with the notion of the Greek writer Isocrates, so influential in Roman rhetoric, that the elements of eloquence are Nature, Education, and

Practice: see Harry M. Hubbell, *The Influence of Isocrates on Cicero, Dionysius, and Aristides* (New Haven, Conn., 1913).

55. This two-part division was not original with Ramus. The *De inventione dialectica* of Rudolph Agricola (1443–1485) makes the same divisions (I.cap.ii). A convenient facsimile of the Cologne 1528 edition, with a foreword by Wilhelm Risse, was published by Georg Olms, Hildesheim, 1976. Agricola also posits two principles about rhetoric that for him limit its parts to Style and Delivery: first, rhetoric deals only with "civil questions" that depend on particular circumstances, and therefore it cannot be a universal art; and second, the fact that there are no Topics (*loci*) which are proper only to Style and Delivery proves that Invention and Arrangement belong only to dialectic. Hence the only function of rhetoric is *elocutionis ornatus* (II.xviii). This is more of an explanation than Ramus gives.

56. "Quaestio igitur est oratio, quae dubium rem quaerit, atque interogat. . . . Quamobrem ubi questio posita est, et eius explicationem doctrina consiliis utimur. . . . Duae igitur (quoniam illic par, idemque que numerus est) inventio iudiciumque" (8:17–20, 8:29–35).

57. Ten of these Ramus elsewhere calls "topics (*loci*)"—the four to be left off this list of fourteen being genus, species, notation, and conjugation—so that Ramus's ten-and-only-ten Topics later become causes, effects, subjects, adjuncts, opposites, comparisons, names, divisions, definitions, and witnesses (testimony). Ong (*Method*, p. 22) lists in addition to Rudolph Agricola and Johann Sturm eight contemporary sources used by Ramus: Johannes Caesarius, Christopher Hegendorph, Franciscus Titelmans, Philip Melancthon, Antonio De Gouveia, Lorenzo Valla, Cornelius Agrippa, and Juan Luis Vives. For an excellent summary of the Agricolan topical logic so critical to Ramism, see James R. McNally, "*Dux Illa Directrixque Artium*: Rudolph Agricola's Dialectical System," *Quarterly Journal of Speech* 52 (1966): 337–47. McNally also translates key excerpts of Agricola's *De inventione* in *Speech Monographs* 34 (1967): 393–422. Nevertheless the Agricola-Ramus relation deserves further study.

58. ". . . quoniam res nil nisi definitur, distribuitur, confirmatur; quae secundi iudicii via est: sed exornationibus amplificatur" (30:30–32).

59. This problem of the place of Memory in Ramism is a vexing one to many modern students, both because the *Rhetoric* of 1548 simply dispenses with what had been a rhetorical canon for fifteen centuries, and because Ramus's dialectical works on the other hand do not seem to provide a satisfactory theoretical statement for his views. On the one hand he often says that dialectic makes memory unnecessary, and yet sometimes (as in *Brutinae quaestiones*, p. 17) he says that dialectic itself consists of the three parts of Invention, Arrangement, and Memory. Memory is thus left dangling between the other arts. Frances A. Yates, in *The Art of Memory*, devotes two chapters to this complex problem: "Ramism as an Art of Memory" (pp. 231–42) and "Conflict between Brunian and Ramist Memory" (pp. 266–86). Ramus clearly distrusted the mnemonic devices of his day, including those of "image" and "figure" inherited from Book Three of the Pseudo-Ciceronian *Rhetorica ad Herennium*. Yates's treatment, which ranges

from Cicero through the medieval mystic Ramon Lull to Descartes and Liebnitz, is indispensable for any serious student of the subject; she disagrees with Ong, incidentally, on the question of "spatial visualization for memorization." See note 67 below.

60. "Volo enim naturae coniuncta semper esse artem, artisque exercitationem: & quoniam total hominus vita nihil aliud esse, quam rationis usus, id est, dialecticae naturalis exercitatio debet" (54:20–29). Agricola (II.xvi) makes a similar statement.

61. 39:18 through 42:39. Ramus cites both Plato and Pythagoras in his discussion of shadows (*umbrae*). Some modern students of Ramus, Yates in particular, find tinges of mysticism in his writings.

62. ". . . interpretationem voco poetarum, oratorum, philosophorum, omniumque artium, & excellentium scriptorum lectionem, auditionem, & ad instituta dialecticae artis explicationem" (44:8–17). Ramus's remark about the *Phaedrus* is on 51:35–40; his complaint is that Socrates pointed out vices but did not "define" anything.

63. 51:28–29.

64. "Scribendi, dicendique exercitatio superest una, & eadem monitione comprehensa" (52:26–28).

65. "Scribendi vero, dicendique prima, facillimaque via est imitatio, que prudenter quos imitari velit, feliget: unus e Latinis in orationibus, in philosophia, in oratoriis institutionibus (quanquam hic authoritate veterum deceptus est) saepe etiam in epistolis multum proderit" (52:46–52).

66. "Quamobrem cum hac interpretationis diligentia puer totam sententiam distinxerit: vel a diligenti preceptore distinctam acceperit: & ex octo & viginti versibus, quator propositioni, sexdecim assumptioni, octo conclusioni tribuerit" (56:24–27).

67. "Exemplum de nostris institutionibus commodissimum hic erit, ut dialectica suiipsius imprimis memoriam confirmet, que aliis opem confirmandae memoriae polliceatur. Figuretur igitur hic artis dialecticae summa & universa partitio, quae (quod dicimus) oculis etiam spectandum proponat" (56:46–52). Father Ong describes this passage as a "dichotomized" outline that opens the era of the "visual" in Ramism; the page is reproduced in Ong, *Method*, p. 181. Ramus himself does not use the term "dichotomy," though here as elsewhere he tends to divide items into pairs. Thus in the chart on the page in question Dialectic has two segments (Invention and Judgment) even though other parts of the page are less clearly marked out as Ramus tries in vain to make neat lineups of types of syllogisms.

68. ". . . hoc artis institutio requirit: hoc sibi deposcit exercitatio" (58:42–44). It is interesting to compare this closing with the final sentence of the Pseudo-Ciceronian *Rhetorica ad Herennium*: "All these faculties we shall attain if we supplement the precepts of theory with diligent practice" ("Haec omnia adipiscemur, si rationes praeceptionis diligentia consequemur exercitationis").

69. That is, his *Prior* and *Posterior Analytics*, *Categories*, *Topics*, *Sophistical Refutations*, and *Interpretations*. For bibliographic details of this edition,

see note 25 above. For remarks on the later reorganizations of the *Aristotelicae animadversiones* see Ong, *Inventory*, pp. 56–57.

70. "Topica in Aristotelea dialecticae inventionis confusione proxima sunt. Sic enim tenebras Aristotelis universas partitus sum, ut inventiones chaos categoriis, & topicis attribuerum" (21:22–26).

71. ". . . cur illa latrocinia permittuntur, ut sophistae sibi vendicent, quod sit grammaticis omni iure debitum?" (32:49–520.

72. ". . . sed exponam tibi meam rationem: tum fortasse ea reiecta Aristoteleus fiam: verum attende, quando syllogismum facis, nonne questionem aliquam probare vis: & eam veram, falsamue iudicares?" (40:13–17).

73. ". . . addidit Boetius Aristotelis discipulos Theophrastum, atque Eudemum secutus, triginta duos concludendi modos in duabus figuris, ex propositionis inequimodis (ut vocat) veros quidem, sed a naturae sensu iudicioque alienissimos, atque ideo prorsus explodendos" (61:29–25).

74. ". . . octavo topico (sicut par fuit) suis aucupiis egegregii concertatores sunt instructi: non enim veri disputatores institutuuntur, sed pertinaces, captiosique, sophistae, & impostores illis artificiis adornatur" (65:52 through 66:4).

75. By contrast Agricola's charges that Aristotle confused the topics, and that Boethius, Cicero, and Quintilian made the matter worse, are delivered in a calm, matter-of-fact tone; see especially *De inventione dialectica* II.i, where all four authors are blamed.

76. 60:15ff.; the subsequent discussion runs over several pages.

77. This may be another debt to Agricola, who concludes his *De inventione dialectica* not with a defense of his brevity (after 405 pages) but with a positive declaration that simplicity of treatment is actually a better way to avoid causing further difficulties: "Rectius itaque credidi, cum possem quidem brevior a dicere, breviore ducere itinere, sed eo aspero difficilisque et impedito, longius potius flexo, sed laeto magis et molliore, minusque spinis obsito circumire." III.

78. ". . . sed si quis liberaliter institutus ad istos accesserit, qui vel poema condere, vel orationem scribere didcerit, primum illud est, ut obliviscatur: indignari siquidem magistri solent si profanis illis (ut iudicant) rebus haec sacra mysteria contaminentur; quid ergo est? quomodo Aristotelei dialectici exercentur?" (66:21–28).

79. ". . . triplex inventio ab Aristotele in rhetoricis descripta est: altera communis ex universis generibus argumentorum, tertia media inter utramque in partibus orationis: quam inconfusionem Cicero Fabiusque autoritatem Aristotelis secuti lapsi sunt" (26:4–12). Despite Ramus's constant reference to the subject of rhetoric, and despite his wide-ranging quotations from Plato, Aristotle, and other Greeks, this is to my knowledge the only time in the works of the 1540s that Ramus even mentions the *Rhetorica* of Aristotle. Later, perhaps after he had studied Greek more carefully, he cites the book more frequently in such revised works as the 1569 *Scholae liberales artes*. However, Latin editions of the *Rhetorica* had been available as early as 1475. On Ramus's knowledge of Greek, see Nancel, pp. 207 and 215.

80. "Problema igitur sumpsit: Quaecumque ab Aristotele dicta essent, commentitia esse." See *Petri Rami vita per Ioannem Thomam Freigium* (text available in *Collectaneae praefationes, epistolae, orationes Petri Rami et Audomari Talaei* [Paris, 1577, and Marburg, 1599] pp. 580–623; this passage occurs on p. 585). Translations vary widely, as do the interpretations; Ong suggests that this exquisitely worded statement (if ever it was made) may be a good example of the type of discussion of tricky problems (*sophismata*) common in the medieval scholasticism then dominant in the university. But Ramus's Boswell, Nancel, never mentions the statement, even though he describes other details of his M.A. ceremony. Nor does Ramus ever refer to it. Even Ramus's enemies fail to bring it up, though they grasp readily at any weapon against him. But Waddington (pp. 28–29) and many others since have simply accepted Freigius's account as fact. Recently Philip W. Cummins has shown that after Freigius the story is not repeated again until 1608, in the *Dai pensieri diversi* of Allessandro Tassoni: see *Journal of the History of Ideas* 39 (1978): 481.

81. As late as 1969 one Renaissance scholar affirms it as a fact: Catherine M. Dunn, "Introduction," *The Logike of the Moste Excellent Philosopher P. Ramus Martyr, Translated by Roland MacIlmaine (1574)*, San Fernando Valley State College Renaissance Editions, No. 3 (Northridge, Calif., 1969), p. xi. Dunn cites Waddington, Graves, and Duhamel, but does not refer to Ong's sceptical discussion (*Method*, pp. 36–41).

82. There is a useful discussion of the "Three Laws" ("Axioms") of Truth, Justice, and Wisdom in Howell, *Logic and Rhetoric*, pp. 149–52; Ong treats them briefly in *Method*, pp. 258–60, and provides a useful chart. Howell is of course interested primarily in the English influence of Ramus, which came about mainly after his death; thus for his purposes Howell's analysis of Ramism can be based on the various versions of the French *Dialectique* of 1555, which by themselves shed little light on developments of the 1540s. All his citations to Ramus's statements on the Three Laws are to works of the 1550s and 1560s. Howell provides a handy summary of these citations in his *Fenelon's Dialogue of Eloquence: A Translation* (Princeton, N.J., 1951), p. 8, note 5.

83. *Dialectici commentarii tres authore Audomare Taleo editi*. Lutetiae [Paris]: Ludovicus Grandinus, 1546. (Ong, *Inventory*, no. 3.)

84. Ong, *Method*, pp. 245 and 246.

85. Gilbert, *Renaissance Concepts of Method*, p. 131. Gilbert sees more influence of Galen and Plato on Ramus than does Ong or Howell; see especially Gilbert's treatment of Galen, pp. 137–142.

86. Ong, *Method*, p. 263.

87. *Ibid.*, p. 264. Ong notes that Ramus also calls Genesis *compositio*, but he does not provide the Latin text of Ramus in which that equivalence is made. It is a logical one, but given the parallel use of *compositio* in grammatical texts it is also a potentially confusing one.

88. Even though the history of Renaissance education remains to be written, the ubiquity—and continuity—of European teaching methods is well documented. Still useful after almost four decades is Thomas W.

Baldwin, *William Shakspere's Small Latine & Lesse Greeke*, 2 vols. (Urbana, Ill., 1944). Some useful observations may also be found in studies of universities by Rashdall, Leff, and Cobban (see above, note 5). For the continuity of the *progymnasmata* or specific classroom exercises, see Murphy, "The Teaching of Latin as a Foreign Language in the 12th Century," *Historiographia Linguistica* 7 (1980): 159–75; and Donald Lemen Clark, "The Rise and Fall of Progymnasmata in Sixteenth and Seventeenth Century Grammar Schools," *Speech Monographs* 19 (1952): 259–63.

89. Ong, (*Method*, pp. 264–65) cites the example of Johann Bisterfield ("the Ramist to end all Ramists"), who divides and subdivides analysis into four levels of application, and then again divides part of one pairing ("logical") into the five types of thematic, topical, axiomatic, syllogistic, and methodic.

90. "Incompetence" is Ong's term (*Method*, p. 24). Ong's view is seconded by historians of logic such as Carl von Prantl and I. M. Bochenski. A frequently quoted study critical of Ramus is Norman E. Nelson, *Peter Ramus and the Confusion of Logic, Rhetoric, and Poetry*, University of Michigan Contributions in Modern Philology, No. 2 (Ann Arbor, 1947); at one point Nelson says: "If a student mastered a real logic, whether Aristotelian, Deweyan, or symbolic, and then read Ramus' logic as logic, he would discover that as a logic it is no good and would infer that a period in which such a farrago of *a priori* nonsense could be taken seriously by 'intellectual leaders' must have been an era of amateurs dabbling in problems which they did not clearly comprehend" (p. 7).

91. Ramus actually published four separate books dealing with orations of Cicero, while Nancel said that ten other commentaries were still in manuscript at the time of his death. Ramus also wrote commentaries on Cicero's *De fato*, *De legibus*, and one 'rhetorical' work—*De optimo genere oratorum*—which is actually a preface to Cicero's lost translation of Demosthenes' *On the Crown*. For details of these works see Ong, *Inventory*.

92. *Petri Rami Veromandui Brutinae quaestiones in Oratorem Ciceronis, ad Henricum Valesium Galliarum Delphinum*. Parisiis: Iacobus Bogardus, 1547 (Ong, *Inventory*, no. 55).

93. For a summary see Donovan J. Ochs in Murphy, ed., *Synoptic History of Classical Rhetoric*, pp. 136–42. Text and translation in Cicero, *Brutus* and *Orator*, trans. G. L. Hendrickson and H. M. Hubbell, respectively, Loeb Classical Library (Cambridge, Mass., 1952).

94. ". . . quae magnorum in republica principum Ciceronis & Bruti de summa regendae reipub. doctrina contentionem explicarent" (p. 6). On p. 4 Ramus speaks grandly of "reipublica gubernacula." The preface is a marvel of name-dropping: Cato, Antonius, Alexander, Esculapius, Abraham, Solon, Saturn, Aeschylus. Dionysius—in addition to the "Aristotle who grievously overturned the arts of rhetoric and dialect" (qui maxime omnium Rhetoricas & Dialecticas artes turbavit").

95. *Brutinae quaestiones*, p. 5. The translation is our own.

96. This too is a complex subject, with implications for the study of humanism from Erasmus to Gabriel Harvey. For the French implications,

now see Marc Fumaroli, *L'age de l'eloquence: Rhétorique et 'res literaria' de la Renaissance au seuil de l'époque classique*, Centre des récherches d'histoire et de philologie de la IVe section, V; Hautes études médiévales et modernes, no. 43 (Geneva, 1980), especially pp. 454–62. The title *Ciceronianus* is one shared by Erasmus, Etienne Dolet, Ramus, and the Englishman Gabriel Harvey (whose work was inspired by his reading of Ramus's book); see Howell, *Rhetoric and Logic*, p. 178.

97. *Audomari Talaei Veromandui Institutiones oratoriae, ad celeberrimam et illustrissimam Lutetiae Parisiorum Academiam*. Parisiis: Iacobus Bogardus, 1545. (Ong, *Inventory*, no. 38.) Ong treats this work in *Method*, pp. 271–74. Its preface is reprinted (as the *Prima* of six rhetorical prefaces of Ramus and Talon) in *Collectaneae*, pp. 14–15.

98. In his *Inventory* Ong lists only nine known copies of the book, and of this total only one is listed for North America (University of Chicago). The work was not printed again after 1548. I have not been able to see any of these editions. Except as it relates to the preface, the following discussion is therefore based on Ong's description.

99. *Audomari Talaei rhetorica, ad Carolum Lotharingum Cardinalem Guisianum*. Parisiis: M. David, 1548. (Ong, *Inventory*, no. 58.) Ong's *Inventory*, pp. 82–90, provides a detailed description of the various forms of this book and addresses the knotty question of authorship.

100. See Murphy, *Renaissance Rhetoric: A Short-Title Catalogue*, pp. 244–46.

101. Nancel, pp. 219–21. The biographer's reluctance to broach the matter was clearly well founded, for Ramus apparently had one manner for the public and quite another for his private colleagues. After praising Ramus for his public forebearance in the face of opposition, Nancel describes his private manners: "At home, on the other hand, among his own people, he was bad-tempered and brutal, attacking now one, now another with his fist, his foot, or a stick, sometimes sending a boy away from him after flogging him within an inch of his life. Consequently he was held in terror by teachers and pupils alike" (p. 247). Nancel also describes an occasion in which Ramus outfaced several armed bandits and drove them away through sheer force of personality.

102. Nancel, p. 193. Later he laments that many manuscripts of unpublished works were stolen from Ramus's study during the looting after his death.

103. Nancel, p. 221.

104. A summary listing of Ramus-Talon texts related to rhetoric may be found in Murphy, *Renaissance Rhetoric: A Short-Title Catalogue*, pp. 242–50.

105. Sharratt, "The Present State of Studies on Ramus," p. 205.

106. It is indeed interesting that the style and vocabulary of the prefaces to all three rhetorical treatises—the Cicero, the 1548 *Rhetorica*, and the Quintilian—seem to have come from the same hand. All are reprinted in the *Collectaneae*.

107. "Rhetorica, est doctrina bene dicendi, ut constat ex origine nomi-

nis: *eirhēkénai* enim vnde et *rhētōr*, et *rhētōinē* dicitur, est dicere et eloqui."

108. "Partes eius duae sunt, Elocutio et Pronuntiatio: hae siquidem solae sunt, et propriae artis huius partes: nam si Grammaticam, Rhetoricam, Dialecticam generales et communes disciplinas: ita, ut ad facile docendum, et perspicue decet, distinxeris, ut non commisceantur alienis inter se preceptis, sed suis et propriis finibus contineantur: Grammatica ex quatuor partibus, etimologia, syntaxi, prosodia, ortographia proprium et purum sermonem prestabit: Dialectica inuentionem rerum, et dispositionem, dispositionisque comitem memoriam suppeditabit: Rhetorica igitur hoc sibi proprium solum retinebit, ut res a Dialectica repertas et collocatas, a Grammatica autem puro et proprio sermone expositas, elocutionis ornamentis magnificentius expoliat, et pronuntiationis et actionis gratia commendet."

109. "Elocutio et eius Species. Elocutio igitur est orationis exornatio, cuius species duae sunt, Tropus et Figura. Tropus est elocutio, qua propria significatio in aliam mutatur: a verbo *xépō*, id est muto. Tropi Genera. Tropi genera quatuor sunt, Metonymia, Ironia, Metaphora, Synecdoche."

110. Figura. Expositio in tropis primo elocutionis Rhetoricae genere, sequitur ut de figura secundo loco dicendum sit. Figura, est elocutio in oratione a vulgari consuetudine mutat: non quod vulgus nunquam his Rhetoricis ornamentis utatur, sed quod ista orationis lumina in hominum imperitorum populari sermone rarius eniteant. Figuram Graeci *sthēma* vocant, id est, habitum et quasi gestum orationis recte et eleganter conformatum."

111. "De Pronuntiatione. Elocutionis, que prima pars est artis Rhetoricae, praecepta in Tropis et Figuris exposita sunt: veniamus ad pronuntiationem, partem alteram institutae artis et doctrinae. Pronuntiatio, est apta concepte elocutionis est doctrina, quam elocutionis: sed illic cogitatur, et concipitur elocutio rebus propositis consentanea, hic qualis cogitatio fuit, talis est pronuntiatio. Pronuntiationis partes. Partes eius duae sunt, vox, unde pronuntiatio: et gestus, unde actio dicitur. Atque earum partium altera ad aures, altera ad oculos attinet, per quos duos sensus ad animum omnis fere cognitio peruenit."

112. Howell (*Logic and Rhetoric*, pp. 166–72) shows how this simply exposed rhetorical doctrine could be followed out in a vernacular language, with specific reference to *La rhétorique francoise d'Antoine Foclin* (1555). Howell's analysis points both to the uniformities of Ramism and to the local variations that probably made it more acceptable in different countries. Also see Roy E. Leake, Jr., "The Relationship of Two Ramist Rhetorics: Omer Talon's *Rhetorica* and Antoine Fouquelin's *Rhétorique francoise*," *Bibliothéque d'humanisme et Renaissance* 30 (1968): 85–108.

113. Ong notes (*Inventory*, no. 69) that the Rheims edition of 1553 included twelve pages of "Tabulae breves in Audomari Talaei Rhetoricam."

114. Understandably there is a considerable Quintilian bibliography. A useful introduction to his career and ideas may be found in the introduction to *On the Early Education of the Citizen-Orator: Institutio oratoria, Book I, and Book II, Chapters One through Ten*, trans. John Selby Watson and James J. Murphy, Library of Liberal Arts, No. 220. (Indianapolis, Ind., 1965), vii–xxx. A good brief biography is that of George Kennedy in the Twayne

Great Author series: *Quintilian* (New York, 1969). There is a recent bibliography of approximately one thousand items by Keith V. Erickson, "Quintilian's *Institutio Oratoria* and Pseudo-*Declamationes*," published in *Rhetoric Society Quarterly* 11 (1981): 45–62; while this bibliography is rather unselective and is listed alphabetically by author rather than by subject or period, it can provide a reader with some useful avenues for further study. Of special importance in Erickson's list are the works of Austin, Clark, Colson, Cousin, Gwynn, Kennedy, Lehman, Little, Marrou, Peterson, Radermacher, Smail, and Winterbottom. Quintilian is invariably treated in any serious study of education, criticism, or rhetoric of the ancient world, and in many dealing with the Renaissance.

115. Text and translation are readily available in the Loeb Classical Library series: *The Institutio Oratoria of Quintilian*, trans. H. E. Butler, 4 vols. (Cambridge, Mass., and London, 1921–1922; reprinted frequently). There is a good critical edition of the Latin text: Michael Winterbottom, ed., *Institutionibus oratoriae libri duodecim* (Oxford, 1970). Quintilian himself tells us that he also wrote a book titled *De causis corruptae eloquentiae*, which is now lost. Two collections of *declamationes* (school exercises in composing fictitious speeches) were long circulated under his name but are now known not to be his. Some editions of single books of the *Institutio* include valuable biographical or analytic data; see especially those of Colson (Book One), Peterson (Book Ten), and Austin (Book Twelve).

116. Charles E. Little, *Quintilian the Schoolmaster*, 2 vols. (Nashville, Tenn., 1951), 2:41. Little presents a detailed analysis of Quintilian's educational principles, his teaching methods, and his sources. Little's book, which has often been overlooked, is to be recommended to any serious student of Quintilian.

117. This passage from the Preface to Marcellus Victorius is taken up for comment by Ramus in the *Rhetoricae distinctiones in Quintilianum*.

118. See especially the preface to Book Six, in which Quintilian laments the death of his wife and their two sons. This is an account of personal loss, but all through the first two books he expresses his solicitude for the students—sons of other men—to whom as master he must strive to be a kind of father.

119. *Institutio* II.xiii.1–2. Citations hereafter will be to the Loeb translation unless otherwise indicated.

120. This concept of a *facilitas* resident in the person may be compared to Aristotle's famous definition of rhetoric as a "faculty" or ability: "Let rhetoric then be defined as the faculty of discovering the available means of persuasion in a particular case" (*Rhetoric* I.2). For both Aristotle and Quintilian the ultimate objective is the capacity of a speaker to adapt to time, place, and circumstances. Ramus does not comment on this basic proposition.

121. It is difficult to pinpoint a single comprehensive modern study of Roman rhetoric that can provide a straightforward, unbiased survey. Some, such as Martin L. Clarke, *Rhetoric at Rome: A Historical Survey* (London, 1953), are clear enough but are prejudiced against rhetoric to the point that

understanding sometimes suffers. George A. Kennedy, *The Art of Rhetoric in the Roman World, 300 B.C.–A.D. 300* (Princeton, N.J., 1972) is good, but detailed and discursive, with as much oratory as rhetoric described. Donald Leman Clark, *Rhetoric in Greco-Roman Education* (New York, 1957), presents a topical survey rather than a chronological history. An extremely brief survey may be found in James J. Murphy ed., *A Synoptic History of Classical Rhetoric* (New York, 1971), pp. 77–182. A reader wishing to absorb both the principles and the tone of Roman rhetoric could do worse than to take up a single ancient text, the Pseudo-Ciceronian *Rhetorica ad Herennium* (see the next note).

122. [Cicero] *Ad C. Herennium de ratione dicendi* (*Rhetorica ad Herennium*), trans. Harry Caplan, Loeb Classical Library (Cambridge, Mass., and London, 1954; reprinted 1964), I.ii.3. The *ad Herennium* treats all five rhetorical canons, providing the first ancient discussion of Memory in a rhetorical work; its lengthy treatment of Style in Book Four, often published as a separate treatise during the Middle Ages, offers definitions and examples of sixty-four "figures" that became a standard set for more than fifteen centuries. The late Professor Caplan spent twenty-six years (1928–1954) perfecting the translation and notes for this splendid Loeb Library edition. The *ad Herennium* was in print in 1470, with at least fifty-two editions prior to the time that Ramus began to publish in 1543 (including a number published at Paris between 1477 and 1538); for the printing history see Murphy, *Renaissance Rhetoric: A Short-Title Catalogue*, pp. 88–94.

123. Cicero included a book called *Topica* among his seven rhetorical works. Text and translation are available in the Loeb Classical Library series: Cicero, *De Inventione. De Optimo genere oratorum. Topica*, trans. H. M. Hubbell (Cambridge, Mass., and London, 1949; reprinted several times). In fact, Cicero makes a statement surprisingly akin to that of Ramus in his *Dialecticae institutiones* of 1543: "Every systematic treatment of argumentation has two branches, one concerned with the invention of arguments, and the other with the judgment of their validity; Aristotle was the founder of both in my opinion" (*Topica* ii.6). There is a summary of the *Topica* by Donovan J. Ochs in Murphy, *A Synoptic History*, pp. 145–49. Cicero claims that his book is based on Aristotle's *Topics*. Cicero's *Topica* was printed frequently at Paris; moreover, Joachim Perion (one of Ramus's first opponents after the 1543 books) published his own commentary at Basle in 1543: *Ioachimi Perionii commentationes in quibis topica Ciceronis cum his Aristotelis coniungit*. Ramus could hardly have been unaware of all this.

124. In his *De inventione*, for instance, Cicero declares: "Every subject which contains in itself a controversy to be resolved by speech and debate involves a question about a fact, or about a definition, or about the nature of an act, or about legal processes" (I.viii.10). The author of *Rhetorica ad Herennium* makes a similar statement (I.x.18).

125. *Institutio* VII.x.13–17.

126. "Dignitas est quae reddit orationem varietate distinguens. Haec in verborum et in sentariarum exornationes dividitur. Verborum exornatio est quae ipsius sermonis insignita continetur perpolitione. Sententiarum

exornatio est quae non in verbis, sed in ipsis rebus quandam habet dignitatem." *Rhetorica ad Herennium* IV.xiii.18. The remainder of Book Four—virtually a third of the entire treatise—is then devoted to definitions and examples of the figures.

127. The complex history of the "figures" remains to be written, and the dominance of Style in rhetoric has waxed and waned over the ages. Howell names "Stylistic Rhetoric" as a major force in Renaissance England (*Logic and Rhetoric*, pp. 116–37); for France see Fumaroli, *L'âge d'éloquence*, especially in respect to "Ciceronianism." There is a major classificatory study by Heinrich Lausberg, *Handbuch der literarischen Rhetorik*, 2 vols. (Munich, 1960), though Lausberg ends his survey at A.D. 600. For an interesting analysis of problems in this area, and especially for the Renaissance period, see Brian Vickers, "Rhetorical and Anti-rhetorical Tropes: On Writing the History of *Elocutio*," *Comparative Criticism: A Yearbook* 3(1981): 105–32; see also the thoughtful analysis in "The Functions of Rhetorical Figures," chapter 3 in Vickers's *Classical Rhetoric in English Poetry* (London, 1970), pp. 83–121.

128. The history of the *Institutio*'s use in the Middle Ages and Renaissance is briefly summarized in the introduction to F. H. Colson, *M. Fabii Quintiliani institutionis oratoriae liber I* (Cambridge, 1924), especially pp. ix–lxxxix. Some further details of the medieval history may be found in Murphy, *Rhetoric in the Middle Ages*, pp. 123–30. Quintilian looms large in any literary or cultural history of the Renaissance; for two examples dealing with France see Terence Cave, *The Cornucopian Text: Problems of Writing in the French Renaissance* (Oxford, 1979); and Robert Griffin, *Coronation of the Poet: Joachim du Bellay's Debt to the Trivium* (University of California Press, 1969). Fumaroli cites Quintilian more than thirty times in his *L'âge d'éloquence*, Vasoli sixty times in his *La dialectica e la retorica dell'Umanismo*. Nevertheless the Renaissance history of Quintilian's use and influence remains largely untold.

129. It is one of the ironies of history that John of Salisbury's *Metalogicon*, designed as a defense of the *trivium* against the boorish "Cornificians" of his day, also presented such a glowing account of Aristotle's dialectical works (then recently translated into Latin) that he helped establish the dominance of the logic that drove rhetoric out of the medieval universities.

130. The German monks of the monastery would not allow Poggio to remove the manuscript, even though they had had so little regard for it that they had piled it into a trunk at the bottom of a tower Poggio says was not fit for a condemned man. On Poggio see Phyllis W. Gordan, *Two Renaissance Book Hunters: The Letters of Poggio Bracciolini to Nicolaus de Niccolis* (New York, 1974).

131. Quoted in William Shepherd, *The Life of Poggio Bracciolini* (Liverpool, 1802), p. 105.

132. For the printing history see Murphy, *Renaissance Rhetoric: A Short-Title Catalogue*, pp. 229–40.

133. *M. Fabii Quintiliani oratoriarum institutionum libri xii. castigati ad*

*fidem optimorum exemplarum, insignitaque lectionis distintione, & additis in marginem adnotationibus percommode illustrati. Addita sunt Petri Gallandii Argumenta singulis omnium librorum capitibus praefixa.* Parisiis, Apud Fran. Gryphium, M.D. XXXVIII. I have used the 1543 edition now in the Cambridge University Library. The *argumenta* are simple, almost pedestrian summaries. For individual books most run fifteen to twenty printed lines, though for Book Twelve Galland furnishes only four lines (and then provides twenty-six lines to introduce Cap. X of that book). Ong (*Inventory*, p. 497) calls this an edition "with commentary" but it is hardly that. One suspects that the marginal notations would have been more useful for most readers. Nevertheless the book does indicate Galland's interest in Quintilian.

134. *Adriani Turnebi in Fabii Quintiliani De institutione oratoria libros XII Commentarii valde succincti et elegantes.* Paris: Th. Richard, 1554. See Fumaroli, *L'âge d'éloquence*, especially pp. 462–65.

135. It is important to note that the reader of later printings of the *Rhetoricae distinctiones in Quintilianum* may have received a quite different impression of the book because of the typographic layout. When it appeared in 1569 and later as part of *Scholae rhetoricae*, the attacks on Cicero and Quintilian were run together as one work; moreover, the combined text was broken up into twenty "books." In the 1569 *Scholae in liberales artes* the original preface to *Brutinae quaestiones* was printed as if it were an introduction to the whole combined double text; at Column 319 the Cicero text ends, and *Liber IX. in Quintiliani lib. i* begins abruptly without further title and without the preface addressed to Charles of Lorraine. Eleven lines of transition connect it to the Cicero text just concluded, and then the new text begins at line 11 of the second section. The unpaginated index of two pages (*Elenchus praecipuorum capitum in scholas rhetoricas*) at the end of the volume treats the two *scholae* as a single work.

136. Gilbert, *Method*, p. vi.

137. See Richard and Mary Rouse, "Biblical *distinctiones* in the Thirteenth Century," *Archives d'histoire doctrinale et littéraire du Moyen Age* 44 (1975): 27–37.

138. One title of the period may be illuminating: Jakob Andrea, *Asinus avis, hoc est metamorphosis nova qua novitius quidam sacramentarius, Marcus Beumlerius, dum tenere in avem falconem transire voluit, ridiculo errore in asinum commutatus est.* Tubingen, 1587. (*Ass Bird, That Is, A Novel Metamorphosis in Which One Novice to the Sacrament, Marcus Beumlerius, When He Wished to Change Himself into a Falcon, by a Ridiculous Error Was Transformed into an Ass.*)

# BIBLIOGRAPHY

Except for certain historical items, essays published in collections of essays are not listed separately in this bibliography, to avoid doubling its size. Readers are encouraged to seek out the collections themselves, whose tables of contents may often be found online. The bibliography is divided up into the following sections: Histories, Quintilian, Renaissance Rhetoric, Educational Background, Biographies of Ramus, Studies of Ramus and Ramism, and General Studies.

## HISTORIES

Bizzell, Patricia, and Bruce Herzberg, eds. *The Rhetorical Tradition: Readings from Classical Times to the Present.* 2d ed. Boston: Bedford/St. Martin's, 2001.

Bochenski, I. M. *A History of Formal Logic.* Trans. Ivo Thomas. Notre Dame: University of Notre Dame Press, 1961.

Clarke, Martin L. *Rhetoric at Rome: A Historical Survey.* London: Cohen and West, 1953; repr. New York: Barnes and Noble, 1963.

Conley, Thomas. *The European Rhetorical Tradition.* New York: Longmans, 1990.

Fumaroli, Marc. *L'âge de l'éloquence: Rhétorique et 'res literaria' de la Renaissance au seuil de l'époque classique.* Centre de recherches d'histoire et de philologie de la IV' Section de l'école pratique de Hautes Études. Hautes Études médiévales et modernes, no. 43. Geneva: Librarie Droz, 1980.

Howell, Wilbur S. *Eighteenth-Century British Logic and Rhetoric.* Princeton: Princeton University Press, 1971.

———. *Logic and Rhetoric in England, 1500–1700.* Princeton: Princeton University Press, 1956; repr. New York, 1960.

Kennedy, George. *The Art of Persuasion in Greece.* Princeton: Princeton University Press, 1963.

———. *A New History of Classical Rhetoric.* Princeton: Princeton University Press, 1994.

———. *The Art of Persuasion in the Roman World (300 B.C.– A.D. 300).* Princeton: Princeton University Press, 1972.

———. *Classical Rhetoric and Its Secular and Christian Tradition from Antiquity to Modern Times.* Chapel Hill: University of North Carolina Press, 1980.

Lausberg, Heinrich. *Handbook of Literary Rhetoric: A New Foundation for Literary Study.* Trans. Matthew T. Bliss, Annemiek Jansen, and Davis E. Orton. Ed. Bry Davis E. Orton and R. Dean Anderson. Leiden, E. J. Brill, 1998.

Meerhoff, Kees. *Rhétorique et poétique au XVI' siècle en france.* Leiden: E. J. Brill, 1984.

Monfasani, John. "Humanism and Rhetoric." *Renaissance Humanism: Foundation, Forms, and Legacy.* Ed. Albert Rabil Jr. Vol. 3: *Humanism and the Disciplines.* University of Pennsylvania Press, 1988. 171–235.

Murphy, James J. *Rhetoric in the Middle Ages: A History of Rhetorical Theory from St. Augustine to the Renaissance.* Berkeley: University of California Press, 1974. Repr. Tempe: Arizona Center for Medieval Renaissance Studies, 2003.

Murphy, James J., and Richard A. Katula, eds. With Forbes I. Hill and Donovan J. Ochs. *A Synoptic History of Classical Rhetoric.* 3rd ed. Mahwah: Lawrence Erlbaum Associates, 2003.

Pernot, Laurent. *Rhetoric in Antiquity.* Washington, D.C.: Catholic University of America Press, 2005.

Pfeiffer, Rudolph. *History of Classical Scholarship: From 1300 to 1850.* Oxford: Clarendon Press, 1976.

Scaglione, Aldo. *The Classical Theory of Composition from Its Origin to the Present: An Historical Survey.* Chapel Hill: University of North Carolina Press, 1972.

Vickers, Brian. *In Defence of Rhetoric.* Oxford: Clarendon Press, 1988.

Yates, Frances A. *The Art of Memory.* London: Wisse, 1966.

## QUINTILIAN

Albaladejo, E. Del Rio, and Caballero, eds. *Quintiliano: historic y actualidad de la retorica.* 3 vols. [Proceedings of a major conference in Spain on the 1900th anniversary of Quintilian's Institutio oratoria] Logroño: Ediciones Instituto de Estudios Riojanos, 1998.

Classen, Carl Joachim. "Quintilian and the Revival of Learning in Italy." *Humanistica Lovaniensis* 43 (1994): 77–98.

Colson, F. H. Introduction. *Institutionis oratoriae liber I.* Ed. F. H. Colson. Cambridge University Press, 1924.

Cousin, J. *Études sur Quintilian.* 2 vols. Paris: Boivin et Cie, 1936.

Cranz, F. Edward. "Quintilian as an Ancient Thinker." *Rhetorica* 13 (1995): 219–30.

Erickson, Keith V. "Quintilian's *Institutio oratoria* and *Pseudo-Declamationes* [A Bibliography]." *Rhetoric Society Quarterly* 7 (1977): 78–90.

Galand-Hallyn, P. F. Hallyn, C. Levy, W. Verbaal, eds. *Quintilien, Ancien et moderne études réunies.* Turnhout, Belgium: Brepols, 2009.

Gwynn, Aubrey o. *Roman Education from Cicero to Quintilian.* Oxford: Clarendon Press, 1926; repr. New York: Russell and Russell, 1964.

Kennedy, George A. "An Estimate of Quintilian." *American Journal of Philology* 83 (1962): 130–46.

———. *Quintilian.* New York: Twayne, 1969.

Katula, Richard A. "Quintilian on the Art of Emotional Appeal." *Rhetoric Review* 22 (2003): 5–15.

Leff, Michael. "Commonplaces and Argumentation in Cicero and Quintilian." *Argumentation* 10 (1996): 445–52.

Little, Charles E. *Quintilian the Schoolmaster.* 2 vols. Nashville: George Peabody College for Teachers, 1951.

Mendelson, Michael. "Quintilian and the Pedagogy of Argument." *Argumentation* 15 (2001): 277–84.

Murphy, James J., ed. *Quintilian on the Teaching of Speaking and Writing. Translations from Books One, Two, and Ten of the* Institutio oratoria. Southern Illinois University Press, 1987.

———. "Roman Writing Instruction as Described by Quintilian." *In A Short History of Writing Instruction from Ancient Greece to Modern America.* Ed. James J. Murphy. Davis, Calif.: Hermagoras Press, 1990. 19–76.

Parks, Brother Edilbert P. *The Roman Rhetorical Schools as a Preparation for the Courts under the Early Empire.* Johns Hopkins University Studies in Historical and Political Science, series 63, no. 2. Johns Hopkins University Press, 1945.

Pennacini, Adriano, ed. *Quintiliano.* Institutio oratoria. Edizione con testo a fronte. [Translations and commentaries by twelve authors] Turin: Einaudi, 2001.

Pujante, David. *El hijo de la persuasion. Quintilian y el estatuto retórica.* 2d ed. Logroño: Instituto de Estudios Riojanos, 1999.

Quintilianus, Marcus Fabius. *Institutionibus oratoriae libri duodecim.* Ed. Michael Winterbottom. Oxford: Clarendon Press, 1970.

———. *Institutio oratoria.* Ed. and trans. H. E. Butler. 4 vols. Loeb Classical Library. Cambridge: Harvard University Press, 1924.

———. *Institutio oratoria. The Orator's Education.* Ed. and trans. Donald A. Russell. 5 vols. Loeb Classical Library. Cambridge, Mass. and London: Harvard University Press and W. Heineman, 2002.

*Rhetorica: A Journal of the History of Rhetoric.* 2 special issues on Quintilian 13 (1995), nos. 2 and 3.

Tellegen-Couperus, Olga, ed. *Quintilian and the Law: The Art of Persuasion in Law and Politics.* Leuven, Belgium: Leuven University Press, 2003.

Ward, John O. "Quintilian and Rhetorical Revolution of the Middle Ages." *Rhetorica* 13 (1995): 231–84.

## RENAISSANCE RHETORIC

### Catalogues of Rhetorical Works

Green, Lawrence D., and James J. Murphy, eds. *Renaissance Rhetoric Short-Title Catalogue 1460–1700.* 2d ed. Aldershot, England, and Burlington, Vt.: Ashgate Publishing, 2006.

Mack, Peter., ed. *Renaissance Rhetoric.* London and New York: St. Martin's Press, 1994.

Murphy, James J., ed. *Renaissance Rhetoric: Key Texts 1479–1602 from the Bodleian Library* [microfiche]. Oxford: Microfilms International, 1982.

Plett, Heinrich F., ed. *English Renaissance Rhetoric and Poetics: A Systematic Bibliography of Primary and Secondary Sources.* Leiden: E. J. Brill, 1998.

Collections of Essays

Malone, Edward A. *British Rhetoricians and Logicians, 1500–1660. Dictionary of Literary Biography.* Farmington Hills, Mich.: Gale Group. *First Series.* Vol. 236, 2001. *Second Series,* Vol. 281, 2003.

Murphy, James J., ed. *Renaissance Eloquence: Studies in the Theory and Practice of Renaissance Rhetoric.* Berkeley: University of California Press, 1983.

Plett Heinrich, ed. *Renaissance Rhetorik-Renaissance Rhetoric.* Berlin and New York: W. de Gruyter, 1993.

## INDIVIDUAL STUDIES

Abbott, Don Paul. "The Renaissance." *The Present State of Scholarship in the History of Rhetoric: A Guide for the Twenty-first Century.* Ed. Lynee Gaillet. Columbia: University of Missouri Press, 2010.

Azibert, Mireille Marie-Louise. *L'influence d'Horace et de Ciceron sur les arts de rhétorique première et seconde, sur les arts poétiques du seizieme siècle en France.* Florence, Mass., 1972; repr. Pau, 1972.

Bayley, Peter. *French Pulpit Oratory, 1598–1650: A Study in Themes and Styles, with a Descriptive Catalogue of Printed Texts.* Cambridge: Cambridge University Press, 1980.

Breen, Quirinus. "The Terms 'loci communes' and 'loci' in Melanchthon." *Christianity and Humanism: Studies in the History of Ideas.* Ed. Nelson Peter Ross. Grand Rapids, Mich.: W. B. Eerdmans, 1968. 93–105.

Classen, Carl Joachim. *Rhetorik in Zeitalter des Humanismus.* Munich: Saur, 2003.

Cogan, Marc. "Rodolphus Agricola and the Semantic Revolutions of the History of Invention." *Rhetorica* 2 (1984): 163–94.

*Contemporaries of Erasmus: A Biographical Register of the Renaissance and Reformation.* 3 vols. Ed. Peter G. Bietenholz and Thomas B. Deutscher. University of Toranto Press, 1984–87.

Cranz, Edward. *A Bibliography of Aristotle Editions, 1501–1600.* Baden-Baden: V. Koerner, 1971.

Davidson, Hugh M. *Audience, Words and Art: Studies in Seventeenth-Century French Rhetoric.* Columbus: Ohio State University Press, 1965.

Donker, Marjorie and George M. Muldrow. *Dictionary of Literary-Rhetorical Conventions in the English Renaissance.* Westport, CN: Greenwood, 1982.

Eisenstein, Elizabeth L. *The Printing Press as an Agent of Change: Communications and Cultural Transformations in Early-Modern Europe.* 2 vols. Cambridge: Cambridge University Press, 1979.

France, Peter. *Rhetoric and Truth in France: Descartes to Diderot.* Oxford: Oxford University Press, 1972.

Gilbert, Neal W. *Renaissance Concepts of Method.* New York: Columbia University Press, 1969.

Gray, Hanna H. "Renaissance Humanism: The Pursuit of Eloquence." *Renaissance Essays from the Journal of the History of Ideas.* Ed. P. O. Kristeller and P. P. Wiener. New York: Harper and Row, 1968.

Green, Lawrence D. *Grammatica movet: Renaissance Grammar Books and elocutio.* Leiden: E. J. Brill, 1999.

Howell, Wilbur Samuel, trans. *Fenelon's Dialogue on Eloquence: A Translation.* Princeton: Princeton University Press, 1951.

Jardine, Lisa. *Francis Bacon: Discovery and the Art of Discourse.* Cambridge: Cambridge University Press, 1974.

Kahn, Victoria. *Rhetoric, Prudence, and Skepticism in the Renaissance.* Ithaca: Cornell University Press, 1985.

Kristeller, Paul O. *Medieval Aspects of Renaissance Learning: Three Essays.* Ed. and trans. E. P. Mahoney. Durham: Duke University Press, 1974.

———. "Philosophy and Rhetoric from Antiquity to the Renaissance." *Renaissance Thought and Its Sources.* Ed. Michael Mooney. New York: Columbia University Press, 1979. 211–59.

———. *Renaissance Philosophy and the Medieval Tradition.* Latrobe, Pa.: Archabbey Press, 1966.

———. *Renaissance Thought: The Classic, Scholastic, and Humanistic Strains.* New York: Harper, 1961.

———. *Studies in Renaissance Thought and Letters.* Rome: Edizioni di Storia e Letteratura, 1956. Repr. 1967.

Kuentz, Paul. "Bibliographie pour 1'études de la rhétorique [i.e., 1610–1715]." *XVIIe siècle 80–81* (1968): 1146.

Lechner, Sister Joan Marie, O.S.U. *Renaissance Concepts of the Commonplaces: An Historical Investigation of the General and Universal Ideas Used in All Argumentation and Persuasion with Special Emphasis on the Educational and Literary Tradition of the Sixteenth and Seventeenth Centuries.* New York: Pageant Press, 1962.

Mack, Peter. *Renaissance Argument: Valla and Agricola in the Traditions of Rhetoric and Dialectic.* Leiden: E. J. Brill, 1993.

———. *Elisabethan Rhetoric: Theory and Practice.* Cambridge: Cambridge University Press, 2002.

McNally, Richard. "Dux *ilia directrixque artium:* Rudolph Agricola's Dialectical System." *Quarterly Journal of Speech* 52 (1966): 3371–47.

———. *"Rector et Dux Populi:* Italian Humanists and the Relationship between Rhetoric and Logic." *Modern Philology* 67 (1969): 168–76.

———. "Rudolph Agricola's *De inventione dialecticae libri tres.:* A Translation of Selected Chapters." *Speech Monographs* 34 (1967): 393–422.

Murphy, James J. "Kristeller and Renaissance Rhetoric." *Kristeller Reconsidered: Essays on His Life and Scholarship.* Ed. John Monfasani. New York: Italica Press, 2006. 205–12.

Padley, G. A. *Grammatical Theory in Western Europe, 1500–1700: The Latin Tradition.* Cambridge: Cambridge University Press,1976.

Patterson, Annabel M. *Hermogenes and the Renaissance: Seven Ideas of Style.* Princeton: Princeton University Press, 1970.

Plett, Heinrich F. *Rhetoric and Renaissance Culture.* Berlin: de Gruyter, 2004.

Rebhorn, Wayne, ed. and trans. *Renaissance Debates on Rhetoric.* Ithaca: Cornell University Press, 2000.

———. *The Emperor of Men's Minds: Literature and the Renaissance Discovery of Rhetoric.* Ithaca: Cornell University Press, 2006.

Scott, Izora. *Controversies over the Imitation of Cicero in the Renaissance. With Translations for Letters between Pietro Bembo and Gianfrancesco Pico on Imitation and aTranslation of Desiderius Erasmus, the Ciceronian (Ciceronianus).* New York: Teachers College of Columbia University, 1910. Repr. Davis, Calif.: Hermagoras Press, 1991.

Seigel, Jerrold E. *Rhetoric and Philosophy in Renaissance Humanism.* Princeton: Princeton University Press, 1968.

Shuger, Deborah K. *Sacred Rhetoric: The Christian Grand Style in the English Renaissance.* Princeton: Princeton University Press, 1998.

Sonnino, Lee A. *A Handbook to Sixteenth-Century Rhetoric.* New York: Barnes and Noble, 1968.

Vickers, Brian. *Classical Rhetoric in English Poetry.* London: Macmillan; New York: St. Martin's Press, 1970.

Weinberg, Bernard. *A History of Literary Criticism in the Renaissance.* 2 vols. University of Chicago Press, 1961.

Wilsdorf, Helmut. *Georg Agricola and seine Zeit.* Berlin: VEB Deustscher Verlag der Wissenschafreu, 1956.

## EDUCATIONAL BACKGROUND

Baldwin, Thomas W. *William Shakspere's Small Latine and Lesse Greeke.* 2 vols. Urbana: University of Illinois Press, 1944.

Clark, Donald L. *John Milton at St. Paul's School: A Study of Ancient Rhetoric in English Renaissance Education.* New York: Columbia University Press, 1948.

———. *Rhetoric in Greco-Roman Education.* New York: Columbia University Press, 1957.

———. "The Rise and Fall of Progymnasmata in Sixteenth and Seventeenth Century Grammar Schools." *Speech Monographs* 19 (1952): 259–63.

Cobban, A. B. *The Medieval Universities: Their Development and* Organization. London: Methuen, 1975.

Denifle, Henricus, and Aemilius Chatelain, eds. *Chartularium universitatis Parisiensis.* 4 vols. Paris, 1889–97.

D'Irsay, Stephen. *Histoire des universités francaises et étrangeres des origines à nos jours.* 2 vols. Paris: A. Picard, 1933–35.

Gabriel, Astrik L. *Student Life in Ave Maria College, Mediaeval Paris.* Notre Dame Publications in Medieval Studies, no. 14. Notre Dame, Ind..: University of Notre Dame Press, 1956.

Grafton, Anthony, and Lisa Jardine. *From Humanism to the Humanities: Education and the Liberal Arts in Fifteenth- and Sixteenth-Century Europe.* London: Duckworth, 1986.

Heath, Terrence. "Logical Grammar, Grammatical Logic, and Humanism in Three German Universities." *Studies in the Renaissance* 18 (1971): 9–64.

Jardine, Lisa. "Humanism and Dialectic in Sixteenth-Century Cambridge: A Preliminary Investigation." *Classical Influences on European Culture, A.D. 1500–1700.* Ed. R. R. Bolgar. Cambridge: Cambridge University Press, 1976. 141–54.

———. "The Place of Dialectic Teaching in Sixteenth-Century Cambridge." *Studies in the Renaissance* 21 (1974): 31–62.

Lang, Robert A. "Rhetoric at the University of Paris, 1550–1789." *Speech Monographs* 23 (1956): 216–28.

———. "Rhetoric in Les Petits-Écoles of Port-Royal." *Speech Monographs* 25 (1958): 208–14.

———. "The Teaching of Rhetoric in French Jesuit Colleges, 1556 to 1762." *Speech Monographs* 19 (1952): 286–98.

Leff, Gordon. *Paris and Oxford Universities in the Thirteenth and Fourteenth Centuries: An Institutional and Intellectual History.* New York: Wiley, 1968. Repr. Huntington, N.Y.: R. E. Krieger, 1975.

Marrou, Henri-Irene. *A History of Education in Antiquity.* Trans. George Lamb. New York: Sheed and Ward, 1956.

Rashdall, Hastings. *The Universities of Europe in the Middle Ages.* Ed. F. M. Powicke and A. B. Emden. 3 vols. Oxford: Oxford University Press, 1936.

Wieruszowski, Helene. *The Medieval University: Masters, Students, Learning.* Princeton.: Van Nostrand, 1966.

## BIOGRAPHIES OF RAMUS

### Sixteenth-Century Biographies

Banosius. *Petri Rami Veromandui, philosophiae et eloquentiae Regii professoris, celeberrimi, commentariorum de religione Christiana, libri quatuor. nunquam antea editi. Eiusdem vita a Theophilo Banosio descripta.* Francofurti apud Andream Wechelem. M.D. LXXVI. Facsimile repr., Frankfurt: Minerva, 1969.

Freigius. *Petri Rami vita per Ioannem Thomam Freigium.* Text in *Collectaneae praefationes, epistolae, orationes Petri Rami et Audomari Talaei.* Paris, 1577, and Marburg, 1599. Facsimile repr. of 1599 ed., with intro. by Walter J. Ong, Hildesheim: Georg Olms, 1969.

Nancelius. "Nicolaus Nancelius, *Petri Rami vita.* Edited with an English Translation." Ed. and trans. Peter Sharratt. *Humanistica Lovaniensia: Journal of Neo-Latin Studies* 24 (1975): 161–277.

### Nineteenth-Century Biographies

Desmaze, Charles A. P. *Ramus. Sa Vie, ses ecrits, sa mort (1515–1572).* Paris, 1864. Repr. Geneva: Slatkine Reprints, 1970.

Waddington, Charles. *Ramus (Pierre de la Ramee), sa vie, ses écrits et ses opinions.* Paris, 1855. Repr. Dubuque, Iowa, n.d.

## STUDIES OF RAMUS AND RAMISM

### Collections of Ramus Studies

*Argumentation* 5 (1991). Special issue. No. 4.

Feingold, Mordechai, Joseph S. Freedman, and Wolfgang Rother, eds. *The Influence of Peter Ramus: Studies in Sixteenth and Seventeenth Century Philosophy and Sciences.* Basel: Schwab, 2001.

Meerhoff, Kees, and Jean-Claude Moisan, eds. *Autour de Ramus: texte, theorie, commentaire.* [Quebec]: Nuit blanche editeur, 1997.

———. eds. *Ramus et l'université.* Paris: Rue d'Ulm, Broche Cahiers V. L. Saulnier, 2004.

———. eds. *Autour de Ramus: le combat.* Paris: H. Champion, 2005.

*Revue des sciences philosophiques et theologiques,* January, 1986. Special issue dealing with Ramism.

Wilson, Emma A., and Steven Reid, eds. *Ramus, Pedagogy, and the Liberal Arts.* Aldershot, England, and Burlington, Vt.: Ashgate, 2010.

### Works of Walter J. Ong, S.J.

Ong, Walter J., S.J. *Ramus, Method, and the Decay of Dialogue from the Art of Discourse to the Art of Reason.* Cambridge: Harvard University Press, 1958; repr. New York: Octagon Books, Farrar, Strauss & Giroux, 1974; repr. Cambridge: Harvard University Press, 1983.

———. *Ramus and Talon Inventory: A Short-Title Inventory of the Published Works of Peter Ramus (1515–1572) and Omer Talon (ca. 1510–1562) in Their Original and in Their Variously Altered Forms with Related Material:. The Ramist Controversies: A Descriptive Catalogue. 2. Agricola Check List: A Short-Title Inventory of Some Printed Editions and Printed Compendia of Rudolph Agricola's "Dialectical Invention" ("De inventione dialectica').* Cambridge: Harvard University Press, 1958.

———. "Hobbes and Talon's Ramist Rhetoric in English." *Transactions of the Cambridge Bibliographic Society* 1, part 3 (1951): 260–69.

———. "Fouquelin's French Rhetoric and the Ramist Vernacular Tradition." *Studies in Philology* 51 (1954): 127–42.

———. "Ramus: Rhetoric and the Pre-Newtonian Mind." *English Institute Essays, 1952*. Ed. Alan S. Downer. New York: Columbia University Press, 1954. 138–70.

———. " Ramist Method and the Commercial Mind." *Studies in the Renaissance* 8 (1961): 155–72.

———. "Ramistic Rhetoric." *The Province of Rhetoric*. Ed. J. Schwartz and J. A. Rycenga. New York: Ronald Press, 1965. 56–65.

———. "Tudor Writings on Rhetoric." *Studies in the Renaissance* 15 (1968): 39–69.

———. "Christianus Ursitius and Ramus's New Mathematics." *Bibliothêque d'Humanisme et Renaissance* 36 (1974): 603–10.

———. Introduction. John Milton's *A Fuller Course in the Art of Logic Conformed to the Method of Peter Ramus*. Ed. and trans. Walter J. Ong, S. J., and Charles J. Ermatinger. New Haven: Yale University Press, 1983.

## Individual Studies

This section is devoted to individual studies not found in the collections listed above.

Adams, John Charles. "Alexander Richardson's Puritan Theory of Discourse." *Rhetorica* 4 (1986): 255–74.

———. "Gabriel Harvey's *Ciceronianus* and the place of Peter Ramus' *Dialecticae libri duo* in the Curriculum." *Renaissance Quarterly* 43 (1990): 551–69.

———. "Ramist Concepts of Testimony, Judicial Analogies, and the Puritan Conversion Narrative." *Rhetorica* 9 (1991): 251–68.

Ashworth, E. J. "Changes in Logic Textbooks from 1500 to 1650: The New Aristotelianism." *Aristotelismus and Renaissance: In Memoriam Charles B. Schmitt*. Ed. Eckhard Kessler, Charles Lohr, and Walter Sparn. Weisban: Wolfenbütteler Forschungen, 1988. 75–87.

Bruyère-Robinet, N. *Méthode et dialectique dans l'oeuvre de La Ramée-Renaissance et âge classique*. Paris: Vrin, 1984.

———. "Le statut de l'invention dans l'oeuvre de La Ramée." *Revue des sciences philosophiques et théologiques* 70 (1986): 15–24.

Duhamel, Pierre Albert. "The Logic and Rhetoric of Peter Ramus." *Modern Philology* 46 (1948–49): 163–71.

Dunn, Catherine M. Introduction. *The Logicke of the Moste Excellent Philosopher P. Ramus, Martyr; Translated by Roland MacIlmaine (1574)*. Ed. Dunn. Renaissance Editions, no. 3. Northridge, Calif.: San Fernando Valley State College, 1969.

Freadman, Anne. "Ramus against Quintilian: A Civil War, Some Readings, and a Couple of Allegorical Divisions." *Southern Review* 25 (1992): 98–152.

Goeglein, Tamara A. "Wherein Hath Ramus Been So Offensious? Poetic Examples in English Ramist Logic Manuals (1574–1672)." *Rhetorica* 14 (1996): 73–101.

Graves, Frank Pierrepont. *Peter Ramus and the Educational Reformation of the Sixteenth Century.* New York: Macmillan, 1912.

Hooykaas, R. *Humanisme, Science et Reformer Pierre de la Ramée, 1515–1572.* Leiden: Brill, 1958.

Hotson, Howard. *Commonplace Learning: Ramism and its German Ramifications, 1543–1630.* Oxford: Oxford University Press, 2007.

Leake, Roy. "The Relationship of Two Ramist Rhetorics: Omer Talon's *Rhetorica* and Antoine Fouqelin's *Rhétorique françoise.*" *Biblothéque D 'Humanisme et Renaissance* 30 (1968): 85–108.

Mack, Peter. "Ramus Reading: The Commentaries on Cicero's Consular Orations and Vergil's *Eclogues* and *Georgics.*" *Journal of the Warburg and Courtauld Institutes* 61 (1988): 111–41.

———. "Peter Ramus as Humanist and Philosophe." *Journal of the Warburg and Courtauld Institutes* 61 (1998): 111–41.

Margolin, Jean-Claude. "Ronsard Collaborateur de la Ramée." *Pierre de Ronsard: Apropos des Amours.* Ed. James Dauphine et al. Cahiers du Centre Jacques Laprade 5. Biarritz: Atlantica, 1997.

Martin, Howard H. "Ramus, Ames, Perkins, and Colonial Rhetoric." *Western Speech* 23 (1959): 74–82.

McKim, Donald K. *Ramism in William Perkins' Theology.* New York: Peter Lang, 1987.

Meerhoff, Kees. "Logic and Eloquence: A Ramusian Revolution?" Argumentation 4 (1991): 357–74.

———. "Agricola et Ramus-Dialectique et Rhétorique." *Rodolphus Agricola Phrisius (1444–1485): Proceedings of the International Conference at the University of Groningen.* Groningen, 1987.

———. "Antoine Fouquelin et Thomas Sebillet." *Nouvelle révue du seizième siécle.* 5 (1987): 59–77.

———. "Bartholomew Keckerman and the Anti-Ramist Tradition at Heidelberg." Ed. C. Strohm, J. S. Freedman, and H. J. Selderhuis. *Späthumanismus and reformierte Konfession. Theologie, Jurisprudenz and Philosophie in Heidelburg an der Wende zum 17. Jarhundert.* Spätmittelalter and Reformation Neue Reihe, 31. Tubingen: Mohr Siebeck, 2006. 169–205.

———. "Galland contre Ramus: le dignité du philologue." *La philologie humaniste et ses representations dans la théorie et dans la fiction.* Romanica Gandensia, 32. Geneve: Droz, 2005. Tome II, 495–526.

———. L'enseignement des lectures royaux pour l'éloquence et la philosophic: de Latomus à Ramus." A. Tuilier (dir.), *Histoire du College de France.* Tome I. *La creation 1530–1560.* Paris, Fayard, 2006. 293–352.

———. "Pédagogie et rhétorique ramistes. La cas Fouquelin." *Rhetorica* 5 (1987): 419–30.

———. Ramus et Cicerón." *Revue des sciences philosphiques et thèologiques* 70 (1986): 25–35.

Miller, Perry. *The New England Mind: The Seventeenth Century* Cambridge: Harvard University Press, 1956.

Moisan, Jean-Claude. "Commentaires sur les Rhetoricae preceptiones, epitome Ramiste anonyme de 1572." *Humanistica Lovaniensia* 39 (1990): 246–305.

Murphy, James J., and Carole Newlands, eds. and trans. *Peter Ramus's Attack on Cicero: Text and Translation of Ramus's Brutinae quaestiones.* Davis, Calif.: Hermagoras Press, 1992.

Nadeau, Ray. "Talaeus versus Farnaby on Style." *Speech Monographs* 21 (1954): 59–63.

Nelson, Norman E. *Peter Ramus and the Confusion of Logic, Rhetoric, and Poetry.* University of Michigan Contributions in Modern Philology, no. 2. Ann Arbor: University of Michigan Press, 1947.

Oldrini, Guido. "Le particolarità del Ramismo inglese." *Rinascimento: Rivista del i'Istituto Nazionale di Studi sul Rinascimento.* 2d series 25 (1985): 19–80.

———. *La Disputa del Metodo nel Rinascimento: Indagini su Ramo e sul ramismo.* Florence: Le Lettere, 1997.

Pomeroy, Ralph S. "The Ramist as Fallacy-Hunter: Abraham Fraunce and *The Lawiers Logique.*" *Renaissance Quarterly* 40 (1987): 224–46.

Reiss, Timothy J. "The Idea of Meaning and Practise of Method in Peter Ramus, Henry Estienne, and Others." *Humanism in Crisis: The Decline of the French Renaissance.* Ed. Philippe Desan. Ann Arbor: University of Michigan Press, 1991. 125–51.

Risse, Wilhelm. "Petrus Ramus and sein Verhaltnis zum Schultradition." *Revue des sciences philosophiques et théologiques* 70 (1986): 49–66.

Sharratt, Peter. "La Ramée's Early Mathematical Teaching." *Bibliothéque d'Humanisme et Renaissance* 28 (1966): 605–14.

———. "Peter Ramus and Imitation: Image, Sign, and Sacrament." *Yale French Studies* 47 (1972): 19–32.

———. "Peter Ramus and the Reform of the University: The Divorce of Philosophy and Eloquence?" *French Renaissance Studies, 1540–70: Humanism and the Encyclopedia.* Ed. Peter Sharratt. Edinburgh: Edinburgh University Press, 1976.

———. "Peter Ramus, Walter Ong, and the Tradition of Humanist Learning." *Oral Tradition* 2 (1987): 172–87.

———. "Recent Work on Peter Ramus (1970–1986)." *Rhetorica* 5 (1987): 7–58.

———. "The Present State of Studies on Ramus." *Studi Francesci.* 47–48 (1972): 201–13.

———. "Ramus 2000." *Rhetorica* 18 (2000): 399–455.

Skalnick, James V. *Ramus and Reform: University and Church at the End of the Renaissance.* Sixteenth Century Essays and Studies, LX. Kirksville, Mo.: Truman State University Press, 2002.

Stegmann, André. "Les observations sur Aristotle du Bénédictin J. Périon." *Platon et Aristote à Renaissance. Actes du XVIième colloque International d 'Études Humanistes de Tours.* Paris: Urin, 1976. 377–89.

Triche, Steven, and Douglas McKnight. "The Quest for Method: The Legacy of Peter Ramus," *History of Education* 33 (2004): 41–54.

Vasoli, Cesare. *La dialettica e la retorica dell'Umanismo: "Invenzione" e 'Metodo" nella cultura del XV e XVI secolo.* I fatti e le idee Saggi e Biografie, no. 174. Milan: Feltrinelli Editore, 1968.

———. "Bruno, Ramo e Patrizi." *Nouvelles de la Republique des Lettres* 14 (1994): 169–90.

Verdonk, Jacobus. *Petrus Ramus en de wiskunde.* Van Gorcum's historische bibliotheek, no. 81. Assen: Van Gorcum, 1966.

Walton, Craig. "Ramus and Bacon on Method." *Journal of the History of Philosophy* 9 (1971): 289–302.

———. "Ramus and the Art of Judgment." *Philosophy and Rhetoric* 3 (1970): 152–64.

Wilson, Harold S. Introduction. *Gabriel Harvey's Ciceronianus, with an Introduction and Notes by Harold S. Wilson and an English Translation by Clarence A. Forbes.* University of Nebraska, Studies in the Humanities, no. 4. Lincoln: University of Nebraska, 1945. 1–34.

## GENERAL STUDIES

Bolgar, Robert R., *The Classical Heritage and Its Beneficiaries.* Cambridge: Cambridge University Press, 1954.

———. ed. *Classical Influences on European Culture, A.D. 1500–1700.* Cambridge: Cambridge University Press, 1976.

Boyle, Marjorie O'Rourke. *Erasmus on Language and Method in Theology.* Toronto: University of Toronto Press, 1977.

Caplan, Harry. *Of Eloquence, Studies in Ancient and Medieval Rhetoric.* Ithaca: Cornell University Press, 1970.

Cave, Terence. *The Cornucopian Text: Problems of Writing in the French Renaissance.* Oxford: Oxford University Press, 1979.

Garin, Eugenio, P. Rossi, and C. Vasoli. *Testi Umanistici su la Retorica.* Rome, 1953.

Gordon, Alex L. *Ronsard et la Rhétorique.* Travaux d'Humanisme et Renaissance, no. 3. Geneva: Droz, 1970.

Griffin, Robert. "Coronation of the Poet: Joachim du Bellay's Debt to the Trivium." *Publications in Modern Philology,* vol. 96. Berkeley: University of California Press, 1969.

Higman, Francis M. *The Style of John Calvin in His French Polemical Treatises.* Oxford Modern Language and Literature Monographs. Oxford: Oxford University Press, 1967.

Howell, Wilbur Samuel. "Poetics, Rhetoric, and Logic in Renaissance Criticism." *Classical Influences on European Culture* A.D. 1500–1700. Proceedings of an International Conference held at King's College, Cambridge, April 1974. Ed. R. R. Bolgar. Cambridge: Cambridge University Press, 1976. 155–62.

Kibedi-Varga, *A. Rhétorique et Litterature: études des structures classiques.* Paris: Didier, 1970.

Kohl, Benjamin G. *Renaissance Humanism. A Bibliography of Materials in English.* New York: Garland, 1985.

Kushner, Eva. "Reflexions sur le dialogue en France au XVI' siècle." *Révue des Sciences Humaines* 37 (1972): 485–501.

Le Hir, Yves. *Rhétorique et stylistique de la Pleiade au Parnasse.* Paris: Presses Universitaires de France, 1960.

Marti, Antonio. *La preceptive ret6rica españiola en el Siglo de* Oro. Biblioteca romanica hispanica. I: Tradados y monografias, no. 12. Madrid: Gredos, 1972.

Noreña, C. *G. Juan Luis Vives.* The Hague: Nijhof, 1970.

O'Malley, John W. *Praise and Blame in Renaissance Rome: Rhetoric, Doctrine, and Reform in the Sacred Oratory of the Papal Court, c.1450–1521.* Durham: Duke University Press, 1979.

Pinto de Castro, Anibal. *Retorica e teorizao literaria em Portugal do Humanismo Neoclassicismo.* Coimbra: 1973.

Rico Verdu, Jose. *Le retorica española de los siglosXVJ y*XVII. Anejos de Revista de Literatura, no. 35. Madrid: Conseja Superior de Investigaciones Cientificas, 1973.

Serrão, Joquim Verissimo. *Antonio de Gouveia e o seu tempo (1510–1566).* Coimbra, 1966.

Topliss, Patricia. *The Rhetoric of Pascal: A Study of His Art of Persuasion in the Provinciales and the Pensées.* Leicester: Leicester University Press, 1966.

Tuve, Roseinond. *Elizabethan and Metaphysical Imagery: Renaissance Poetic and Twentieth Century Critics.* Chicago: University of Chicago Press, 1947.

Warrick, Barbara. "Fénelon's Recommendations to the French Academy Concerning Rhetoric." *Communication Monographs* 45 (1978): 75–84.

# PETER RAMUS

## OF VERMANDOIS

## *Arguments in Rhetoric against Quintilian,*

Dedicated to
CHARLES OF LORRAINE,
*Cardinal Guise.*

PARIS,

*From the press of Matthew David, on the via amygdalina, near the college of Rheims, by the sign of Truth.*

1549.

# PETER RAMUS

## OF VERMANDOIS

## *Arguments in Rhetoric against Quintilian,*

Dedicated to
CHARLES OF LORRAINE,
*Cardinal Guise.*

MOST EXCELLENT Maecenas, the Greeks have a wise proverb which teaches that each man should practice the art which he knows. Although I have been engaged in the study of rhetoric and dialectic for many years, I should not, like other people, care to boast about them; rather I feel ashamed to look back upon them due to the very meager results they produced. And so do I not seem to have some justification if in my studies of these arts I engage rather frequently in the very same argument? I have a single argument, a single subject matter, that the arts of dialectic and rhetoric have been confused by Aristotle, Cicero, and Quintilian. I have previously argued against Aristotle and Cicero. What objection then is there against calling Quintilian to the same account?

Aristotle's logic both lacked many virtues and abounded in faults. He left out many definitions and partitions of arguments; instead of one art of invention embracing the ten general topics—causes, effects, subjects, adjuncts, opposites, comparisons, names, divisions, definitions, witnesses—he created unfathomable darkness in his two books of *Posterior Analytics* and eight books of *Topics* with their confused account of predicables, predicaments, enunciations, abundance of propositions, and the invention of the middle term; in his treatment of simple syllogisms he did not collect the rarer ones; he gave no instruction on connections; he was completely silent about method; in a loud sophistic debate over quite useless rules he handed down to us nothing about the use of the art as a universal, but only as a particular. We have added to the art the virtues it lacked; we have uncovered these various faults and, I hope, have abolished them; we have revealed its true use and have shown it to be common to all things. Consequently, we have fought this dialectical contest over the art and its use with vigor and intelligence.

Our second contest was against Cicero. For he had transferred to rhetoric almost all Aristotle's obscurity concerning invention and arrangement, and indeed also style, confusedly making one art from the two, and then applying it confused in this way to the legal process of civil suits. Some time ago we had taught the virtues of invention and arrangement. By means of a defined, organized and illustrated classification of subjects, my close colleague Audomarus Talaeus cast light on style and delivery and pointed out their deficiencies. To this extent therefore we have here expelled the darkness.

Yet now Quintilian follows Aristotle's and Cicero's confusion of dialectic and rhetoric. Indeed he makes it worse by fabrications of his own, and by including in his teachings all the disputes concerning all the arts he had read or heard something about—grammar, mathematics, philosophy, drama, wrestling, rhetoric. We shall distinguish the art of rhetoric from the other arts, and make it a single one of the liberal arts, not a confused mixture of all arts; we shall separate its true properties, remove weak and useless subtleties, and point out the things that are missing. Thus, just as I previously attacked the Aristotelian obscurity in Cicero, so now in almost the same way I shall attack it in Quintilian. But since the same subject has already been handled in my attack on Aristotle and Cicero, I shall discuss the numerous points more briefly and less rigorously.

Finally, we shall rely on the supreme help of unwavering reason in our attempt to establish the true description and practice of the arts on which, up to this time, I have placed my energy and enthusiasm. For how many days, indeed how many years and ages do we suppose are wretchedly spent on false conjectures about these disciplines? I wish I had not known the wretchedness of wasting so much of my youth in this way. I wish that the scholars of rhetoric and dialectic would heed my advice and would sometimes think of the truth and usefulness of their subjects instead of tenaciously and obstinately quarreling over matters which they have naively accepted at a first hearing, without ever giving them proper consideration. As a result, if the arts were taught with greater conciseness they would certainly be more easily understood, and once the true method for their use was revealed, they would be more easy to practice.

But suppose someone should say, "By almighty God, do you attribute such greatness to yourself that you think you have seen faults or virtues in these arts which have escaped this array of such great men?" Indeed, Maecenas (for I address you and those like you, pure-minded judges unclouded by prejudice), if I were to say that Aristotle was a failure in philosophy, and Cicero and Quintilian each a failure in style, I would seem to be not quite sane. Therefore let us allow Aristotle as sharp an intelligence in various subjects and branches of knowledge as any Aristotelian could imagine, for I admit that that philosopher had an amazing fecundity of talent. Thanks to the generosity of Alexander, he compiled a natural science from the inventions and books of all nationalities; in his logic he questioned all philosophers, physical as well as moral and political; sometimes he showed as much syllogistic reasoning in judgment and as much method in arrangement as could be sought in the best of philosophers.

If you wish, attribute to Cicero these equal ornaments of dialectic, invention, and arrangement. I shall not demur. In fact I shall not only gladly but also perhaps truly admit that of all the men who are, have been, and will in the future be, he was the most eloquent. One could scarcely hope for such excellence of style (which we see in his books) and of delivery (which we learn from stories about him).

I would be acting impudently if I were to admit anything similar about Quintilian. For although he showed a certain shrewdness in the ability to conduct civil suits and although he usefully collected certain examples, nevertheless he differs vastly from Cicero in his style, which is possibly his chief virtue. For in individual words Quintilian does not possess the same purity, appropriateness or elegance. In consequence there is such a great difference that Cicero seems to have spoken in an age of gold, Quintilian in an age of iron. But nevertheless, compared to the eloquent men of that time, he was without doubt counted among the eloquent. I probably could not be like him, even if I should wish so; but in fact if I could, I would not even wish so. Such then were the qualities of Aristotle, Cicero, and Quintilian, and such was their stature. However, must those who excel in one or many virtues necessarily excel in them all? And is it necessary to think them not men, but gods in all things?

At present I am not inquiring after the supreme virtues of other kinds, such as those accorded the Apollos or the Jupiters. I am discussing now the precepts of dialectic and rhetoric, which I admit were almost all in fact either first discovered by those men, to the great glory of their names, or certainly were collected from others. Yet I add the observation that if they had applied as many months as I have years to judging these precepts accurately and to arranging them in order, I certainly do not doubt that they would have left us arts that are far truer and more distinct.

But the writings of these scholars reveal that while they indeed collected a lot of material, they did not evaluate it sufficiently, for in some places I look in vain for a syllogism. And they did not arrange it in a sufficiently fitting order, for elsewhere I find a lack of method. I confidently state that I have truly judged and correctly organized this same material in my teachings. Why so? Because the dialectical and rhetorical arts of Aristotle, Cicero, and Quintilian are fallacious and confused in their treatment of the dialectical and rhetorical usage of reason, and then of speech—the usage, I repeat, which one observes in their books. Mine are truthful and distinct, as both the art and its practice prove when they have been thoroughly investigated. This is the first, the middle, and the final support of my argument. I do not make evil use of the testimonies of men who can lie, but I establish my argument by the truthfulness of unwavering, natural usage, the usage, I repeat, which I have been following for so many years with the greatest effort through daily practice and by experience in the subject.

And so, Maecenas, since I am relying on the very pleasant knowledge of your most just wish, I would be embarrassed if I never wrote what I know about those arts. I shall explain them especially to you since you are not so much my patron as a mutual appreciator of good literature, sent by the grace of God to our France. But we delay too long on the threshold: let us take up the rhetorical controversies.

# PETER RAMUS

## OF VERMANDOIS

## *Arguments in Rhetoric against Quintilian,*

Dedicated to

CHARLES OF LORRAINE,

*Cardinal Guise.*

IT WILL PERHAPS seem to some people an enormous and very difficult task which I propose to undertake against Quintilian, for I shall undertake to teach that his instructions on oratory were not correctly ordered, organized, described—especially so since he seems to define an orator brilliantly at the start, then to divide elegantly the parts of the subjects covered by the definition and finally to delineate the property and nature of each part with extreme care and accuracy. Thus he seems to have looked at everything with especial thought, to have evaluated all things critically and to have organized them methodically. In this disputation, however, I shall, as far as I may, apply dialectic, the mentor of speaking with truth and constancy, in order that I may evaluate the subject with more incisiveness and wisdom. And so, all you dialecticians—that is, whoever can form a judgment about this question with truth and constancy—come here, pay attention, sharpen your wits, drive far away from you (in case passions of this kind have been ready to seize your minds), drive far away, I say, love, hate, prejudice, levity, fickleness, and rashness. Listen to me with willing and impartial minds to the extent that unwavering reason will convince, to the extent that certain conclusion will establish, finally to the extent that truth itself—which cannot be refuted or disproved—will hold firm.

And so first of all let us put forward the definition in which Quintilian outlined for us his ideal orator, and let us refer to this point of dispute everything relevant from all parts of his *Institutiones*. "I teach," he says, "that the orator cannot be perfect unless he is a good man. Consequently I demand from him not only outstanding skill in speaking but all the virtuous qualities of character." This is the type of orator that Quintilian constructs for us. Afterwards in the twelfth book, where he defines him in similar terms as a good man skilled in speaking well, he identifies those virtuous qualities of character as justice, courage, self-control, prudence, likewise knowledge of the whole of philosophy and of law, a thorough acquaintance with history, and many other attributes worthy of praise.

What then can be said against this definition of an orator? I assert indeed that such a definition of an orator seems to me to be useless and stupid: Why? Because a definition of any artist which covers more than is included in the rules of his art is superfluous and defective. For the artist must be defined according to the rules of his art, so that only as much of the art as the true, proper principles cover—this much is attributed to the artist, and nothing further. For a definition is not only a short, clear explanation of a subject but also it is so appropriate to the subject which is being defined that it perpetually agrees with it and is consistent within itself. The grammarian is defined as skilled in speaking and writing correctly; he is not defined as skilled in speaking, writing, and singing. Why not? Because grammar provides no precepts about the last. The geometrician is not defined as skilled in measurement and medicine. Why not? Because there is no precept in geometry which teaches how to cure illnesses.

Therefore let us hold to our axiom and let us lay down this first proposition of a syllogism:

> The definition of an artist which covers more than is included within the limits of the art is faulty.

Then let us add to the first proposition we have put down:

> But the definition of the artist of oratory handed down to us by Quintilian covers more than is included within the limits of the art.

For rhetoric is not an art which explains all the virtuous qualities of character. Moral philosophers speculate appropriately and judiciously on the numerous problems involving the moral virtues and the virtues of intelligence and the mind; mathematicians deal with arithmetic and geometry; men of learning and wisdom, not rhetoricians, discuss separately through their individual studies the remaining important branches of learning including the virtuous qualities of character. I conclude therefore:

Quintilian's definition of the orator is as a result defective.

But suppose Quintilian should say that moral philosophy and the very theory of virtues are proper to rhetoricians, not to philosophers. Then the perfect orator is fashioned who cannot exist unless he has attained all the virtuous qualities of character. However, what if each of these statements is inappropriate and false? Shall we not then confirm the chief point in the conclusion of our syllogism? Accordingly, let us investigate whether instruction in virtues can be considered a part of rhetoric.

Is it because the orator ought to control the state and its citizens that moral training will therefore be a proper part of rhetoric? Undoubtedly it seems this way to Quintilian since he says:

> But I would not grant this, that (as certain men have thought) the principles of a good and upright life should be the responsibility of the philosophers since it is that citizen who is fitted for the administration of public and private matters, who can guide cities by his counsels, fortify them with his laws, and correct them with his judgments, who is assuredly none other than the orator. Accordingly, although I admit that I shall make use of certain things which are contained in the books of the philosophers, nevertheless let me argue that these truly and rightly fall within my field and properly belong to the art of oratory.

This is what Quintilian says, and consequently when he wishes to give a name to a human being who is an ideal leader in the republic and is perfect in every virtue and branch of knowledge, he calls him an "orator"—as if to make him a god rather than just a man skilled in a single art. Yet at this point Quintilian has proposed that he should give instructions about one certain art and virtue, not about perfection in every art and virtue. He thinks rhetoric is one of the liberal arts, not in fact a common art, and yet at the same time he deems rhetoric to be an art, a science, and a virtue. For in these books on oratory he has not described any science of civic skills, any theory of life and its duties, nor finally, in the sections dealing with rhetoric, any instruction in those virtues which he claims are parts of the art of oratory.

Quintilian decrees that there are five parts to the art of rhetoric—I shall talk about these afterwards—invention, arrangement, style, memory, delivery. He thinks there are no more and no less. Yet in no one of these parts does he fit in the moral philosophy which he now attributes to rhetoric. In fact this man was sadly lacking in a knowledge of dialectic. If he had learned from it that in every art and branch of knowledge one must seek out the true, proper, and primary causes of the subject, he would have decided that an orator should be defined quite differently, and he would have learned that he should speculate quite differently on the proper qualities of the arts.

There are two universal, general gifts bestowed by nature upon man, Reason and Speech; dialectic is the theory of the former, grammar and rhetoric of the latter. Dialectic therefore should draw on the general strengths of human reason in the consideration and the arrangement of the subject matter, while grammar should analyze purity of speech in etymology, syntax, and prosody for the purpose of speaking correctly, and also in orthography for the purpose of writing correctly. Rhetoric should demonstrate the embellishment of speech first in tropes and figures, second in dignified delivery. Next, from these general, universal so-called instruments other arts have been formed: arithmetic with its numbers, geometry with its diagrams, other arts with their other subjects. If these arts have been kept separate and enclosed within their own proper limits, then certainly what grammar will teach in its rightful province will not be confused with rhetoric, and dialectic will not encroach upon what each of the others has clearly described. In use these should be united, so that the same oration can expound purely, speak ornately, and express thought wisely. However, the precepts of pure diction, ornate delivery, and intelligent treatment must be kept separate and should not be confused.

Therefore, from this dialectical distinction of subjects, Quintilian should have defined rhetoric so that first of all he would grasp as a whole the material belonging strictly to the art and distinct and separate from all other art's material; then, when it was separated into parts, he could explain it. Thus to conclude this line of reasoning, I shall recall again two syllogisms:

> If moral philosophy were a part of rhetoric, it would have to be expounded in some part of rhetoric.
>
> But in fact Quintilian does this nowhere, nor should it be done at all.
>
> And therefore it is not a part of rhetoric.

Likewise,

> The parts of the material which belong to the art of rhetoric are only two, style and delivery.
>
> However, the parts of the art of rhetoric are the parts of its subject matter and they correspond completely to one another.
>
> Therefore there are only two parts of rhetoric, style and delivery.

But Quintilian will persist, as in fact he does, in the same proposition, and indeed he will urge even more keenly that rhetoric is a virtue—this is in the second chapter of the second book—and that no one can be an orator unless he is a good man (this is in the first chapter of the twelfth book) and for this reason, I believe, he will conclude that instruction in virtue is a part of rhetoric.

Nevertheless it must be seen that each of these statements of Quintilian's opinion is false. For although I admit that rhetoric is a virtue, it is virtue of the mind and the intelligence, as in all the true liberal arts, whose followers can still be men of the utmost moral depravity. Nor is rhetoric a moral virtue as Quintilian thinks, so that whoever possesses it is incapable of being a wicked man. Yet some Stoic philosophers seem to Quintilian—as he points out in the second book—to come cleverly to the following conclusions:

> To be self-consistent as regards what should or should not be done is a virtue, which we name prudence. Consequently, to be self-consistent as regards what should and should not be said will be a virtue. Likewise if a virtue is something whose rudiments have been provided by nature, rhetoric will be a virtue, because its rudiments are provided by nature.

But each one of these supposedly ingenious conclusions is twisted and false. For prudence is not a moral virtue but a virtue of the intelligence and mind. Therefore rhetoric will not be a moral virtue.

Moreover it is absurd to think that these things are moral virtues whose their origins are from nature, as if vices instead of virtues did not rather have their origins in nature. Thus these philosophers deceive Quintilian in that they fabricate a fraudulent sophism instead of a sound syllogism.

For all that, Quintilian continues and maintains his own opinion that since dialectic is a virtue, so therefore is rhetoric. Quintilian should turn the whole thing around and should more correctly conclude that since dialectic is not a moral virtue which can shape a good man, so neither is rhetoric.

"An orator," he then adds, "cannot succeed in panegyric if he is not well versed in the distinctions between what is honorable and what is disgraceful; he cannot succeed in the law courts if he is ignorant of the nature of justice; and he cannot succeed amidst the turbulent threats of the people if he is timid." What then, O Quintilian? Is he who knows what is honest and just, himself honest and just? How few are the spendthrifts and cutthroats who do not know what is honest and just? If the orator should be fearful in the case of Milo, you say he will not speak well. What then is the result? Will rhetoric therefore mean bravery? Undoubtedly the grammarian will not be able to speak correctly if he is frightened, because when he is upset by fear he will pronounce syllables as long instead of short, or short instead of long. And because of his confused memory he will produce impurities of diction and solecisms. Is grammar therefore a moral virtue? Of what sort will the relationship between the two be? Indeed it is one thing to be something that is necessary to the other—quite another thing to be a part, a limb of it. I shall not object to your opinion that moral virtue is undoubtedly useful and suitable for the use of all arts, but in no way shall I admit that any art is a moral virtue.

Finally Quintilian scrapes together the most stupid trifles, saying that since virtue exists in beasts, and courage exists in robbers, it is therefore no wonder that eloquence is a moral virtue. But Quintilian no longer seems to be inexperienced and ignorant only of dialectic but rather of the whole of philosophy, especially of that main branch of philosophy which gives instruction in virtue. O Quintilian, although you say that moral virtue fashions good, respectable, and praiseworthy followers, nevertheless you do not give sufficient thought to what you say when you attribute moral virtue to beasts and robbers. For the future I expect better words than this, or you should think up better advice.

But Quintilian does not let the matter rest, for in the twelfth book he drifts back to that same problem and accumulates similar worthless ideas.

"An evil mind cannot have leisure to devote to rhetoric," he says. Or again, "The greatest part of rhetoric concerns goodness and justice," and "Virtue's authority prevails in persuasion." Of these the first two are absolutely ridiculous and absurd, while the third is like his statement that a timid orator will not plead well. However, let us pass these things by. Meanwhile let us maintain that moral philosophy is not a part of rhetoric, nor is rhetoric itself a moral virtue at all, as Quintilian thought.

Let us come rather to that part where he now says that he intends to fashion the perfect orator; such a man cannot exist unless he is equipped and embellished with all the virtuous qualities of character. Consequently moral philosophy is a part of rhetoric, and virtue must be included in a definition of the orator. It is in this last statement that this entire error can be checked. For truly, suppose that in the name of the perfect orator a politician is now imagined who can handle the public and private cases of his citizens by speaking, who by the authority of his virtue and by the smoothness of his oration can direct the minds of his audience wherever he wishes, who is indeed such a man as the poet describes:

> Then if by chance they have noticed some man grave with his sense of duty and his merits, they fall silent and stand around him with ears pricked; he rules their minds with his words and charms their hearts. [Virgil, *Aeneid* I.xv.1–3]

If, I say, that politician equipped with every art and virtue is the man defined by Quintilian, then Quintilian would have had to expound and describe not merely the one art of rhetoric from among so many arts and virtues, but all the arts and virtues (since that political ability is made up of these)—grammar, rhetoric, dialectic, mathematics, the whole of philosophy. But Quintilian did not do this.

Therefore Quintilian does not fashion the perfect orator about whom he talks, but, as I have said before, he examines only one of the liberal disciplines. In order to make it appear more admirable he confuses it in the following way and deceives himself by this line of reasoning: An orator cannot be perfect without philosophy; therefore philosophy is a part of rhetoric. But I point out—and I blame him for it—that Quintilian has erred here on two accounts, first because he so unwisely uses a false argument and then because he follows it with a fallacious proof. For it is not true that rhetoric cannot be practiced, nor, within reasonable limits, be perfected without moral philosophy. For even before a knowledge of moral philosophy has been acquired, the whole doctrine of style in both tropes and figures, and likewise the whole variety of delivery in both voice and gesture can be explained. At first those excellent qualities of oratory can be revealed and expounded by set examples from the orators and poets. Next, through the exercise of imitation they can be expressed first in writing and next in speaking; finally they can be generally handled and practiced as a whole in whatever kind of exercise you please.

However, those two parts, style and delivery, are the only true parts of the art of rhetoric, as I have demonstrated before. And the order in which the arts should be taught is as follows. The first is grammar, since it can be understood and practiced without the others; the second is rhetoric, which can be understood and practiced without all the others except for grammar.

Moreover, just as the perfect grammarian, one who is outstanding and exceptional (for there is nothing completely perfect either in nature or art or practice even though it is by these things that the art is perfected), just as I say again that the grammarian who has achieved every perfection in his art is to be called perfect, just so the orator who has acquired the consummate, fully developed virtues of oratorical theory clearly must be deemed perfect.

But if you were to add more arts, undoubtedly the man who masters them will have a greater perfection, though the perfection of each separate art will not be greater but the perfection derived from many arts will be joined. Perfect, consummate skill in arithmetic does not mean perfection in geometry, for perfection in the arts must be evaluated and measured from the arts themselves, not summoned outside from alien material. Therefore that pupil who in speaking has learned to vary and embellish his oration with tropes and figures, and likewise to declaim with voice and gesture in harmony, will be my perfect orator—if anything can be considered perfect in the arts—because he has grasped all the perfections of the art of oratory including its virtues and praiseworthy qualities.

In book two Quintilian confirms this very point—but how unwisely he does it! He says that the goal of the orator is not to persuade, because that depends on a chance result for which the art by its own power cannot be responsible, but rather to speak well. Consequently, although the orator may not win, still, if he has spoken well he has achieved his goal, because he has lived up to the ideals of his art. "For," he says, "the pilot wishes to reach port with his ship safe; if, however, he is swept out of his course by a storm, he will not on that account be a bad pilot, and he will utter the familiar saying, 'As long as I can keep a steady helm.'" Here Quintilian truly and generously realizes that the goal of rhetoric, complete perfection, is not found in alien and external matter but in the proper scope of the art itself. Therefore Quintilian should not be ashamed of being reprimanded for his great error—if not by us, then certainly by Quintilian himself. He says at the beginning that rhetoric is not perfect without philosophy; yet afterwards he says that the whole of rhetoric is directed towards itself, and that its goal of perfection does not depend on anything external but is completely and fully contained within the art itself. Therefore let us conclude that rhetoric can be perfected and completed without philosophy. Yet see how great is the advantage which the fairness and soundness of our judgment provides for us.

I have proved by so many arguments the falseness of the argument by which Quintilian was misled. At the same time I admit and allow that all this could be considered most true and certain if what Quintilian wishes could be accomplished in the following way.

Suppose therefore that the practice of rhetoric could not be perfect and complete without the remaining arts and virtues, especially philosophy—will it be right then to agree that whatever is useful and suitable to it is an integral part of rhetoric? Suppose we apply to the dialectician and the arithmetician what Quintilian says about the orator. Neither the dialectician nor the arithmetician can be perfect without a knowledge of all subjects, since the practice of all the arts which concern humanity is linked by a certain common bond and connected by a sort of kinship. Yet who believes that the dialectician and arithmetician are correctly defined if they are called "good men skilled in debate or in calculation" and perfect in every branch of knowledge and virtue? It is one thing to be something that is necessary, another to be an actual property. A house cannot be roofed without a foundation, without the soil of the land, and finally without God; therefore in defining "roof" shall I include all those things? This error would be too absurd. And so Quintilian errs both in argument and in proof.

And yes, as you may remark, I admit that the people labeled the orator according to Quintilian's conception, and I acknowledge that the stupidity inherent in this definition of the orator was due to the stupidity of the inexperienced common people. First of all he was called *rhetor* in Greece; then in Italy the orator was the man who conducted civil cases, like those we now call Advocates. And rhetoricians were named after rhetoric, grammarians after grammar, because at first rhetoric gave instruction in tropes and figures and in those subjects which are the property of rhetoric and common to no further discipline. Then, although the rhetoricians joined to their discipline the subjects of the dialectician—invention, arrangement and memory—and mixed in also many other things, they kept the name *rhetorician*. Finally, under the very same name, law, and philosophy, and the arts of mathematics, and history and the virtues were heaped together so that whoever had joined all these things with eloquence was called an orator.

But I believe that in treating the arts one should follow not the wavering error of the mob but the fixed law of truth. Therefore let us agree that Quintilian's definition for fashioning our orator is redundant and defective; let us agree that moral philosophy is not a part of rhetoric since it is not related to any part of it and is contained in no part of the relevant subject matter; let us agree that the Stoics' reasons are false and deceptive; finally let us agree that that magnificent definition of the orator is full of vain airs and devoid of truth. But enough about the definition of an orator. Although so far Quintilian does not seem to be sufficiently sharp-witted or to argue with sufficient accuracy, yet perhaps he will be sharper and wiser in the partition which follows.

Now the main partition of the work designed by Quintilian for creating an orator is its division into twelve books:

> My first book [he says] will contain those subjects which are preliminary to the task of the rhetorician. In my second I shall deal with the rudiments of the schools of rhetoric and with

> problems concerned with the essence of rhetoric itself. The next five books deal with Invention, and also with Arrangement. Four will be given over to Style, to which are joined Memory and Delivery. There will be one final book in which the orator himself is to be delineated so that, as far as I am able, I can discuss his character, the rules which guide him in undertaking, studying, and pleading cases, the type of style, the time at which he should cease to plead cases, and the pursuits he should follow afterwards.

In Quintilian's partition here, as indeed in his definition, I see his scrupulous care. For he has gathered together into one place everything which the Greeks and Romans handed down about the orator. However, I look in vain for sound judgment. I firmly assert that with the exception of a very few passages dealing with the theory of style and delivery, all the rest of his partition is partly false and partly stupid; certainly everything is confused, out of place, and lacking the illumination of dialectic.

The first book (he says) contains those subjects which are preliminary to the task of the rhetorician. These things therefore, I say, are alien to the art of rhetoric and, since the subject about which he is writing is rhetoric, they should not be placed among its precepts. Yet in these subjects alien to rhetoric Quintilian describes four forms of training for shaping the pupil who is to become an orator.

The first type of schooling, discussed in the first three chapters, concerns the first education of the infant boy: his nurses, parents, companions, proctors, the time, place, and method of learning Greek and Latin letters, and finally, the rudiments of the arts he will soon learn from the order of letters, from writing, from reading, from memory, and from delivery. Although among these there are some true and noteworthy things that are necessary to the first form of training in boys' education, and although so many Latin and Greek writers have produced numerous works dealing with this first education and schooling for boys, who has ever said that this belongs to instruction in rhetoric? Who has included this in rhetorical instructions as something proper to them? Is this method equally appropriate for the senator, the general, and the lawyer as well as for the orator? Arts must be fashioned not only by true but also by proper rules. It is one thing to be something useful, true, and praiseworthy, and another to be the property of some art.

Therefore this form of training has nothing to do with the art of rhetoric, and neither has his thought and understanding of the matter here. But Quintilian failed to analyze and to reason syllogistically, for this one conclusion could have annulled all those things:

> What should be included in the precepts of the arts are their properties;
> These things are not the properties of rhetoric;
> Therefore let them not be included here.

Nor should we keep coming back to this point, that an orator cannot exist without this boyhood education, for this cause is too remote from its effect. Perhaps a doctor cannot be perfect without the same training, yet I do not hear the doctor giving instructions in medicine that derive from that boyhood elementary schooling.

In the next nine chapters the subject of the second form of schooling, the grammatical school, is treated. First of all the same thing should be known about this as about the schooling discussed before. These instructions may be true, they may be useful, they may be necessary to the future orator, but what then? Should they therefore be mixed in with the teachings of oratory? Surely the same studies in grammar are necessary for the philosopher? But who would put up with a philosopher stammering in philosophy about the arts of the grammarians? Of course, the orator should not ignore the grammatical arts—I do not deny it. Indeed they are investigated by the grammarians, and once known are carried over into rhetoric. Let the same syllogism be the judge of this error as of the previous one. This training is not proper to the orator; therefore, let it be removed from the art of oratory.

But nonetheless, in this training Quintilian offends more deeply than in the first. For I say that here things are not only out of place and inappropriate, but that they are false both in the art and in the practice of the art. For in grammar Quintilian makes an almost equal and identical error as in the whole of rhetoric. He makes grammar have two parts, method (*methodicen*) and literary interpretation (*historicen*). To the former he attributes skill in speaking and writing correctly, to the latter interpretation of the poets. In that first part he gives some instructions—confusedly however—on the accent of letters and syllables, on the etymology of the parts of speech, on syntax, and on spelling. These are the complete and only parts of grammar. In addition to the regular subject of its second part (the task of interpreting the poets), he assigns to the grammarian history, music, astrology, philosophy, and finally rhetoric itself, whose handmaiden he wishes grammar to be.

This error arose from the mistaken notion of the unskilled common people—just as we said about the orator. For grammarians were once commonly said to be those men who instructed boys in letters and interpreted the poets for them; in this capacity they would use their knowledge of the various arts beyond grammar. However, the common people did not realize that the scholar who taught various arts in the course of explaining the poets was also a historian, a musician, an astrologer, a philosopher, a man skilled in rhetoric, and thus not merely a grammarian. Indeed in explaining the precepts of theory, Quintilian ought to have made a sharper distinction among these things than the common people could; and so he should have realized that literary interpretation—as he calls it—is no part of grammar. For if that teacher in explaining a poet not only practices the arts of etymology, syntax, prosody and orthography for the purposes of speaking and writing purely and correctly, but adds ethical knowledge in order to explain morality, adds astrology in order to demonstrate the rising and setting of stars, and adds other arts in order to explain matters related to them, certainly he will do this not by virtue of his skill in grammar but by virtue of his skill in those other disciplines. Quintilian almost says the same thing in chapter one of book two, but because of his lack of wisdom he confuses many things. In sum—so that I may be silent about several other things in these six chapters—that division of grammar into method and literary interpretation is false, just as that school on which he has spent so many chapters has nothing to do with rhetorical teaching.

From such an elegant, even dialectical description of the art of grammar Quintilian passes to its practice: that is, the interpretation of authors by the grammarian, the duty of the teacher, and the writing of the pupil. However, he orders the grammarian to lecture to his pupils on only the poets, especially Homer and Virgil. Here I strongly disagree with him. For although I believe that the reading of the poets serves both to arouse the still tender intelligence with various emotions and to make clear the rules of prosody (since the quantity of syllables is understood from the laws of verse), these however are only small and unimportant matters. For the purpose of acquiring an abundant vocabulary for speeches, a deliberative and forensic use of style, and an appropriateness and elegance of diction, I would prefer the pupil to read the letters of Cicero rather than the elegies of Ovid, and the stories of Terence (which are almost like daily speech) rather than the eclogues of Virgil.

Indeed, there is one style for poetry and another for oratory. And perhaps this display of irrelevant instruction explains why Quintilian's oratory was so vastly different from Cicero's, since he believed he should imitate the poets' style, not Cicero's and his followers'. Here therefore Quintilian makes his first mistake, in prescribing only the poets for his pupils.

Next he orders that in teaching and explicating a poet, the grammarian should grant importance to even those lesser functions of methodology such as the proper quality of metrical feet and the meaning of words. However, he says, "He should teach tropes and figures of speech and thought with greater care. Especially he will fix in their minds the value of proper arrangement and of graceful treatment of the subject matter, and he will show what is appropriate to each character, what is praiseworthy in thoughts and in words, where richness of style is to be commended, where restraint."

From what Quintilian says here about the duty of the grammarian, we see that of the two parts of grammar which he has made, methodology, the only real property of this art, is almost despised—while literary interpretation, which has nothing to do with grammar, is especially commended. But indeed, O Quintilian, this teacher should postpone and reserve those subjects—which, though more outstanding, are out of place—for the time when the pupil studies them in the proper sphere of the rhetoricians and philosophers. However, he should handle and practice with every diligence and care those subjects which do belong strictly to his discipline. Here he should spend time; here he should dwell. He should embellish this task in every way: he should explain the primary, original meaning in each expression; then he should illustrate the rules of diction and style with examples; he should constantly examine the sounds of letters, observe accent, and pay attention to spelling; finally he should realize that his sole, total responsibility is to teach the pupil committed to his training how to speak and write correctly. However, he should use those greater and more exalted subjects which you here so strongly recommend, only as far as is helpful for carrying out the methodology which you spurn.

Indeed, once the pupil has diligently practiced all the parts of grammar by speaking and writing, he will then use the wisdom of rhetoricians in tropes and figures, and the wisdom of philosophers in the remaining virtues. Quintilian himself says the same thing later, but, as so often elsewhere, he imprudently contradicts himself, saying as follows in the seventh chapter of this book:

> These parts of speaking and writing correctly are the most important; I do not indeed take away from the grammarians the two remaining parts of speaking with elegance and significance, but since I still have to deal with the tasks of the rhetorician, I am reserving these for a more important part of the work.

Then afterwards, in chapter one of book two, he complains that the duties of the rhetoricians have been taken over by the grammarians.

Quintilian says that grammar is the theory of speaking and writing correctly. Yet the same Quintilian also directs the grammarian to teach how to speak and write, not correctly, but rather decoratively by means of tropes and figures, and wisely and appropriately by means of planning, judgment, and prudence. But the first alone belongs to grammar, while the rest belongs to rhetoric and philosophy. Therefore Quintilian does not describe the proper duties of the teacher of grammar, but very unwisely mixes in those that are not proper and are out of place; he has fallen again into the snare of his previous error.

"The final part in the practice of the art of grammar," says Quintilian, "is that the pupil should analyze the verses of the poets he has been prescribed; next he should explain their meaning in different words; then with more boldness he should turn to a paraphrase; he should abbreviate certain lines and embellish others; and he should explain set aphorisms when the general scheme has been given."

But how will the Roman pupil who has been entrusted to the teacher of grammar explicate Homer in different words when he was not able to understand Homer's own words in the first place without his teacher's explanation? For the Roman pupil is not handed over to the instruction of a Greek grammarian in order to use his native gift of speech for other subjects—for where did the young child's native gift come from?—but in order to pursue the gift of speech by hearing, reading, imitating. And this third error as regards practice is equal to the second. For Quintilian imposes on the learner of grammar as well as on the teacher of the same art the functions not of grammar but of rhetoric, both its clearly established theory and its practice. And so Quintilian errs far more seriously in this second prescription than in the first. For there he recorded things that were out of place, whereas here he also muddles together things that are false, both in the art of grammar, of which he makes literary interpretation a part, and in its practice, first because he prescribes that only poets should be read, and then because he instructs the teacher and the pupil in that method. I am not saying here that Quintilian lacked care in seeking out and finding material, but I do very much long to see in him wisdom in judgment and syllogistic reasoning.

In the remaining three chapters of the first book two new fields are described for Quintilian's orator. In one of these he should learn mathematical arts, and in the other he should study teachers of comedy, tragedy, and wrestling in order to acquire dignity of voice and gesture. Such instructions concerning mathematics in the rhetorical arts are even more amazing than those concerning grammar, even though Quintilian says very little more on the subject. Nevertheless, if you imagine that Quintilian teaches mathematical arts separately, what sort of a sequence will this be for educating youth? Rhetoric in its rules of style and delivery, and dialectic in its instructions on invention and arrangement, are more general and common than all the mathematical arts, and from those universal sources of the sciences the mathematical arts, like fountains, have flowed separately. Therefore rhetoric and dialectic go first in the order of learning, and every branch of mathematics follows. On the other hand one cannot say on Quintilian's behalf that at one time the arts were handed down to pupils in this way. For mathematics were for a long time the first and only arts, and no others could be treated before them because there were none. For, as long as language was basic, there was virtually no grammar, and before Isocrates absolutely nothing was taught about rhetoric. But since subjects can not only be taught and understood, but can be easily taught and understood when the arts for this purpose have been discovered, I believe we must now inquire into what at this time ought to be done, not into what once was usually done. As if with one voice, all the schools of every master teach that progress and instruction in the arts develop from universals to particulars. Consequently grammar, rhetoric, and dialectic must go first; mathematics must follow. I pursue the fundament of truth, not the error of custom.

Quintilian sends us from the mathematicians to the comedians and tragedians and wrestlers. They could be useful if we lived in Quintilian's time, because then those men took great pains to develop properly the voice and body, though not in a manner suitable for the writer of an art. For arts ought to consist of subjects that are constant, perpetual, and unchanging, and they should consider only those concepts which Plato says are archetypal and eternal. There was, and will be, however, no time and no place in which refinement of voice and gesture could not be elegantly produced or studied. There were and will be many times and places, when there were, and will be, no comedians or tragedians or wrestlers. Therefore Quintilian does not act correctly when he hands over a constant and unchanging art to such impermanent teachers.

Now in all these remarks so far, we see that there is no lack of variety and abundance of subject matter, but rather that it is the rationale of the syllogism and of judgment that is missing. Quintilian has thrown together here whatever he believed would be useful to the orator, without considering whether those things were true properties of this branch of education.

We should refer all these teachings to dialectic and we should abide by its judgment: the first kind of training in infancy has nothing to do with rhetoric; the second concerning grammar is not only alien to rhetoric but is false in many parts; the third and fourth likewise are completely alien and muddled in a variety of ways. What therefore should we expect the opinion of dialectic to be except an order to drive out and abolish from rhetorical teachings all those studies which are not only inappropriate but are false and awkwardly confused? So much then for the first book.

In the second book, Quintilian says, he treats the first principles taught by the teacher of rhetoric and inquires into the very essence of rhetoric. But first of all, before anything is said about the first exercises in rhetoric, come three fulsome, expansive chapters about the age at which a boy should be sent to the rhetorician, about the character and duties of the instructor, and about whether the best instructor should be employed straight away. I grant that such things are dependable, true, praiseworthy, useful; but how can I grant that they are true properties of this art and doctrine, described to direct the pupil towards a short, clear way of speaking? Suppose Donatus investigated similar things in the treatment of his art, such as when the pupil should be taken from teaching at home to the grammarian, what kind of character the grammarian ought to have, and whether the best grammarian should be employed straight away; investigation of these problems would be as useful in grammar and every branch of learning as here in rhetoric. But not everything which can be investigated with truth and usefulness can also be investigated with strict appropriateness and relevance to the matter taught. The best teacher ought to follow a short, easy path in his teachings. Why then is such a thorny, such a twisty path with diversions and side tracks undertaken? I acknowledge here Quintilian's very great care and diligence in gathering together subject matter, but I acknowledge no dialectical skill at all in his discrimination and judgment of that subject matter.

In the next four chapters there is a completely muddled discussion about rhetorical training. First of all, the pupils should be given practice in the recounting of fictional and realistic narrative and of historical fact, by means of corroboration, refutation, praise, and blame. I denounce Quintilian's precept not wholly but in part, because it is not put in the right place or order. An art should first of all be described, and then the method of practicing the art, first in writing, secondly also in speaking, should be made clear. But nevertheless let us look at the entire instruction concerning practice which Quintilian recorded in this place.

Previously Quintilian had assigned only the poets for grammatical exercises. Now for rhetorical studies he prescribes first the historian and then the orator, so that pupils receive lectures on the poets first, then on the historians and finally on the orators. I previously spoke about the poets, and I am really surprised that it occurred to Quintilian to think that poets and historians were more suitable than orators for fashioning an orator, especially since Quintilian warns in his very own teachings that the orator should avoid several of the virtues of the poets and historians, not to mention their frequent rather licentious and loose treatment of their subjects. Will Livy or Sallust fashion the orator better than Cicero? Indeed in the shaping of a poet I would prefer Virgil and Homer and the other outstanding, famous poets, to any orator. Likewise in educating an orator I would prefer Cicero by far to all the historians and poets. Indeed, does an orator seem more at home among historians than among orators? Consequently I judge that this whole chapter is not only out of place but that its advice is false.

The next two chapters about the division of subject matter and about speaking are useful—let us hope they are also true! But as in the chapter above, these two are not put in the right place or order. Previously, Quintilian talked first about the art of grammar and then about its practice, and in this he was correct. For an art must be described and learned before its practice is discussed. However, the art of rhetoric has not yet been described by Quintilian; therefore his instructions on its practice are unsuitable at this point. Here as before I look in vain for judgment and syllogistic reasoning from Quintilian.

The next seven chapters contain investigations of learning, of the pupil's task, of the method of teaching the pupil, of the usefulness of declamation, of whether knowledge of the art is necessary, of the reason the uneducated often seem to the mob to have more talent, and of what boundary the art possesses. All these subjects are even more alien to the prescriptive description of the art of rhetoric than those we have discussed so far. The last part about the limit of the art seems especially true, namely that the teachings of rhetoric are not universal but changeable according to the variety of time, place, character, and case. But if the art of rhetoric were properly understood by its parts, style and delivery, this would be flagrantly wrong. For rhetoric will be an art almost as fixed as arithmetic or geometry, and its precepts concerning style and delivery will be as unchanging as Euclid's theorems of the plane and line. But Quintilian calls his teachings—which are a tightly packed, confused mixture of various arts aimed at Roman rules for forensic and civilian cases—the art of rhetoric; nor is it surprising that we say about such an art that its rules must not be trusted, since they are so deceptive and false, as well as inharmonious with every place, time, and character. Thus in the first book and in the thirteen chapters of the second book Quintilian treats things that are outside the main body of rhetoric.

Then, in a section rather like another preface, he says that the remaining eight chapters of the second book concern the essence of rhetoric; and without doubt in the fourteenth chapter the essence of rhetoric is treated to a certain extent. However, Quintilian does not go far enough when he appears to wish to explain the origin of the word *rhetoric*, for a person does not at all reveal its etymology by saying that in Latin *rhetoric* is translated as "oratoria" or "oratrix," but by explaining what the origin of the word is and from where it derived its meaning.

He divides the entire following theory into three parts so that he discusses the art, the artist, and the work—a totally ridiculous and senseless division. The second and the third part are understood from the definition of the first. In grammar the grammarian is not defined, nor the work of the grammarian. In arithmetic and geometry neither the instructors nor their work are defined because the art reveals what the artist and the special work of the art should be like. And so I look in vain here for Quintilian to give us dialectical rules of division.

Moreover, all the other points about the various disputed definitions of rhetoric—for instance, that rhetoric is a useful skill, what art it is and of what kind, that art bestows more than nature, whether rhetoric is a virtue, and what its subject matter is—these points are so confused and wordy that they are clearly the work of a teacher who wishes to scare away, break down, or deceive the ignorant novices of this art. Nevertheless, at the start of the eighth book Quintilian in fact strongly condemned this kind of teacher; in the same place he applauded the teacher who by a different way, simple and short, wishes to lead to the practical application of the art.

But what is the use of piling up, so to speak, the mistaken notions of so many people concerning the definition of rhetoric, its usefulness, and its art, and even of mixing in false notions such as the idea that the gift of art more than nature is responsible for the orator of consummate skill? For if, as is fitting, nature, art and practice are kept separate in this investigation of the perfect orator, then undoubtedly we would attribute the first importance to nature (as Cicero correctly realizes in the second book of *De oratore*), the second to practice, and the third and least to art. And we shall show that Quintilian's following sophism is false: when he says that instruction has more bearing on perfection than nature, he covers nature, art, and practice (under the art's single name), although nevertheless he compares nature with art in this investigation. Here there is not even a single grain of dialectical salt. This teacher can make no distinctions, no evaluations with any genuineness and constancy: in dialectic he is without doubt totally leaden.

Quintilian's arguments on the question of whether rhetoric is a virtue are quite ridiculous; but since these were discussed at the beginning it is not necessary to discuss them again.

In the final chapter Quintilian is completely preoccupied with investigating the subject matter of rhetoric and makes various remarks about the different opinions concerning this subject. In the end he concludes that the subject matter of rhetoric is everything which is brought before it as a subject of speech. This statement is hardly sound, complete or clear, first of all because the material of the art is one thing, the material of the artist truly another. The art of rhetoric assigns to itself natural usage observed in the examples of good stylists and explained by precepts; the artist, that is the orator trained in the art of rhetoric, assigns to himself everything that can be embellished by speech. In the same way the subject matter of the grammarian is everything which is laid down before him for speaking or writing correctly; the subject matter of the dialectician is everything which is laid before him for correct debate; the subject matter of the arithmetician is everything which is laid before him for calculation; the subject matter of the geometrician is everything which is laid before him for measurement. But then I do not deny that sometimes we talk figuratively—*tropikôs*—of the material of the art instead of the material of the artist. Hence this definition of subject matter does not receive sufficient explication; nevertheless, I approve and accept it as teaching appropriate to true rhetoric. In the two first books of the instructions in oratory, out of the many forms of training—domestic, grammatical, mathematical, with comic and tragic actors, with wrestling instructors, and finally with a rhetorician—there are only two statements which can be praised and approved of in true rhetoric. Rhetoric is the science of speaking well; the subject matter of the orator is whatever is laid before him as a subject for speech. Although indeed the many other things are true and useful in some places, nevertheless in an accurate description of the art of rhetoric they are all either completely out of place, or patently absurd.

My dispute with Quintilian's first two books has up until now dealt with the part where grammar in particular is confused. In the next five books the discussion concerns dialectic, specifically invention and arrangement. Therefore we must discuss these parts next, as well as the separate chapters. And so in the first chapter of the third book Quintilian gathers together the discoveries of all the Greek and Latin teachers about this art, and with intense but useless diligence he reviews the teachers themselves by name. For this list of so many names sheds no light on the theory of rhetoric, no more than if in grammar, through his love of vanity, he were to seek out by name all the writers about grammar; this catalogue, I say, sheds no light on the theory. A lack of judgment and of syllogistic reasoning has caused his vanity to overflow.

The next chapter is the same. Here Quintilian does not separate with sufficient sharpness rhetoric's cause and origins, its nature, its usefulness, its art, and its practice. What is the problem? Were Plato and Cicero wrong? Or was Quintilian himself wrong when in the fifth chapter of this book he teaches that rhetoric is perfected and completed by three things: nature, art, and practice? How is usefulness different from those three causes and origins? For nothing either conceived by nature, described by art, or handled by practice is futile and without some usefulness. This is a dialectical nicety of division indeed, that what you ought to explain in three parts you expand into four by a new creation.

In the third chapter rhetoric is separated into five parts: invention, arrangement, style, memory, delivery. I am now not at all surprised that Quintilian is so bereft of dialectic in this division, for he was unable to recognize that here he has confused dialectic itself with rhetoric, since invention, arrangement, and memory belong to dialectic and only style and delivery to rhetoric. Indeed, Quintilian's reason for dividing rhetoric into these five parts derived from the same single source of error as did the causes of the previous confusion. The orator, says Quintilian, cannot be perfected without virtue, without grammar, without mathematics, and without philosophy. Therefore, one must define the nature of the orator from all these subjects. The grammarian, the same man says, cannot be complete without music, astrology, philosophy, rhetoric and history. Consequently there are two parts of grammar, methodology and literary interpretation. As a result Quintilian now finally reasons that rhetoric cannot exist unless the subject matter is first of all discovered, next arranged, then embellished, and finally committed to memory and delivered. Thus these are the five parts of rhetoric.

This reasoning of Quintilian's often deceived and misled him without any need (as some men report). I propose rather—as I have already said—that we should argue and deliberate quite differently the questions concerning the proper nature and the true divisions of the arts. I consider the subject matters of the arts to be distinct and separate. The whole of dialectic concerns the mind and reason, whereas rhetoric and grammar concern language and speech. Therefore dialectic comprises, as proper to it, the arts of invention, arrangement, and memory; this is evident because, as we find among numerous dumb persons and many people who live without any outward speech, they belong completely to the mind and can be practiced inwardly without any help from language or oration. To grammar for the purposes of speaking and writing well belong etymology in interpretation, syntax in connection, prosody in the pronunciation of short and long syllables, and orthography in the correct rules for writing. From the development of language and speech only two proper parts will be left for rhetoric, style, and delivery; rhetoric will possess nothing proper and of its own beyond these.

And here I am not arguing like Quintilian on the basis of the *sine qua non* for the subject, but by a proper, legitimate line of reasoning:

> In every art one should teach as many parts as exist in its proper, natural subject matter, and no more.
>
> To the subject matter of the art of dialectic, that is to the natural use of reason, belongs the skill of inventing, arranging, and memorizing.
>
> Therefore it should deal with the same number of parts.

Likewise,

> To the subject matter of rhetoric pertains only the ascribed skill of style and delivery.
>
> Therefore it should deal with the same number of parts.

Likewise,

> The parts of another art should not be intermingled with the art of rhetoric.
>
> Invention, arrangement, and memory are parts of another discipline, namely dialectic.
>
> Therefore they should not be intermingled with rhetoric.

However, in other places Quintilian shows us with his very own testimony that those parts belong to dialectic. For in the last chapter of the fifth book he speaks as follows about dialecticians: "Those learned men, seeking for truth among men of learning, subject everything to a detailed, scrupulous inquiry, and they thus arrive at the clear, acknowledged truth so that they can claim for themselves the parts of invention and judgment, calling the former *topiké*, the latter *kritiké*." Here Quintilian says that the dialecticians lay claim to invention and judgment (which contains a large part of arrangement in the conclusions of each argument and in syllogisms). And finally in the second chapter of the eleventh book he says that if memory belongs to any art, then it belongs completely to arrangement and order. Therefore he should say that the dialecticians could rightly claim this part also, because in dialectic that has been rightly described, one should teach the truest theory of order and arrangement according to the precepts of the syllogism and method.

In this chapter Quintilian disproves the various opinions concerning the number of these five parts, but he does this in such a way that he himself makes far worse mistakes than do those whose mistakes he censures. Some men added that judgment is rather different from invention and arrangement. Quintilian correctly censures these men, not however with a correct argument but with one that is very clumsy and ignorant of what true judgment is. Quintilian thinks that judgment is so inextricably mixed in with invention, arrangement, style, and delivery that it cannot be separated from them by theory or precepts; he does not recognize any theory of judgment at all but, as he explains later in the last chapter of the sixth book, he considers that judgment can no more be transmitted by art than can taste or smell.

In this way Quintilian reveals himself to be quite ignorant of dialectic, for he has either not heard or not read anything about the role of judging, and about the many types of syllogisms, both simple and complex. He has not remembered that Cicero said the following about the Stoics, that as long as they labored in only the one part of dialectic, they did not reach the arts of invention, and yet they did diligently follow the paths of judgment.

Nor indeed should we consider it possible that rhetorical judgment is one thing and dialectical judgment another, since for evaluating whether something is truly useful, suitable, fitting, or has the qualities it seems to have, there is one faculty of judgment which the syllogism alone executes and accomplishes. For something to be understood as true or false by the rule of the syllogism is no different than it would be for a subject of control and debate to be spoken truly or falsely. Why should I say here that Quintilian knew nothing of the theory of judgment or of the teaching of the syllogism when he himself denies that any at all can exist? Why should I now make a case with many arguments that Quintilian has no training in dialectic? For he not only confesses what I argue, but openly declares it. He says that two arts are claimed by the dialecticians—one invention, the other judgment—but he does not believe what he says, because he maintains that there is no art of judgment.

Therefore let us continue, and let us still use the art of judgment against this rhetorician who lacks the art and theory of judgment. Let us refer his opinion about the remaining subjects to the standard of dialectical judgment. His next instructions are indeed wonderfully confused.

In the fourth, fifth, sixth, tenth, and eleventh chapters he discusses the orator's subject matter and its separation into parts. Let us therefore first of all take up the debate over this question. First Quintilian decrees that there are three classes of causes, demonstrative, deliberative, and forensic. He uses Aristotle as the author of this division, the very man who—to repeat what I have already taught in my "Observation against Aristotle"—was virtually the sole author and inventor of all the obscurity in this art, who was the first to mix dialectical invention in with the art of rhetoric, and who organized his inquiries so awkwardly and so ridiculously.

I say first of all that this partition is false, since there are countless questions which are not contained in any part of these classes. Quintilian saw this when he said,

> But then a feeble attempt was made, first by certain Greeks, then by Cicero in his books of the *De oratore*, and now almost forcibly by the greatest authority of our times, to prove that there are not only more than these three kinds but also that they are practically countless. For if we place the task of praise and denunciation in the third division, in what kind of oratory shall we seem to be engaged when we complain, console, pacify, excite, terrify, encourage, instruct, explain obscurities, narrate, plead for mercy, give thanks, congratulate, reproach, vilify, describe, command, retract, express our desires and opinions, and so on? As a result I must ask pardon, so to speak, for remaining an adherent of the older view, and I must ask what were the motives which caused earlier writers to confine so closely a subject of such variety.

He recites these things with a certain grandeur, so that he appears to have solved a difficult matter; he does not seem to have understood the force of the argument which he uses against himself but, content with a fallacious, faulty solution, he has ensnared and deceived himself.

Quintilian, however, thinks he meets this objection in the following way: "In the course of a thorough examination of all these things," he says, "the following line of reasoning helped, that the entire task of the orator is either in the law courts, or outside the law courts." Agreed: and so? "The type of the objects of investigation in the law courts is obvious," he says. I admit this; what then? "Those matters which do not come before a judge either deal with past or future time," he says. Why, I ask? Can there not exist any question, any dispute, any occasion for speaking that deals with a contemporary subject? When there is an investigation of this syntax, this square, this star, this wound, this rhetoric, or countless matters of this kind, does the investigation concern a past or future rather than a contemporary matter? Consequently this is false.

But go on, nevertheless. "We praise or denounce past action," he says, "we deliberate about the future." But cannot the opportunity also be offered for investigating, consoling, pacifying, exciting, terrifying and doing countless other things that concern past and future? Thus Quintilian here concludes nothing, solves nothing, but confuses himself.

But another clear proof is added to the one above. "All subjects of speech," he says, "must either be certain or doubtful." What then, O Quintilian? What will you achieve by this division? "We praise or blame what is certain, according to each person's inclination," he says. Yet, like Cicero and Caesar in the Cato debate, we do praise and blame many uncertain things, and of course without either praising or blaming we treat many certain things, such as the almost limitless functions of the subjects covered by the liberal and practical arts. Therefore, part of this division is false.

"In some cases," he says, "dubious matters require deliberation, in other cases, litigation." Truly I look in vain here for the same statement as in the previous section, that the things which are doubtful to the ignorant are the countless subjects covered by the arts. Should a man who is ignorant of those arts guide the deliberation of the people or the judgment of the law courts according to Quintilian's precepts, instead of employing and seeking information from a learned, experienced man? O capricious and artless proposal! By this devious argument has Quintilian refuted the objections thrown against him? Has he in this way opposed the greatest author of his times? Yet his method is not to refute false arguments by true arguments, but rather to confirm true arguments by false sophisms.

Quintilian adds to this last quasi-solution one other. He abridges all those other species into the three kinds, but in a quite insolent manner that is inappropriate for a writer of the art. Indeed he wished to overrule us by the force of his authority, since he can prove nothing true by reason. I look in vain here for dialectical wisdom in his partition. Now I am saying not only that Quintilian errs without the art of judgment but also that he rambles on without any understanding of invention.

Partitions of questions of a similar but far greater uselessness follow in the whole of chapters five, six, and eleven. I have decided not to use up the greater part of my discourse against these by teaching that they are stupid and false, but rather I have decided that I should use one comprehensive refutation for so many foolish statements. I say therefore that the whole partition and division of these questions is clearly futile not only in the art of rhetoric, which is composed truly and appropriately from the parts of style and delivery, but also in this confused art of Quintilian's which is thrown together from the parts of invention, arrangement, style, memory and delivery. Since we indeed feel this way, let us repeat this line of argument from our "Observations against Aristotle."

> A theory common to the subjects laid before it for treatment seeks no partition of these subjects.

For instance, in grammar there is no division of the subjects laid before grammar for treatment, because grammar is a common art that deals with all aspects of writing and speaking.

> Rhetoric, though confused by Quintilian into five parts, is a theory completely common to the subjects laid before it for treatment.

For there is one art common to memory, delivery, and style, and their parts are not variously adapted to various questions—unless I do not know what is taught concerning the quality of style, and about the classification of arguments as either demonstration, deliberation, or adjudications; even then, there is not another art of tropes and figures, but another use. I shall demonstrate my proof concerning invention and judgment in their place.

But indeed I shall instead agree with Quintilian's opinion that rhetoric is defined as the science of speaking well, not about this or that, but about all subjects.

Rhetoric therefore requires no partition of its areas of investigation.

Here I am not using fallacious or obscure proofs, but I am explaining the first and most important reason for dividing a question. If a question were to be divided in rhetoric, this would happen because some fixed arts are suited to fixed questions; not all parts of those arts as a whole would agree with all questions. But I contend that this is false, and I hold this to be plain and obvious first of all in respect to the three parts, style, memory, and delivery; in respect to the other two parts, invention and arrangement, I hold the same position about those things necessary for speaking.

Indeed the chief point of the whole confusion is in invention alone. The theory of memory and delivery is not repeated very often and is not confused in so many ways; it is dealt with once, and in one place only. The teaching of style through tropes and figures is not muddled by the same repeated and confused classifications; although Quintilian burdened this part with many unrelated subjects, still he did handle it altogether in a single place over the eighth and ninth books. In various places Quintilian says many things about the teaching of arrangement, proofs, questions, and the parts of a speech; he infers no universal and general (if I may use his word) precept. I say again that the chief point of this rhetorical confusion occurs entirely in invention; the reason for this we can see from reason and from the developments of history.

For I see that the scholars and teachers of this art have spent greater zeal in collecting the instructions of the ancients and in thinking up new instructions than they have used judgment in discriminating among their own and others' discoveries. The purpose of the early rhetoricians before Aristotle was not to record some general theory for speaking eloquently about all subjects, but only to draw up for forensic and civil cases some advice concerning the rules for amplification through tropes and figures. Other writers suggested other things about how to move the audience to anger, pity, envy, indignation, and similar passions, and about the classification of causes (demonstrative, deliberative, and judicial). Later Aristotle collected all their material together with great eagerness and care, and he mixed up these first arts with the universal, common topics of dialectical invention; he also gave some thought to delivery; later memory was added to rhetoric. Thus he entangled the arts of invention in as many ways as we have them now, despite the fact that only one general theory—separated into the ten topics of causes, results, subjects, adjuncts, opposites, comparisons, names, divisions, definitions, and witnesses—could be adapted to make clear most easily and plainly all questions, all parts of a speech, and finally all subjects.

But someone will say that in the classification of causes and the parts of a speech these lesser arts of invention are described for uneducated novices, whereas the more important and more common arts belonging to the universal topics are described for the pupils who have already made some progress in those studies. I hear them, I say, and I know that this is said in the second book of Cicero's *De oratore*, for there Antony speaks as follows about these topics of invention:

> If, however, I should wish that someone quite unskilled should be taught to speak, I would instead hammer with undivided zeal on the same anvil night and day, and I would thrust all the tiniest morsels, everything chewed very small, as the nurses say, down the young pupil's throat. But if he is generously instructed in the theory and already familiar with some usage, and if moreover he seems to be of sharp enough intelligence, I would snatch him away, not to some remote, landlocked rivulet, but to the source of the mighty, universal river. This site, as the home of all proofs, would reveal them to him through brief illustration and verbal definition.

Thus Cicero spoke there in Antony's voice.

Here I wish to lay down a comprehensive rebuttal to Cicero—namely, that in his rhetorical precepts there is almost nothing of Ciceronian judgment or intelligence; rather, he dealt merely with the rules of teachers and rhetoricians whom he had heard or read, Aristotle in particular. Cicero did not become eloquent from these rules, and his eloquence can easily be seen as splendid, not because of his own mixed-up rules but because of our own rules, which we make conform to his achievements. There is yet another point in respect to the authority of Cicero: Do we wish the authority of any man in a debate concerning an art to be superior to the truth of the case? Consider some similar proof in another body of instruction for an art. Suppose the grammarian should define a noun and should expound as a whole all the circumstantial adjuncts of the noun and its accidents. Because this is comprehensive, because it is general, we consider it sufficient for all nouns. We look for no lesser arts, nor could any particular art be more easily explained than that general one. The same proof obviously holds for the theory of invention.

Our instructor teaches that all the things which one can say about anything are either causes, effects, subjects, adjuncts, opposites, comparisons, names, divisions, definitions, or witnesses, and he carefully explains these things; indeed he explains the theory of all reasonings and of all arguments. No instruction trimmed so closely could be more appropriate, nor is there any better or easier way taught for deliberating on and discovering what should be said about a subject brought forward for treatment than these many forms of appraisal which Quintilian uses in the areas of investigation and in the parts of a speech.

For this reason there is no way an excuse can be permitted for such a great muddle.

But let us turn to these arts of invention which Quintilian teaches in the classification of causes, in the divisions of a speech, and in the common topics. Let us teach that nothing apart from our ten topics should be included in them, and that nothing better can be shown for teaching and helping youth. For I allege and assure you that these ten topics are the only ones, and that apart from these there is nothing taught in the numerous inventions of Quintilian that can be truly referred to the rationale of theory.

The seventh chapter deals with demonstration. What topics of praise different from ours does Quintilian handle here? None. Instead he makes a muddle of four of ours and does not adopt them as complete in themselves as causes, effects, adjuncts, and witnesses. For he teaches that the source of demonstration derives from parents and ancestors who in our topics are the procreative causes; likewise it derives from discoveries, exploits, words, and deeds, which are effects; likewise it derives from the condition of mind, body, and fortune, which are adjuncts; likewise from divine witnesses; no classification of argument beyond these is of any concern.

Here therefore Quintilian reveals nothing about invention that is not more useful and suitable in our topics, but here is not even made distinct and separate. He adds a few things about arrangement, namely that we should follow either a chronological order or the distribution of various characteristics. We ought to follow the latter in every dispute which proceeds along straight and orderly lines. We can, however, apply the second to the first, and for the sake of clear understanding we ought to do this. Florus did this in his praise of the Roman people in which he follows a chronological order and yet divides the complete work into four parts. Livy had done the same thing in his complete history composed in gradual stages. And so Quintilian has shown nothing here that is the true property of demonstration, and the things he thinks are separate can best be joined. For this art of universal invention is likewise also suited to demonstration.

In the chapter dealing with deliberation Quintilian fails to write about the topic of invention, or to make clear any method of arrangement; he expands the whole subject with mere trifles. Moreover, Quintilian taught nothing separately about the judicial classification; he referred to its theory in books four and five. However, these things concerning the parts of a speech, and likewise concerning the common, general topics of invention, are generally taught by other rhetoricians. And so let us conclude first of all that Quintilian in his classification of causes does not describe any arts that are proper to invention; as a result there should be a division of classes into questions and causes. Next let us likewise conclude this, that although I admit that arts of invention for praise or deliberation were shown, none was relevant apart from the one species of causes, the results, the adjuncts, and the divine witnesses. Our ten topics explain all these things thoroughly. For if there is a question concerning praise and advice, without doubt our instructions will open all those sources of dialectical wisdom in the classification of causes, in results, in the many parts and manners of subjects, adjuncts, and opposites, and in the abundant and brimming topics for the remaining arguments. A choice of subjects and a method will almost be difficult for you, since such an abundance of material will be offered.

And so what sort of a dialectician do we acknowledge here, one who says that there is no theory of judgment, and who when he decrees that the art of invention is threefold, puts forward such a useless and sterile art of invention as this first one in the classification of causes? The second art of invention which follows is placed by Quintilian among the parts of a speech. Since he argues first about the number of those parts, we must therefore say something about them.

And so in the ninth chapter Quintilian constructs two duties for a judicial case—the bringing and rebutting of charges—and five parts for a speech—the introduction, the statement of facts, the proof, the refutation, and the peroration—as if in demonstration and deliberation there were not an argument over the interpretation of an action that leads to either some charge or a rebuttal; as if also these five parts of a speech could not be identified in other questions; and as if all these things, whether duties or parts proper to the judicial question, were not common to all questions.

But we must say a little more about the parts of a speech. For with the exception of this division there is not a spark of true and artistic arrangement in the whole of Quintilian's rhetoric. The dialectical method (as I have stated in my teachings) gives the following instruction: that in a great debate which we wish to conduct along straight and orderly lines, the matter in its entirety should be put in the first position and then divided into parts and species; and we should follow to the limit each separate part and its lesser divisions (by proof and explanation) so that the universals go first, and the particulars follows. Some rhetoricians point out that as a second order of method and arrangement there are two parts necessary for pleading (although if the question were simple it would not have parts), namely the statement of facts and the proof; and that two parts which are not necessary can nevertheless be sometimes adopted, namely the introduction and the peroration. Aristotle is the source of this opinion. Others wanted a speech to have four parts, introduction, statement of facts, proof, peroration; Cicero subscribed to this opinion in his *De partitionibus oratoria*. Still others had named five parts, like Quintilian here. Some people named more than five parts, although they all had some grasp of the rules for that artistic order by which the subject as a whole would precede the treatment of its parts. Thus a summary of the subjects is usually placed in the exordium, and they are generally treated by division in the parts that follow.

But nevertheless the instructions of these rhetoricians were confused in this respect, that in their description of order they failed to distinguish between the topics of invention and the methods of style. This is not surprising; since these men had no separate arts of dialectic and rhetoric, and since they handled the same subjects repeated and confused by a thousand obscurities, why was it surprising that they generated such variant and clashing opinions about these subjects? Wherefore we shall omit any dialectical praises for the third book in its division of questions and its explanation of the inventions of demonstration and deliberation. I have learned how great a dialectician Quintilian was! How perceptive and careful he was in investigating the causes of things! And in showing the practical application of his theory! Let us see how great a philosopher he was, and of what sort, when he brought forward for the parts of a speech an invention which described new kinds of arguments in the exordium and the statement of facts. He reserved for the other remaining parts of a speech the general topics of teaching, arousing and delighting, and dealt with no topics proper to each one.

I am afraid, however, that many people may not pay sufficient attention to what I am arguing against Quintilian concerning this second art of invention. Quintilian identifies five parts of eloquence: invention, arrangement, style, memory, and delivery. Therefore, I say that Quintilian must refer all his instructions in eloquence to one of those parts. He teaches nothing about memory and delivery in the exordium and statement of facts; he confuses the very few instructions concerning style and arrangement. And so I say that a theory of invention is left, which not only has nothing that could be referred to the true art of invention, but is one which I declare to be completely unreliable, sophistic, pedantic, and utterly puerile.

Let us first of all seek the reason why special inventions are prescribed for two parts of a speech, the exordium and the statement of fact, for then we will argue truly when we deal with the proper, true issues. I see that the reason for the exordium was in fact threefold, to make the listener well disposed, attentive, and ready to learn. But what is attributed to the exordium as its property is not its property; surely it would be more dangerous if the listener were not well disposed, attentive, and ready to learn in the middle of the speech when the debate is at a serious pitch, than in the exordium. Moreover it is untrue that an exordium is composed merely for those reasons; it is contrary to actual practice, for in Cicero's many speeches not one exordium is composed simply for these banal reasons. Rather, in every surviving speech the exordium straight away informs the listener himself plainly, briefly, and credibly about the case; it does not merely make him well disposed, attentive, and ready to learn.

Yet come, there must be some rationale for the assignment of good disposition, eagerness to learn and attentiveness to the exordium. Let us see whether this is achieved better by Quintilian's confused special topics than by our ten common topics. According to Quintilian, a good disposition emanates from persons, or from cases, or from matters related to each of these—as if indeed the person who is accused of something were not a part of the case; as if so many of the things which this wise rhetorician has collected concerning the topics of persons and cases were not adjuncts of persons; and as if we did not clearly teach concerning the topic of adjuncts all these things that Quintilian has here confused. Rhetorical theory—so help me God—could be treated, entire and complete, with greater brevity than this fulsome theory of *exordia* is handled by Quintilian. Here there is no sound theory of invention such as I explain in my ten topics. But let us look at the topics of the statement of facts, and at the same time let us seek here the chief reason why the art of that statement is described by its attributes.

Quintilian says that there are three qualities according to which the topics proper to the statement of facts should be described; that is the statement of facts must be brief, clear, and plausible. But Aristotle rightly scoffed at the first; in addition the remaining two are more vital in the proof than in the statement of facts. For if something is not sufficiently plausible when the facts are stated, it finally becomes credible through treatment and proof. Since both invention and arrangement are related to the whole of dialectic, and both style and delivery are related to the whole of rhetoric, as we point out clearly and plausibly, it is therefore patently absurd that he attributes those virtues which are common to all speeches only to one part of a speech as if its property alone—and then as well that he tacks on the arts of clarity and probability as if those arts in their entirety could reveal and achieve something through their precepts.

But, after all, which ones are the proper topics of invention which Quintilian talks about here? He mentions and mixes together instruments from cases, from place and from time, and from adjuncts—but mentions beyond these nothing at all. And so Quintilian had no reason for adulterating invention here; nor is it anything except foolish, vain technicalities instead of true art. However, amidst these stupid notions there is one thing alone that is especially proper to the dialectical art. Quintilian teaches that one should use arguments in the statement of facts but should not actually argue any points there. Consequently let us jeer at every dialectician and let us scorn any dialectic which teaches us that no speech capable of some application of reason is without an argument; that, however, the whole revelation of an argument is argumentation; and that there is virtually no speech which does not involve some argumentation. Actually Cicero has no statement of facts which does not lay down arguments and reasons for the subjects and which does not also apply syllogisms and argumentations. Thus Quintilian records for us paltry falsehoods, not precepts derived from actual practice.

There are so many other things in this chapter that if I were to pursue them I fear that I myself would be foolish. What indeed shall I say about Digression? Although Quintilian, despite some hesitation, nevertheless places it among the figures and says here that it is not a part of a cause, he nevertheless devotes the whole third chapter to Digression. In case he might appear to have omitted some of the rhetorician's trifles and tricks, he shows himself to be utterly devoid of training in the art of dialectic. He is still like this in the fourth and fifth chapters about proposition and partition, for although the proposition is either the very question which is advanced or is the basis of the syllogism and argumentation, and although the partition is the place for invention, nevertheless Quintilian here explains nothing of its theory, such as the number of types or methods. Clearly he handles this second theory of invention in the parts of a speech in such a way that the cases, the adjuncts, and the partition are confused; he refers nothing at all to the general and common usage of speech. But by immortal God, let us with greater accuracy get rid of the obscurity of this partition into four, or five, or even more parts of a speech; let us seek for causes; let us use conclusive proof; and let us see what ought to be the correct partition of a work fashioned by art!

For I say that we must emphatically reject this partition of a speech into four, five, or even more parts. If anyone should wish to distribute the praises and virtues of pure speech (the task of the art of grammar), he must undoubtedly return to the universal causes of the art, not to one part of the art; and he should not say that there are two parts of speech, noun and verb, because these parts are looked at in order and syntax. For that reason he should not confine grammar for us to these two parts; but indeed, if he wishes to consider all the good points of speech, he should of course examine etymology in each of its parts and syntax in their connection, prosody in the accent and quantity of syllables if the concern is recitation, and orthography in the formation of letters and syllables if the concern is writing. Finally he must examine the parts of the grammarian's task according to the parts of the art of grammar.

If also anyone should wish to divide out the parts of a debate, the task of the art of dialectic, he should consult the common parts of the art of dialectic, invention, and arrangement, not some minor particle of it. Neither should he decree the existence of three parts of a debate, major proposition, minor proposition, and conclusion; nor the proper roles of the major proposition, the minor proposition, and the conclusion; nor their proper positions as first, last, or intermediate. Nor should he create for us this unfathomable dialectical confusion. Why not? Because the major proposition, the minor proposition, and the conclusion belong to the art of arrangement, not to the whole of dialectic.

How therefore should a dialectical debate be suitably divided? I believe strongly that if anyone refers to the parts of invention and arrangement, the true and only parts of the dialectical art, his division of the dialectical task will be correct and complete. He should say that a debate consists of two things: arguments, because they are supplied by the art of invention; and likewise the syllogism (and sometimes also method) because they are comprehended within the arrangement of dialectical order. I repeat, then, that we shall understand the virtues and parts of the work to the extent that we consult the legitimate and real parts of the art. The art is just as different from the work as results are from causes; for art is the skill of creating, and the work is the creation of the art. Thus Aristotle, who found so many of those obscurities—or at any rate collected them—teaches that the analysis of a dialectical work is different from the creative agent, which he calls genesis.

Therefore let us first of all posit the following:

> The partition of a work constructed by art ought to be derived not from some part, but from the whole of the art.

And next let us add,

> A speech is some work constructed by art; namely (as is Quintilian's opinion) by the art of invention, arrangement, style, memory, and delivery.

Finally let us conclude,

> Therefore the partition of a speech should be derived not from a single part—for instance, from arrangement and order

divided into exordium, statement of facts, proof, refutation, peroration—but from the whole of the art divided into invention, arrangement, style, memory, and delivery (since Quintilian attributes these parts to the art of rhetoric). Thus we remove this partition and the great confusion over the exordia and statements of facts found in these petty precepts.

I come now to Quintilian's third form of invention. We have discussed the invention of causes; we have argued over the invention of exordia and statements of fact; there remains one invention that is common to causes, to parts of speech, and generally to everything. However, Quintilian seems to have placed it in the third part of a speech, that is, in the proof, because he thought that there is no place for arguments in the exordium and the statement of facts, but only in the proof. For if he thought otherwise, why does he attribute to one part what he should reckon common to all? Come then, let us tackle this problem.

I propose, however, that his theory of universal invention is just as careless and as useless as the one above, the specialized invention in causes and in the parts of a speech. Quintilian, following Aristotle, divides proofs into two kinds, so that some are "inartistic" and others are "artistic." He calls those inartistic which are outside art and which the litigant receives from outside himself, such as the decisions of previous courts, rumors, evidence from torture, documents, oaths, and witnesses. Quintilian errs in this along with Aristotle. First, since there are countless questions about those subjects and arts which use the evidence of scholars and learned men although they do not come into the forum, in what way can they be called inartistic? Again, how can we call something inartistic which is taught by the precepts of art? Surely the precepts and arts concerning these arguments are well known. In fact, as the matter stands, I would prefer to call these reasons inartistic because they contain no art at all, because they have only the tiniest particle of true proof from all available arguments, and because on the whole one does not believe the evidence but rather trusts in the causes of the evidence. Therefore Quintilian is misled by a false line of reasoning.

Next he divides the artistic proofs in a rather superficial and foolish fashion so that they concern either a thing or a person, and derive from things preceding, subsequent, or opposite, from past, present, and future time, and from something greater, equal, or less; likewise so that some proofs are necessary, some credible and others not impossible; or so that because one thing is, another thing is not; or because one thing is, another thing is; or because one thing is not, another thing is; or because one thing is not, another thing is not. What can be more idiotic than this whole category of partitions? Granted that he may fashion out of the most trifling details such infinite sections for every subject, what usefulness has this in any case either for recognizing the nature of the arguments or for dealing with actual practice?

"Therefore all artistic proof," says Quintilian, "consists either of signs, arguments or examples"—as if examples and signs were not arguments! O sharp and dialectical divider! Let us look at the differences between signs and arguments which Quintilian suggests, so that we can see this marvelous distinction between examples and signs, and arguments.

"Signs," he says, "are not discovered by the orator but are brought to him along with the case." But this is false, for what he calls signs are actually the effects or adjuncts that are visible to the eye; the orator probing into every problem can seek and discover them. But if we suppose that the orator does not discover them but that they are brought to him, they are therefore, I say, inartistic, and consequently not parts of artistic proofs, as you, O Quintilian, make them. In this way you fall into a more serious error of syllogistic judgment.

Quintilian sets out another difference between argument and sign, and enfolds it in an amazing double proposition.

"If signs are infallible," he says, "they are not arguments, because where they exist there is no room for question; even if they are doubtful, they are not arguments because they themselves need the support of arguments." But signs, I insist, are either infallible or doubtful; arguments therefore—if I may conclude for you—are neither. But truly, O Quintilian, the clearer the arguments the more they remove the problem and the more they prove it, so all the more are they arguments. But you yourself a short while later define an argument as infallible; therefore the first part of your double proposition is false. This one place can indeed prove just how sharp was Quintilian's judgment, for he makes such feeble arguments, he draws such trivial and inconsistent conclusions, and he deliberates contrary to all dialectical reason.

For from this handsome double proposition you should conclude that no proof is an argument, as follows:

> If a proof is infallible, it is not an argument because there exists no room for question. If it is doubtful, it is not an argument, because it needs the support of arguments.
> And yet a proof is infallible or doubtful.
> Therefore no proof is an argument.

This is the dialectic of Quintilian. But let us look at the definition of an argument, for perhaps this will provide a clearer difference. "Argument," says Quintilian, "is a process of reason providing proof, which enables one thing to be inferred from another and which confirms facts that are uncertain through facts which are certain." But this definition of an argument suits both sign and example. His entire partition of artistic proof into sign, example, and argument, where two species are placed along with their class as if they were different classes, is clearly both false and stupid. Almost the whole theory of proofs outlined by Quintilian in the fifth book is the same.

However in the general theory of arguments—which we handle completely in our ten topics of causes, effects, subjects, adjuncts, opposites, comparisons, names, divisions, definition, and witnesses—Quintilian confuses and muddles the topics as if they were general (even though he treats them not only as general but separates them into sections). He confuses, I repeat, those topics drawn from person, such as birth, nationality, country, sex, age, education, physical appearance, fortune, condition, natural disposition, virtue, occupation, previous deeds, previous words, and name. For our teachings cover these many topics and separate them into the two topics of effects and adjuncts.

Next, Quintilian's greater weakness concerns effects. For he put these forward in the topics of persons, yet here once again he repeats them as if they were now different. He does the same with time, place, and chance event, which belong to adjuncts, and yet once again he puts adjuncts afterwards as if they were different. He does the same with opportunities, instruments, and methods, treating them as if they were not causes or adjuncts. He does the same with definition, class, species, and proper difference, as if a property were different from adjuncts, or difference were not an opposite.

However, Quintilian does talk about this later. He does the same with division, as if class or species, indeed mentioned shortly before, were somewhat separated from the topic of division. He does the same with removal, where Quintilian prates quite childishly in thinking that the removal of parts is a class of argument different from division. He does the same with beginning, amplification, and climax, three topics which provide no universal class of argument but are mixed in with the others. He does the same with similarities, differences, opposites, adjuncts, and references, where Quintilian most ignorantly subordinates adjuncts to references. He does the same with causes and results, which however he enumerated previously. And he does the same with conjugate arguments which Quintilian laughs at, because, he says, "There is no need for proof when a man has the common right to send his cattle to graze in a common pasture." Quintilian shows the same dialectical judgment here as he did when he previously distinguished signs from arguments: there is no need to prove that because an animal is rational, it is a man. Is anything, O Quintilian, further from dialectic than that judgment according to which a definition is not an argument? What could be more bereft of philosophy? The same can be asked about the major and minor terms.

But at last he draws together the countless topics, variously confused, into a sum total of confusion, so that he draws every argument from persons, causes, places, time, opportunities, means, definition, class, species, differences, properties, removal, division, beginning, amplification, climax, likes, unlikes, contradictions, consequents, efficients, effects, results, conjugates, and comparison. He adds to these the supposition he calls "hypothesis," which can be drawn from all arguments because there are just as many fictitious species as there are true.

Here Quintilian cannot be called negligent in seeking out so many items from all over, but certainly he can be seen as quite ignorant of dialectic and without experience of the syllogism, for he does not see that this "hypothesis" is the proposition of a connected syllogism according to which nothing can be argued, proved, or concluded unless a minor proposition, either expressed or understood, is joined to it. I repeat, he does not understand that invention is a process which supplies arguments, whereas arrangement is a different process which organizes arguments. But that "hypothesis" is part of a connected syllogism; it arranges the argument along with the question, and it can grasp every type of argument which a syllogism can. A syllogism, however, is not an argument, nor indeed is the proposition of a syllogism an argument. And although Quintilian mixes these falsehoods so unwisely and confusingly with the general, universal topics, he nevertheless alleges that he can write about many more topics of invention. In this he deceives himself, for there is no class of arguments outside the ten topics of causes, effects, subjects, adjuncts, opposites, comparisons, names, divisions, definitions, and witnesses. In our teachings all the things covered here have been very clearly distinguished according to their classes and parts.

There is a similar confusion over examples. "All arguments," says Quintilian, "must either be from things like, unlike, or contrary." A little later, however, he clearly incriminates himself by also adding arguments from greater and lesser things and from historical authorities. What he thinks are examples of contraries, such as Marcellus' restoration to the Syracusan enemies of the works of art which Verres took from them when they were allies, are in fact unlikes, not contraries.

He says a lot of things that are partly false, partly true, about the use of arguments. He also adds some things about arrangement which have nothing to do with syllogism and method since they concern a certain type of artistic arrangement. Although Quintilian orders that a speech should not descend from its most powerful to its weakest point, afterwards in the first chapter of the seventh book he will say the opposite, for there he will teach that the strongest argument against the accused must be refuted first before the weakest can be dealt with.

In the chapter concerning refutation, there are similar trivialities, with an utter lack of any instruction concerning invention. Finally Quintilian collects many things about the enthymeme and the epicheireme; by this he proves again what was evident in so many previous places—namely that in dialectic he is without doubt a lightweight. His discussion of the syllogism is clearly rather a description of what he has either heard or read from some author. Quintilian here has Aristotle as the source of his mistake. He separates dialecticians from orators not according to practical use but according to the false fabrications of Aristotle, who taught that the former use syllogisms, whereas the latter more freely use loose-knit speech. This man does not realize that, like grammar, dialectic through all its parts of invention and arrangement has common use in every speech; and that dialogues, lectures, debates, poems, and finally speeches—of whatever kind they may be—are all more dialectical than oratorical. Virtually no speech is without reason and argument, or without the organization of reason and argument which belongs to dialectic. But Quintilian, following the vain imaginings of Aristotle, who made a foolish distinction between dialecticians with their scholastic disputes and rhetoricians with their forensic and civil debates, thinks that orators use the syllogism less frequently than dialecticians; as if in fact the reasoning in the dialogues of Plato were not connected to both dialectic and rhetoric, and as if we do not find as many syllogisms in Cicero's forensic cases as in even the thorniest sophisms of Aristotle. If Quintilian had recognized that the arts of invention and arrangement are distinct, and if he had evaluated Cicero's speeches according to their standard, he would have found more frequent syllogisms in Cicero's speeches than could be observed in any philosophical writings. This mistake by Aristotle deceived Quintilian, for he simply followed Aristotle's fabrication here and never considered whether it was a true statement. For if he had examined it, most obviously he would have discovered the error of those things upon realizing that the books of poets and orators use and handle dialectic as much as those of philosophers. Such are his statements about the invention of arguments in the third, fourth, and fifth books.

The whole of the following sixth book is taken up with the arts for stirring the emotions and causing delight; here nothing is the property of dialectic or of rhetoric. Since rhetoric and dialectic are general arts, they should therefore be explained in a general fashion, the one in respect to style and delivery, the other in respect to invention and arrangement. Many rivulets arise from these universal fountains, but they should not be intermingled with the precepts of these arts. Three arts of invention are taught by Cicero and Quintilian: for the purpose of teaching they describe topics in the classes of causes, in the parts of a speech, and finally, those that are common to all questions. Secondly, they also lay down some instructions for stirring the emotions, and then for causing delight. But in invention one who is teaching should explain only the topics, since arousal and delight do not have any proper arts. However, they are drawn in common from those topics of invention, and likewise from style and delivery. They are especially drawn from moral training, where you learn to recognize what is virtue, what is vice, what things please honest men, what things delight the wicked, and likewise what offends each. Cicero often provides proof of this, for in his writings on oratory he alleges that this part is therefore most necessary of all parts of philosophy for the orator; and Aristotle, who was responsible for this great confusion of dialectic and rhetoric, alleges that rhetoric by reason of the emotions and passions is in a certain sense part of moral philosophy; he refers the whole art of stirring the emotions to that moral philosophy. For this reason Quintilian himself said in his first book that moral philosophy was a part of rhetoric.

In the last chapter of the sixth book Quintilian discusses the difference between common sense and judgment, and he thinks that judgment, as I said before, can no more be transmitted by art than can taste or smell. Here I do not find Quintilian lacking in care in his collection of material, but I long for prudence in his making of judgments. Previously he stated that there are two parts of dialectic, invention and judgment. Now, as if dialectic were not an art, and as if his instructions concerning judgment in syllogisms were inartistic, he says that judgment cannot be transmitted by art. And yet this theory is so full, so wonderful, and so divine that the man who knows all the other arts but does not know this one from precepts or from some observation seems to have understood nothing truly and to have learned nothing surely. And so these matters concerning invention have been confused by Quintilian.

Quintilian seems to wish to explain the theory of arrangement in the next book, the seventh. If he had done this, he would have taught all the modes of the syllogism, and the correct ways of method, theory, and prudence, just as our teachings have explained. But in the beginning Quintilian declares that there is no fixed art of arrangement which can be formulated for all matters; here he is seriously wrong. For there is a fixed theory of syllogism and artistic method, common to everything which can be treated with order and reason. And so how many things must now be said against this man concerning the art of arrangement, for he not only is ignorant of it but believes that none can exist!

Indeed the countless things which Quintilian writes in the whole of this book under the heading of arrangement in fact concern merely the rules for civil cases and for the practice of litigation in the Roman forum in his own times. But all such things, not being very stable or enduring, merely provide instruction for those specific rules of the Roman forum. Moreover he drags back to this place all those sophisms in the third book concerning types of status, conjectural questions, definition, quality, deed, the letter of the law, its intention, opposing laws, syllogism, and ambiguity—in none of which is there any general precept for arrangement. Also he confuses some precepts for invention in conjecture and definition where they concern causes, deeds, and advice, so that one can most truly allege that in five books (the third, the fourth, the fifth, the sixth, and the seventh), Quintilian does not formulate an art of invention and arrangement; rather he overwhelms the theory of each part with many false, alien, and useless matters.

Therefore now we may conclude this whole debate on invention and arrangement, and we may put our teaching on a footing with Quintilian's teaching, our usage with his usage, so that in the end we can understand more fully and exactly what it is possible to decide about this subject. We ourselves rightly attribute the arts of invention and arrangement to the art of dialectic, as its proper parts. Quintilian falsely subordinates the theory of dialectic to rhetoric. We define a question and give advice about its parts whatever may be relevant to the use of invention and arrangement; Quintilian does not define the question, and he proposes no use for it; rather, he confuses this part of the theory with sophisms of all kinds. We define invention, we separate its classes, we deal with each species and part of the classes, and we illustrate by excellent examples. Quintilian does not illuminate invention, the classes of invention, the species of the classes, or its parts, with any light at all of true definition and partition, but instead of one brilliant invention that is common to all subjects, he accumulates three most inane and disordered arts—the first dealing with the classes of causes, the second with the parts of a speech, and the third with the general topics common to all causes as well as to all parts of a speech.

We have pursued all the virtues of syllogism and of method, that is of universal arrangement; in this case Quintilian did not in any way perceive any fixed and enduring precept. In the clearest and most suitable order for comprehension we have organized the general rules first, and then the particular rules; in what way, with what order, by what rule of dialectical method did Quintilian put together his whole confusion of so many arts? Plato compares a methodically and rationally organized speech to the perfect figure of a fine animal, whose very head rears above, whose feet stab the ground below, and whose chest, belly, and remaining limbs have an orderly arrangement in the places in between. He believes that a speech, arranged thus by dialectic, covers the universal subjects in the first, most important place, the particulars in the least important place, and in between the subjects first of all that are subsidiary to the univerals, and then the subjects that are more important than the particulars. As a result a debate is guided from its head through its parts to the final, particular details. But indeed what sort of a monster would we think the animal whose feet were raised above, whose head was thrust down below and along with the stomach was swallowed up by one foot as if by some vortex? Such undoubtedly is Quintilian's triplicate organization of invention: the feet are the particular arts of causes which are in the first, most important place; the stomach is the parts of a speech which are common rather than demonstrative arts, and deliberative causes which are less common than the general topics—while the head is the topics common to all questions; but this theory of speech and common topics is confused in one class of judicial cause, that is, in one foot.

Thus, in his whole explanation of the art Quintilian did not only make all too many absurd mistakes in the subjects themselves, but we see how confused and muddled he was in order and arrangement. Yet what do we think will happen if we seek for practical application of such foolish, useless confusion? Like any other discipline, the theory of invention and arrangement must be practiced in two ways: first, in order that by its means we should through external examples learn common sense from argument, judgment from the manner of conclusion, and complete prudence from the method of arrangement and order; secondly, that by means of the same art we should devise similar examples in speech and writing. But suppose we take some speech of Cicero and investigate invention and arrangement according to Quintilian's arts: of what use first of all for this system of practice is that whole technical doctrine of status that deals with whether the question is reasonable or legal, whether it inquires if something is complex or definite, what it is, or of what sort; whether it arises from an ambiguous basis or is of a syllogistic type, whether it involves contradictory laws, the letter or the spirit of the law, or whether it involves transference—what use, I repeat, will these things be to me for the system of invention? None. For the system of arrangement? None. Indeed, which arts of Quintilian shall I now apply to explain Cicero's intention here and the type and probity of the argument he used; I repeat, which arts of invention shall I apply here? Shall I attack again the classes of causes, shall I abolish the countless teachings on the parts of a speech, and shall I refer here the whole system of common topics? For, good God, why should there be such a great, mixed-up confusion, when the whole matter is very clear and easy?

Do you wish to recognize and to evaluate the wisdom in the speech of Cicero that is set before you? Refer its arguments to either part of the question, consider what its arguments are, whether cause or effect, subject or adjunct, opposite, comparison, rule of name, division, definition, or witness, then follow up the results by a short, easy way—something which you can barely do, and not even barely, by the annoying roughness of Quintilian's road. Finally, granting that there is the same danger in Quintilian's arts concerning arrangement, how shall I come to know Cicero's judgment and his method? But Quintilian is so far from teaching any theory of judgment that he alleges that none at all can be formulated. He is so blind to the entire art of arrangement that he professes there can be no such art common to all subjects. Aristotle's error is almost equal in foolishness to Quintilian's; in his *Topics* the former denies that a common invention can be formulated, but he entwines it in all the many obscurities that I have pointed out in his books. The latter states with truth that judgment is a part of dialectic, and yet the same man, apparently dreaming, says that there is no theory of judgment and no common theory of artistic arrangement. Accordingly, here I shall now once more ask a question: How can the second system of practice be handled according to Quintilian's arts? Neither wisdom nor judgment nor method in set authors can be understood from them; how therefore will we be able through those arts to pursue the same virtues in writing and speaking?

At this point, then, since the art of invention and arrangement is so carelessly and so senselessly laid out by Quintilian, since nothing is perfectly defined, divided, valued, or arranged, since the true use of these parts cannot in any way be elicited from those teachings—it is for you to decide, O dialecticians whom I summoned at the start as judges of my debate—to decide, I repeat, what sort of dialectician you now reckon this rhetorician to be!

Up until now we have used dialectical procedures against Quintilian in the dispute over the dialectical theory of invention and arrangement. Next follows Quintilian's teachings on style, which are almost as overblown and confused as his teachings on invention and arrangement in the preceding five books. As before in this discussion, I shall apply myself to the principal points of the subject even as I bring his teachings to account. Here likewise I shall search for dialectical prudence from this teacher—how he defined, how he divided, how he clarified, what sagacity, what reasoning, what judgment, and what wisdom he possessed as a scholar, and finally what sort of a dialectician he showed himself to be.

Rhetorical style ought to have been defined and explained by those precepts to which nothing grammatical or dialectical would be added. Thus first of all purity of speech would be delineated by grammatical decrees, subtlety and wisdom in reason by dialectical decrees; then the remainder—dealing with embellishment by means of tropes and figures and with grace and dignity of voice and gesture—would be explained by definitions, divisions, and examples. But Quintilian, true to form, mixes and jumbles grammar and dialectic together in his precepts concerning rhetorical style.

"Style," he says in the first chapter of the eighth book, "is revealed in individual words and in groups of words." What next? "As regards individual words we must be sure that they are pure, clear, elegant, and fitting. As regards groups of words, we must be sure that they are faultless, well-placed, and adorned with suitable figures." We should consider what dialectic this division of Quintilian's possesses. For first of all elegance of pure and faultless speech has nothing to do with rhetoric but belongs completely to grammar, for the absence of barbarism and solecism is a virtue of grammar. Thus so many of these things in this division are redundant, and they reveal the total absence of dialectic here, because when you argue about rhetorical style it will surely not be honest to mix in grammatical matters.

In a certain sense Quintilian admits this when he says, "But I have said all that is necessary on the method of speaking purely and faultlessly, already, in my first book where I talked about grammar." Here in truth, though, Quintilian is the same as he was before, without dialectical wisdom, without syllogism, without judgment. "But," he says, "there I gave instructions only to prevent faults in diction, whereas here it is not out of place to warn that our words should have nothing provincial or foreign about them." But O Quintilian, when you talked about grammar in your first book you not only put down the same things as you say again in this book, but there you also said far more than here. And yet through your great care in collecting material you clearly reveal that you are oblivious and unmindful of dialectic, and, I maintain, without experience in it.

We must acknowledge the same thing concerning clarity and propriety of subject, for they have almost nothing to do with rhetoric, whose province is completely confined to verbal style and delivery. In the second chapter clarity is produced from appropriate words; however, propriety is quite ridiculously divided into eight forms. Every meaning of a word—as I shall later demonstrate—is either appropriate or is altered by some class of trope through metonymy, irony, metaphor, and synecdoche. Thus, if we wish to dictate true instructions, there is a single rule and a single form for propriety in a word.

But Quintilian says that words are called appropriate in the first form when their primary quality is comprehensibility and meaning; this is true. In the second form a term is called "appropriate," he says, "which, among many of the same name, is the original word from which all the others have been derived." But, O Quintilian, this second form is not different from the first. Every utterance has some appropriate meaning; however, this meaning is often changed by some trope to mean something else. But if that term from which all others are derived alone is appropriate, all the other terms are used *tropikôs*—that is, as tropes. Therefore, with the use of the light of dialectic you can see that that second form of propriety is no different from the first.

"The third form of propriety occurs when a thing which serves many purposes has a special name in some particular context." But, O Quintilian, synecdoche is this form of propriety, for whenever you separate species in meaning from its class, you define this later as synecdoche. Why then do you wrongfully insert a trope in this place, and why do you not rather teach in the theory of tropes that a modification of meaning, if it is necessary, is also appropriate?

"The fourth form occurs when a term which is common to other things is especially applied to one thing." This error is not merely like the one before but clearly is identical with it. The fifth type is that in which "the name is more significant than any other." But either the name is appropriate, so that there is no difference here from the first form, or it is modified; thus he teaches nothing here.

The sixth form of propriety is in those words which have been skillfully turned into metaphors. But why are these things about metaphor thrown in here rather than taught in the proper, correct place for tropes? The seventh form is in those words which are "the special characteristics of an individual," but sometimes the word is appropriate so that this form agrees with the first, at other times it is altered. The eighth form occurs when "words mean more than they say." Quintilian, however, prefers to call this "emphasis."

Thus he manufactured eight kinds of propriety which did not exist at all in any well-formulated rhetoric. Grammar governs the rules of appropriate words, rhetoric the rules of modified words; thus, appropriate words should be separated from modified words. However, from two classes of meaning, appropriate and modified, Quintilian made eight classes of the appropriate, with such subtlety and nicety that the second kind is no different from the first; the eighth is rejected by Quintilian himself; the third, fourth, and sixth are the tropes synecdoche and metaphor; and the fifth and seventh belong to the first or to some trope. So here, while I see scrupulous care in the gathering of material, I see no dialectical judgment and no dialectical syllogism.

I am passing over a multitude of false and witless things because my task would be endless if I attacked every single one. Quintilian contrasts obscurity with clarity and handles some of its forms in individual words, others in groups of words. But, O Quintilian, just how oblivious are you, how truly forgetful are you of what you have said! You divided style according to individual words and to groups of words; you placed clarity among individual words. But now you make this theory also penetrate groups of words, and you teach that you yourself are very confused in your definition and separation of the arts.

There is a similar wavering and confusion in the third chapter concerning ornament, where the introduction is extremely awkward on account of its length. At long last the theory of ornament follows, applied to both individual words and groups of words even though in the first partition Quintilian placed ornament only in individual words. I shall first of all unmask that dialectical consistency! Ornament, he said previously, resides entirely in individual words. Next he says there are two kinds of ornament, one that resides in individual words, the other in groups of words. He divides the individual words into three kinds, either appropriate, newly coined, or metaphorical. But previously Quintilian made metaphor a subdivision of propriety—now he separates it from propriety as if it were different. He repeats some things concerning newness of words that were confused in his first book; about metaphorical words he says nothing here. Thus Quintilian concludes his theory concerning the ornament of individual words in such a way that he promises us magnificent things but never delivers them.

The ornament of groups of words, it appears, is distorted into an equal or even greater muddle. First of all it is divided into two parts, our ideal of style and our mode of expression. There he says that we must think over what we wish to amplify or minify—a field in which the whole of dialectic and rhetoric is included—lest we should come to the opinion that such a great teacher accomplishes nothing. He deals rather with what tropes, figures, maxims, and rhythms we should use; here once more the whole of dialectic from premises is jumbled together with style, with its tropes, figures, and rhythms. So superbly does Quintilian outline this theory that without applying even a grain of dialectical salt he spouted forth whatever came into his mouth. And what is even more absurd is that he follows up neither of the divisions he has proposed, but he scrapes together from grammarians everywhere unspeakably despicable faults; moreover he spends the rest of this long-winded chapter on embellishment, which he makes different from these two parts. But here he assigns illustration to embellishment, even though in the ninth book he makes illustration a figure. He does not realize that this illustration has no separate body of precepts but can be produced from all the parts of invention, arrangement, and style. Moreover, all the examples of illustration which Quintilian uses here are from effects, adjuncts, and comparisons; here he is so blind, so poor, and so deficient in dialectic, that he does not understand the art of the examples which he uses and even names one kind instead of another. For instance, in the following example from the *Pro Archia*, he thinks a comparison of minor points is a simile: "Rocks and deserts echo his voice, even huge beasts are swayed by his song and stand still, yet are we, who have been given the best instruction, not moved by the voice of poets?"

He made brachylogy a subdivision of illustration, without realizing that the example which he provides—"Mithridates, armed to match his huge stature"—is actually a simile, which, however, he had made a subdivision of illustration in the previous type. Then he made emphasis a subdivision of illustration, part of which, reticence, he quite ridiculously makes a figure. Finally he heaps together here from all sides everything he can—simplicity, sublimity, imagination, finish, repetition, and vigor—not only without art but without any species of art at all.

The next two chapters concerning amplification and the classes of aphorisms are of this sort, for in these chapters Quintilian has no grasp of any art at all. In this book he gives instructions on style, but these classes of amplification and aphorisms result not from the style of words but from the invention of material, and the classes of amplification which Quintilian thinks are different are almost the same. For the first and second originate from the one topic of comparison. Indeed augmentation, the rising from lesser to greater, is the same as comparison, though Quintilian thinks the art of comparison is different from this art of augmentation. Reasoning and accumulation belong to no fixed art; they can be drawn from all classes of arguments. However, the classes of aphorisms which Quintilian surveys are from opposites, comparisons, or some figure, and they are truly confused contrary to every rule of art.

O philosophers, O dialecticians, O true judges of these matters, consider what these things are, and of what kind, that I talk about and put forward! For I am ashamed, I am ashamed to talk of and point out such verbosity, as senseless and disgusting as it is, and I deem it sufficient to warn against it. It is the task of a good judge to recognize from his knowledge of laws and justice the merits which make each subject worthy: I put forward the fact, you make a decision about the quality.

And so from the three parts of the whole eighth book two entire sections in the five chapters discussed have been thrown together from some grammarians, dialecticians, and rhetoricians, but in such a way that there is no semblance of the art of grammar, or rhetoric, or dialectic. In respect to rhetorical style, Quintilian promises that he will provide instructions: but he formulates nothing about the art of tropes and figures which comprises the entire art of style when it is truly described.

In the remainder of the eighth book Quintilian promises us the theory of tropes. As a matter of fact he does define a trope in the beginning, and separates its parts; sometimes he even follows the path of dialectical method. But if we wish to give a correct judgment, he defines nothing accurately, he separates nothing distinctly, and he organizes nothing on straight, orderly lines.

"A trope," he says, "is the skillful change of a word or phrase from its proper meaning to another." But a trope resides entirely in individual words and has nothing joined in a phrase. For when forms of speech are changed they are figures, not tropes. Those changes of speech which Quintilian thinks to be tropes are not tropes, as I shall teach in the proper place. Therefore, first of all that definition is false.

Quintilian identifies twelve classes of tropes: metaphor, synecdoche, metonymy, antonomasia, onomatopoeia, catachresis, metalepsis, epithet, allegory, periphrasis, hyperbaton, and hyperbole. But there are only four classes of tropes—metonymy, irony, metaphor, and synecdoche—as I shall make clear when I talk about each one. Quintilian's theory is likewise false in this part, and we see that he is as outstanding a dialectician in defining as in dividing.

First of all, Quintilian discusses metaphor without defining it; besides that, he separates it in such a way that it was better not to be separated. And so let us pass by his empty, ridiculous divisions, according to which metaphor is used either for necessity, for meaning, or for decorative effect—as if these things were not interconnected and some metaphor were applied out of necessity and not also for the sake of the meaning. However he adds to the three kinds a fourth form for avoiding obscurity, so he says, as if this form were not for the sake of decorative effect.

Let us pass by another division of similar clumsiness, according to which metaphor substitutes one living thing for another, something inanimate for something else inanimate, inanimate things for living things, living things for inanimate things. Leave him to conjure up such countless partitions which have absolutely no artistic usefulness. And since metaphor is a species of similitude—for metaphor is a trope marking like from like—since, I repeat, it is a part of similitude which can be drawn not from this or that class of subjects but from the whole nature of things, it is as vain and useless to wish to pursue lifeless species here as if anyone were to try to teach the origin of class, of species, of opposites, and ultimately those first dialectical sources of subjects. I keep this first class of trope; otherwise I reject all the trifles and blunders which Quintilian collected in this place.

Quintilian makes synecdoche the second class. He surveys its many types, such as the substitution of a number for a number, the whole for the part, the genus for the species, antecedents for consequents, and vice versa. The last of these has nothing to do with style; for instance this example,

> See, the oxen bring back the ploughs hanging from their necks

is an argument from adjuncts, indicating that noon and night are approaching. Quintilian realizes these things, but even so he confuses them. Quintilian does not understand that the one class of division covers the rest. Thus synecdoche is correctly defined as the substitution of the part to signify the whole, or vice versa. For a species is part of a genus, and a genus is the whole of a species, and a plural number compared to a single number is something whole compared to a part.

The third class of trope for Quintilian is metonymy. It is defined, quite wrongly however, as the substitution of one name for another. For every trope involves the substitution of another name for the proper name. Metonymy, says Quintilian, has the power to substitute for plain speech the cause of the speech. But this is not always the case. For often this trope also indicates the causes from the effects, not only the effects from the causes, and likewise the adjuncts from the subjects, or vice versa. And so that we may understand how unskillful and confused this art of tropes is, I shall refer Quintilian's examples to these four topics. Causes indicate effects when one says "Ceres and Bacchus" instead of grain and wine, for those gods are imagined to be the inventors and originators of these products. On the other hand, effects indicate causes, as in the example of "pale death, sad old age," for they themselves are not pale and sad, but they make man pale and sad. Subjects indicate adjuncts, as in the substitution of "well-mannered cities" for citizens, and the "devouring of men" for the dissipation of their patrimony; and finally the same is true whenever we talk of the container instead of the content, the owner instead of the possession, and the principal instead of the subsidiary subject. On the other hand, adjuncts indicate subjects when one says "sacrilege" instead of a sacrilegious man and "audacity" instead of an audacious man. Notwithstanding, the whole confusion about this trope is eradicated by this one true definition: namely, that metonymy is a trope indicating effects from causes, adjuncts from subjects, or vice versa. Although Quintilian makes some conjectures about a certain similarity between synecdoche and metonymy, he is on the wrong track. And so in this category I keep the true theory, I set it in order artistically, and I take away the darkness.

Quintilian makes antonomasia the fourth class of trope. He defines it as the substitution of something else for a proper name. This definition is very similar to that of the previous trope. For the substitution of something else for the proper name fits every trope. These definitions of Quintilian are of such a kind that they define nothing; yet Quintilian fails even more seriously. For what he imagines to be antonomasia, or in fact synecdoche, occurs when "son of Peleus" and "son of Tydeus" are substituted for Achilles and Diomedes. For general names or some explanation is substituted for particular names, as in the definition of Jupiter in this example:

> Father of the gods and king of men.

The same thing occurs in the definition of Scipio in this example: "Destroyer of Carthage and Numantia." And so this type is deleted from the list of tropes because either it has nothing different from the others, or it is not a trope at all.

Quintilian's fifth class of trope is onomatopoeia, as to moo, to hiss, or the like. But there is no change of meaning here, for these words never indicated anything else and this meaning is their primary one. Therefore there is nothing of the trope about it.

Quintilian makes catachresis the sixth class of trope, and defines it as the application of the nearest available term to things lacking their own name. But this definition fits all tropes, and so catachresis, like antonomasia, is placed among the tropes by the same error. This trope overlaps with others, or is not a trope at all. The line of verse

> They *build* a horse by the divine art of Pallas

is a metaphor marking like from like—difficult, I grant, but nevertheless possible—for we talk in this way both of building ships and of constructing speech, and the like. Now I do not object to this more difficult metaphor being called catachresis if so desired, but it should be understood that in its class it is not different from metaphor. "The lion will give birth" is a sufficiently difficult metaphor, just like parent for father, because to give birth is a feminine activity, yet this latter metaphor is quite common. Synecdoche involves substituting parricide for murderer, and boxwood casket for a casket of any material, that is, substituting species for genus. This synecdoche too can be called catachresis, if you wish. But Quintilian tries to separate metaphor from catachresis on the grounds that we have "abuse" when a name is lacking but we have metaphor when another name exists. Each solution, however, is false. For metaphor is sometimes used for the sake of necessity, as Quintilian himself said previously, and catachresis is sometimes used when there did exist a name such as parricide for murderer, parent for father. Therefore let us get rid of this class, for it is a subdivision of metaphor or synecdoche or some other trope altogether. We should not call it a separate species of trope. And also, if we wish to speak truly, every trope is catachresis, for it does not give expression to a subject by its own, proper meaning but uses something quite different.

The seventh class of trope is metalepsis, and it is defined as the trope which provides a transition from one thing to another. This definition is common to every argument; therefore it is wrong. Here there is no genus of trope whatsoever; moreover, Quintilian thinks it has virtually no use. Therefore let us do away with it, first because it involves no change of meaning and thus is not a trope; and second because it has no use.

The eighth class of trope is the epithet, thrust in here through an error even greater than the one above. For what is more inherent in epithets than their proper meaning? For example, warm fire, solid land, clear air, wet water. Sometimes however the meaning is changed and it is a metaphor, for instance, "unbridled greed." Thus no new theory is needed here. It is not therefore a trope because it is an epithet, but because it is a metaphor, or synecdoche, or metonymy, or irony. Let us therefore remove epithet from this theory.

The ninth class of trope for Quintilian is allegory, defined as an inversion showing one thing in words and another, sometimes absolutely opposite, in meaning. The first part of this definition fits every trope; the second is the property of irony. For if allegory is produced from a series of metaphors, it is not a new class of trope, no more than if metonymy or synecdoche were often strung out in a series. For in this case one would not talk of different classes of tropes but of multiple metonymies and multiple synecdoches; likewise in the former case there would be multiple metaphors, not a different class. If, however, you prefer to talk of allegory rather than a series of metaphors in speech, I do not object; but be sure that in describing the art you do not inexpertly substitute what is not the class for the class itself:

> Oh ship, new waves will bear you back to sea.
> Oh what are you doing? Come courageously to harbor.

In these lines there are many metaphors: a ship for the republic, the waves of the sea for the civil wars, a harbor for peace. And if we were to call all those metaphors allegory, we would not be distinguishing allegory from metaphor in kind.

When something is obscure we call it a riddle, quite correctly named. However, Quintilian thinks that the riddle is a species of allegory, and he thinks so falsely. While every allegory consists of tropes, there are many riddles without tropes, such as this one which Quintilian mistakenly reviews among the tropes,

> Say in what land—and you will be my great Apollo—
> The breadth of the sky is not more than three ells wide.

Everything in this riddle is handled by proper words, with no modification. And here, where there is no trope at all, even men ignorant and unskilled in the arts may produce such obscure maxims, drawing on all the arts.

Quintilian also believes that allegory sometimes does not have tropes, as in the lines of Virgil:

> Yes indeed I had heard that where the hills
> Begin to run downwards and the ridge starts to sink with
> gentle slope
> As far as the water and the tops of the ancient beech, now
> broken,
> You, Menalcas, had saved everything by your songs.

If this were true, there would certainly be no trope, because there was no change in a word from its proper meaning. But there is a metaphor in the word "Menalcas" which indicates Virgil instead of a shepherd; however, there is no allegory here.

Quintilian listed irony as a subdivision of allegory; here he is wrong. Irony itself is a separate class of trope. In every allegory like is indicated by like; in irony the opposite is indicated by its opposite. Even more wrongly he appended sarcasm, urbane wit, contradiction, and proverbs (sneerings) as subdivisions. For here nothing whatever concerns a trope, since all these things can be expressed by their proper words.

Quintilian makes periphrasis the tenth class of trope. But periphrasis can be devised in all cases through proper words. For this reason it does not involve any trope at all but a class of argument from the dialectical topics of definition.

Quintilian makes the eleventh class hyperbaton, in which, since there is no change of meaning, there will also be no trope. If one can say anything about hyperbaton in relation to rhetorical style, one can most suitably say it consists in "composition," thanks to which some words are postponed while others are placed first.

Quintilian makes hyperbole the twelfth and final class. If it resides in a word, it is in fact almost a metaphor, indicating like by like; it is also often metonymy; yet it is one in which more is included if a subject is amplified, for instance, "to soar with desire for glory," or "crime" instead of the criminal—or less is included if a subject is diminished, as for instance, "He could not endure the grating voice of the true, brave tribune of the plebs." Nevertheless if hyperbole does not reside in a word, it can be drawn from all arguments and therefore is not a trope.

Therefore, out of the twelve classes confused by Quintilian in this theory, none—namely antonomasia, onomatopoeia, metalepsis, epithet, the many species of allegory (irony excepted), periphrasis, hyperbaton, and hyperbole outside individual words—none is a trope. I do not find Quintilian lacking in care here, for instead of a few classes of tropes he has accumulated many classes of trivialities, but I do miss judgment and prudence. If he could have formulated this one syllogism, he would never have confused so many things:

> Every trope is a change of meaning.
> Antonomasia, onomatopoeia, metalepsis, epithet, the many species of allegory except irony, periphrasis, hyperbaton,

hyperbole outside individual words, involve no change of meaning.

Therefore none of these is a trope.

Again I say, if Quintilian could have reached this conclusion from his definition, he would never have fallen into such fruitless ignorance. But he seriously lacked a knowledge of dialectic, which he confused so greatly in his writings.

And in addition, so that it may be more firmly understood that there are only four classes of trope—metonymy, irony, metaphor, and synecdoche—I shall explain the reason for this more clearly and openly, using the topics of dialectical invention.

Every change in its proper meaning from causes to effects, from subjects to adjuncts, from opposites to opposites, from comparisons to comparisons, from whole to part, or vice versa, involves metonymy, irony, metaphor or synecdoche.

For metonymy is a change in meaning from causes to effects, from subjects to adjuncts, or vice versa; irony is a change in meaning from opposites to opposites; metaphor is a change in meaning from comparisons to comparisons; synecdoche is a change in meaning from whole to part, or vice versa.

However, every trope involves a change of the proper meaning in a word from causes to effects, from subjects to adjuncts, from opposites to opposites, from comparisons to comparisons, from whole to part, or vice versa.

For the remaining classes of subjects, which seem to be able to indicate meaning by a simple word, have nothing distinct from those. For etymological connections and derivation are a question of name, not of the meaning of a thing. Definition and witness are not signified by a simple locution.

Therefore every trope is either metonymy, or irony, or metaphor, or synecdoche.

But perhaps I am wrong, and, led on by an ill-considered zeal for probing the truth, I am advancing further than the limits of dialectic and sound judgment require. Quintilian has made tropes into twelve classes; I teach that there are only four. I do not think that antonomasia, metalepsis, epithet, the many species of allegory (except irony), hyperbaton in groups of words, and hyperbole are tropes, because they require no change of a word's proper meaning.

But at the start of the ninth book Quintilian makes a distinction between a trope and a figure, and does it so cleverly that he retains all the species of tropes which he proposed. "A trope," he says, "is a word transferred from the place where it properly belongs to another place where it does not properly belong; a figure is a certain fashioning of speech removed from the ordinary and obvious." This is the difference between a trope and a figure that Quintilian puts forward. I admit that it is true, certain, and necessary. For ornament of style involves a change in speaking from the proper but common manner to some more elegant and brilliant one. Ambiguity in a single word is a trope, but in speech it is called a figure—this is a very just distinction.

But Quintilian will not be able to maintain such a true statement for long. Soon he obscures that syllogistic distinction, that firm judgment, by some fallacy or another. The syllogistic distinction runs as follows,

> A trope is a change in a word.
> A figure is not a change in a word, because it is a change in speech.
> Therefore a figure is not a trope.

Nothing, I say, could be truer and more certain than this syllogism. What then, Quintilian? A little later he makes a fallacious attack on this syllogism and teaches a great number of sophisms. A short while earlier he defines a trope as a word transferred from its proper place; he therefore realizes that antonomasia, allegory, hyperbole in general, and periphrasis do not exist in single words. As a result he begins to speak differently and reasons as follows:

> In tropes some words are substituted for others.
> In figures some words are not substituted for others, for a figure can be produced by proper words.
> Therefore figures are not tropes.

He offers the proposition by induction: In tropes some words are substituted for others, as in metaphor, metonymy, and antonomasia. But Quintilian, what are you doing? This antonomasia here is not a word transferred from its proper place, as in "the parent of Roman eloquence" for Cicero, or in "the father of the gods and the king of men" for Jupiter: a phrase is not a word. Therefore antonomasia is not a trope. Next I shall convict Quintilian by means of his second fallacious syllogism. He assumes that some words cannot be substituted for others in figures, because every word can be proper. But in Quintilian's example of antonomasia ("destroyer of Carthage and Numantia"), everything is explained through its proper words. Thus, relying on each of Quintilian's syllogisms, I shall separate antonomasia from the class of tropes.

But let us look at the remaining assumption, namely that tropes involve the substitution of some words for others. If metalepsis substitutes one word for another, it is actually metonymy, irony, metaphor, or synecdoche. I have said enough about how catachresis and allegory were included among tropes. "Onomatopoeia," says Quintilian, "is substituted for another word which we would have used if that one had not been invented." But what words, O Quintilian, would we use in expressing the proper animal passions if we did not invent the following: chuckle, wail, roar? What kind of reasoning is this, how wretched, how remote from dialectical judgment?

"Periphrasis uses many words in place of one," Quintilian says, "therefore it is a trope." What is this? O Quintilian, do you make your judgment here? How far do you stray from your definition? But I come to a far different judgment and conclusion, I construct a far different syllogism:

> Every trope is a word changed from its meaning.
> Periphrasis is not a word changed from its meaning.
> Therefore it is not a trope.

Consider, O Quintilian, how false your conclusion is, but how reliable and sound is this one of mine.

"Epithet," you say, "becomes a trope through its connection with antonomasia." But neither antonomasia nor epithet is a trope. Use your own judgment and use your own syllogism against yourself:

> A trope is a word changed in meaning.
> An epithet is often proper and has no changed meaning.
> Therefore epithet is not a trope.

And so, by means of this syllogism, I cast off and throw out all the false species of tropes jumbled together by Quintilian in this theory.

Even beyond that, Quintilian gets into serious difficulties in the first chapter of the ninth book when he creates problems for himself which he cannot solve. He wishes to retain the opinions of the Greek and Latin rhetoricians, but he realizes that his examples do not agree with their definitions. In the end he tries to break this Gordian knot which he cannot untie. "Figures and tropes," he says, "are often called by the same names and give rise to the most technical debate, but such matters have no bearing on my present task." But to the contrary, O Quintilian, the trope and the figure are completely distinct in name, definition, and class. If you could have followed the truth, you would never have wanted to appear so vain, so gloriously diligent, and you would not be involved in that technical debate.

Quintilian collects various meanings and definitions for "figure." But instead of so many petty items a single true, proper, and clear definition would be helpful. He identifies two classes of figures, blaming both those who made fewer classes and those who made more. I wish, O Quintilian, you had taken less delight in such Greekish vanity. Arts should consist of a canon of useful, reliable teachings, instead of a collection of everybody's errors and faults.

Next you inquire how many figures belong to each class. You recite verbatim two important passages from Cicero, although they contradict one another. For in the third book of *De oratore* Cicero designates forty-three figures of speech, whereas in the *Orator* he puts down only seventeen. In the former work there are forty-eight figures of thought, in the latter forty-five. But what does this citation of Cicero add to our theory, especially since he is inconsistent and contradicts himself? I think that you should have dispensed with Cicero because you were about to disagree with him. But, O Quintilian, how did Cicero excuse himself in the *Orator* when he disagreed with his own statements in the third book of *De oratore*? Is it not really unbecoming, O Quintilian, to defend someone else's error and false opinion while describing an art, so that in the meantime you delay and betray the truth? And deceive and cheat the pupils whom you undertake to teach? You blame certain rhetoricians because they said that figures were emotions; Cicero says this too when he describes anger, curses, and conciliation as figures. But Cicero seems to you to have made no mistakes, since the authority of such a great man, I suppose, prevents you from freely admitting such a thing. Oh what a modest, kind critic! But I would prefer a dialectical critic; I would prefer one that was reliable; I would prefer one that was truthful.

In the second chapter Quintilian deals with figures of thought, but he does not define what a figure of thought is. It is in fact the fashioning of a whole expression in a complete thought which therefore remains even when the words have been changed. Indeed I do not know as yet of any definite classes; however, there are certain points in common among these figures which can be noted.

For example, there are a good many figures in interrogation and reply. I give the name interrogation to the process of seeking out and questioning something; in interrogation by itself, when something is sought after, there is desire, entreaty, doubt, and communication. Reply includes permission and concession. In both classes there is prolepsis and subjoining. In a fictional case there are personification and apophasis; in purposeful breaking-off there are digression, turning away from the theme at hand, reticence, and correction; in intensification of the emotions there are exclamation, suspense, and license. One could identify some species of the art if it were outlined in this way. But Quintilian does not define nor divide a figure of thought; instead, in his usual way he again mixes up and confuses what pertains to such a figure.

He counts interrogation and reply among the figures, and he distinguishes them from emotions; however, neither interrogation nor reply nor emotions is of itself a figure, although some figures are observed in them. For all of these can be *aschemata*, that is, straightforward and non-figural.

Quintilian calls it subjoining when we reply to our own questions, for he thinks that prolepsis is different in class from it. But he is wrong, because in every prolepsis there is some question and reply to the question—in other words, subjoining. I shall not track down types of prolepsis invented by Quintilian: he allowed himself to invent countless of this sort in all the figures, but without theory and without practical application.

He also mixes in correction with these figures, as in his example, "although that was not a punishment but merely a prevention of crime." But there is another function of correction, separate from prolepsis. He makes a similar mistake in respect to hesitation, consultation, permission, and concession, for those first two figures always reside in interrogation, the second two always in reply. For when we express doubt or consult, we are in fact asking something and making an inquiry; in permission and concession, by assuming that we have made the inquiry and asked the questions, we permit and concede by replying. Similarly, in a certain kind of inquiring and asking we find desire and entreaty—but about these Quintilian utters not a word.

Likewise suspense, exclamation, and license are figures always placed in intensification of the emotions. But Quintilian removes the last two from the class and number of figures. Yet because they are forms of speaking removed from the common, everyday mode of speaking they must surely be figures. Here he accumulates nameless figures that are suitable for intensifying the emotions. But neither emotion nor simulation is a figure, for irony is a trope, not a figure; it is a change in meaning from opposite to opposite, even in the examples which Quintilian treats among these figures: "Rejected by him, you decamped to your close friend, that excellent gentleman Marcus Marcellus." Irony is in the single word "excellent," not in the whole sentence. And it is the same even in the other examples, such as the quotation from the *Pro Sulla*: "Unless you thought there were a few who might try or hope that they could destroy such a great power." For irony is in the word "few"; however, one can join together many ironical words, as in the example from *In Clodium*: "Believe me, your integrity has cleared you of blame, your modesty has snatched you from death, your previous life has saved you." Here, as in allegory, there is not one figure but many tropes.

In the breaking up of a speech the figures are digression, turning away from the matter at hand, reticence, and correction. But, as I have said, Quintilian makes no separate mention of correction. He thinks illustration is a figure, yet at the start of this chapter he had not considered it a figure in Cicero when he reeled off those Ciceronian luminosities which he himself did not regard as figures. Truly illustration is not a figure, but it can be created from all arguments and figures.

Quintilian supposes that concession, confession, and agreement are three figures distinct in class. I think that two of them combined make one class, and I realize that concession is very closely related to confession. On the other hand Quintilian separates impersonation from prosopopoeia or personification. But in no way can it be separated.

Indeed the crowning point of such a long chapter—which speaks about figures of thought—is taken up by an exceptionally long discourse on emphasis, which he says occurs when "some hidden meaning is extracted from some phrase." But this, O Quintilian, is part of the process of reasoning and of reaching a conclusion; it has nothing to do with a figure. For it does not involve a new form of speech, but rather a careful, keen power of thought. And when this class was well established due to Quintilian's word, it was then especially adopted in the schools of rhetoric.

Finally, so that Quintilian should not seem to have been careless, or not to have brought together all men's inanities into his teachings, he collects forty-three new figures apart from the figures he has tested and apart from the figures of Cicero he has already mentioned. Why? So that we could not look in vain for diligence just as we look in vain for judgment and prudence anywhere in Quintilian. He took great pains, he investigated, he read, he observed, and finally he heaped together as many things as possible—but he could not judge and distinguish the good, the useful, the true, the proper things. At the start of this book he could not separate a trope from a figure; in actual fact, he cannot define a figure, nor can he detach figures from those that are not figures. Quintilian lacked one instrument, but an absolutely essential one for the teaching of his art—the syllogism, I repeat, the syllogism; and in actual fact he was also radically deficient in method. He spent many years in the forum and he trained the youth in his school, but he did not grasp the art of teaching—or at least he did not apply it in these books.

Nevertheless his figures of speech remain, and they are even more confused than his figures of thought. Let us therefore take on this subject. Truly, I see in these figures such a massive confusion—greater than any up till now—not only in Quintilian but among all the rhetoricians. Nothing has been handled with art; a figure of speech has not been defined as a whole; a distribution of classes has not been made; many false figures have been mixed in in place of true ones; the same species have nonetheless been separated by examples as if they were distinct; finally—the crux of the confusion, no slight one—the originators of this art have so mixed up the figures by name that very often some figures are called by the names of others.

But now let us deal with Quintilian, who at the start of the third chapter says truly enough that figures are liable to frequent change. This may be true, but look at the sort of thing which Quintilian says for proof: "The ancients," he says, "and especially Cicero, would say 'to envy something,' (with the accusative) instead of 'to be envious to something' (with the dative.)" But, O Quintilian, not only does Cicero not talk in that way, but he even admits in the *Tusculans* that Accius rendered the following poem in bad Latin,

> Has anyone envied the promise of my children?

And so this section can warn us how carelessly this man was versed in his reading of Cicero, for he not only suggested that he himself should not imitate any of Cicero's words or phrases, but he did not even observe or analyze what Cicero's own usage was like.

Next Quintilian makes two classes for the figures of speech, grammatical and rhetorical, not even remembering the area of inquiry which he has undertaken to explain. He calls his teachings rhetorical, but he ought to have called them "gramma-dialectorical," because in them he intermixes grammar, dialectic, and rhetoric. For a grammarian should teach grammatical figures and a rhetorician should teach rhetorical figures; grammatical figures should not be mixed in with rhetorical figures. And at this time that fine defense should be removed—that since the orator must use these figures they are therefore written down here—for the orator can also use them when he has learned them from the grammarians.

On the other hand, what are these grammatical figures that Quintilian supposed he should mix together with the others here? For through them I shall prove that Quintilian was as bad a grammarian as the bad rhetorician I have up till now taught him to be.

*Metaplasm* is the term usually used by grammarians for the situation in speech when there is irregularity of class or number and some parts are substituted for others. Here Quintilian again shows that he has not represented any man's form of expression, let alone Cicero's. "It is well known," he says, "that Cicero disapproved of saying 'to make an insult' (*facere contumeliam*) instead of the usual 'to be afflicted with an insult' (*affici contumelia*). But, O Quintilian, Plautus and Terence said "to make an insult" before Cicero did. The former says, "You should not say that you make someone an insult." The latter, however, says, "You may make him insults according to the new idiom." Although it was more customary to say "afflict" an insult than to say "make" an insult, nevertheless "to make" an insult was also perfectly good Latin. His desire to blame Antony took Cicero a little too far. Therefore, Quintilian again makes a mistake in the category of style and diction.

Next Quintilian makes similar mistakes as he points out examples of obsolete archaism in Virgil:

> Verily when he boasts that he trembles at my taunts.
> Forsooth a new race was rising from Trojan blood.

He seems to ignore the fact that Cicero also used both forms of archaism as accepted idioms and in a similarly elegant fashion. "Verily because it was written in the same decree," he says in the *Pro Flacco*. "Forsooth, he has not only talent but also natural virtue," he says in the *Pro Archia*.

Next Quintilian mixes in among the grammatical figures one from the figures of thought, apostrophe; however, he had treated it before in its proper place among the figures of thought. And this whole passage about grammatical figures is so confused that it utterly unmasks Quintilian's dialectic.

Next, from grammatical figures he turns back to rhetorical figures. He makes the first class those figures that are produced by the repetition of the same word, and he reels off figures of repetition without their names: epizeuxis, epanalepsis, anadiplosis, epanados, anaphora, epistrophe, and symploce; among them he confuses polyptoton and gradation, both of which involve reciprocal change, not repetition of the same word; and asyndeton, which involves omission, not repetition. He also throws together a lot of things about accumulation, which he calls metabolè, and about distribution and synonymy of words and thoughts, which do not belong to any species of figure.

Then follows the second class, which Quintilian says is drawn from omission. Here he lists five species. First is ellipsis, which is a metaplasm so far from being a figure that it is more often permitted in poets than it is ever praised in any orators. He adds asyndeton and *synezeugménon*, which are grammatical rather than rhetorical figures. Next *synoikoíōsis* and distinction, where the former connects contrary things, and the latter differentiates among similar things. They have nothing at all to do with style, nor for that reason with any figure.

The third class is in three parts: resemblance, equality, and contrariety of words. But all the rules of contrariety belong to argument, and have nothing to do with style; therefore, contrast cannot be a figure. In the first segment, resemblance, he makes paronomasia a figure from that figure of speech which he previously called polyptoton. For instance, the variation of case in "a woman unskilled at everything, unlucky in everything," produces a polyptoton. Likewise he here mistakes paronomasia for connection, as in his example "To private individuals, this law might not seem to be a law." He also mixes in *ántanáklasis*, as in his example of a son's speech to his father, "Father, I am not waiting for your death." And the father on the other hand says to the son, "Well then, I'm asking you to wait." In this example there is no figure but rather sarcasm arising from the ambiguous meaning of the verb. For in the former case "to wait for" means "to long for," but in the latter case simply "to wait."

And since by these two names *pleonomasía* and *paronomasía* nothing is meant except a figure in which a word is used altered or changed slightly for a variation in meaning—as in the examples "not emitted, but admitted" or "not orator, but arator (ploughman)"—this figure ought to be explained succinctly and clearly. But I remind you that even though nothing else than that is meant, here the longest and clumsiest speech is scraped together so that despite it nothing new is taught.

Next Quintilian proposes four types of resemblance—parison, homoeoteleuton, homoeoptoton, and isocolon—but since the first and fourth are the same and each one is produced from equal clauses, they are not different at all. Quintilian also falsely thinks that homoeoteleuton occurs in the following example, "Lust conquered shame, boldness fear, madness reason."

He makes antithesis the last of the figures of speech and he is wrong to do so, for an argument is not a figure; antithesis is of course an argument from unlikes and therefore it is not a figure.

Quintilian collects to the absolute limit all the inanities and trivialities of rhetoricians, with the intention, I believe, that we should not look in vain in any part of Quintilian's rhetorical teaching for his diligence, though not his prudence.

Finally, Quintilian separates artistic structure from figures, but quite without skill or thought. For what is a figure, O Quintilian? You say it is a fashioning of style removed from everyday usage. But, I say, structure and rhythm are a fashioning of style removed from everyday usage; therefore each is a figure. If, however, you had learned this rule for reaching a conclusion through the syllogism, and if you had applied the law for describing an art and organizing a theory, you would have never babbled forth such ill-considered remarks, O Quintilian. Truly this rhetorician has an amazing talent, for when Quintilian is about to give instructions on structure he makes no definition at the start, then he makes no divisions, but he does employ the longest and wordiest introduction in which there is no theoretical system—just as he did in the previous chapter about ornament.

When he has at last concluded his introduction he follows with a theory of structure in which first of all he creates three very foolish divisions. The first divides a speech into either a close-knit or a loose style. For what is this, O Quintilian? You take upon yourself the responsibility of laying down instructions concerning the virtues of style, yet here you organize style according to the structure of good and faulty points, so that the structured style is praiseworthy and good whereas the unstructured style is reprehensible and faulty. However, you correct yourself by saying that in dialogues and letters the rhythms are looser rather than nonexistent, so that any kind of speech ought to be structured; this undoubtedly is as true as in the case of the remaining ornament of a speech. Indeed tropes and figures exist in every speech, but ornament is increased or diminished in accordance with the nature of the subjects which are treated and the persons who are taught.

The second division is into the comma, the colon, and the period; this is not a structural division. For a speech can be separated into all these parts, and yet be most awkwardly structured. And all this deserves the consideration of grammar, since in grammar a pupil must be taught how he should divide a speech with punctuation and how he should mark off the clauses.

The third partition is the most fatuous of all, for the nature of artistic structure is split into three: into order, connection, and rhythm. In the first place, structure itself and rhythm are clearly the same; indeed rhythmical and structured speech are the same, for no speech that is structured is not rhythmical, or vice versa. Although all that he says about the remaining parts is essential for structure, he could more fittingly say this in the section dealing with rhythm.

The instructions on order that Quintilian gives here are false. A speech should not continually grow in force, as Quintilian says, but since degrees of diminution should be equal to degrees of amplification, a speech should decrease in force as often as its subject has to be narrowed down.

"There is another order called natural" says Quintilian; "for instance, one says 'men and women,' 'day and night,' 'rising and setting,' rather than the reverse." But if, as usually happens, a dignified order must be observed, certainly it should be observed from the subjects themselves, not from the order of the words. But very often the chronological sequence which we follow is in reverse: "We should say 'brother twins,'" says Quintilian, "not 'twin brothers.'" But Livy—whose smooth-flowing brilliance this teacher himself so greatly admires—says "twin brothers" and "triplet brothers" in his first book. This slipshod dispute over the order of parts of a speech is really as ridiculous and silly as the dispute in the section on connection over the hiatus of vowels and the harshness of consonants; here Quintilian's carelessness—or perhaps I should say ignorance—is really to be wondered at.

He discusses the faults in structure which can occur with vowels and consonants; he utters not a word about the virtues which he should of necessity describe. For all the value, the joy, the splendor, the obscurity, the magnificence, the subtlety of each word, and the whole virtue of every rhythm, springs from the natural excellence of letters rather than from the measurement of beats in syllables. Nor is it enough to advise what feet start or end a rhythm smoothly. For there is a great difference in feet between long and short vowels. If long vowels have been placed in first and third place, do we imagine there is no difference between their sounds? Or do we believe that there is no addition to the sounds of vowels when they unite with consonants? But indeed one rhythm can be more or less pleasing than another. It is not that distinction of beats through the syllables which creates rhythm, but rather tunefulness, euphony.

Finally, how does Quintilian divide rhythm, the third section of structure he treats? "Rhythm," he says, "depends on equal balance, as in the case of the dactyl; or one part may be half as long as the other, as with the paean; or twice as long as the other, as with the iambus." What an awkward, senseless partition! First of all, what usefulness does this partition have, even if it is true? Then what part of structure or what rule of theory has any bearing on that comparison of equal, three to two, and two to one? None at all. Next, is it not truly ridiculous and tasteless to form a partition in such a way that you leave our more parts than you cover? But the comparison of greater with lesser has five different classes: *pollaplasion*, from which comes the rules of double time; *èpimoríon*, from which comes three to two; and *èpimerè, pollaplasiepimórion, pollaplasiepimerè*. Quintilian mentions nothing here about these last three classes, and he mentions only one of the first class, since amphibrachys from short, long, short, is of the same class, for it belongs to the multiple, triple rule; and if the dochmiac foot which Quintilian later remembers is made up of short–two longs–short–long, so the space is divided in the middle, it will create the form *èpimerè*. And so that whole partition obviously must be abolished and sent back to the sophistic subtleties of Aristotle from whom Cicero and Quintilian took it in the first place.

But to continue: next Quintilian teaches special differences between metre and rhythm. "Metre," he says, "consists of order, rhythm of length of time; thus the former deals with quality, the latter with quantity." He seems to suppose that there is no order in a prose speech and that it is not highly important whether long or short syllables should follow. The second difference is equal in wisdom to the first. "In rhythm it does not matter," says Quintilian, "whether the dactyl has its short syllables first or following; in verse the anapaest or spondee cannot be substituted for the dactyl." What is the result then, Quintilian? If there is no order for long and short syllables in prose and if it does not matter whether three syllables (of which one is long, two are short) make an anapaest or a dactyl, why is it that afterwards you discuss so many things about the order of longs and shorts in the linkage of feet? Why do you make so many observations if it is of no importance whether shorts or longs go first?

Other distinctions similar to these two follow: for instance, that metre deals with words, rhythm with the movement of the body, as if indeed the following verse,

> Weeping thus, he speaks, and gives the fleet its reins.
> [Virgil, *Aeneid*, vi.1]

is contained within individual words rather than within the whole six-footed rhythm. Oh what an expert teacher of theory you show yourself to be! But let us pass by so many absurdities and give thought to the rest.

In loose-knit prose you should avoid a complete verse; at the beginning of a speech you should avoid the start of a verse; at the end of a speech you should avoid the end of a verse. You may structure a speech from all syllables of every kind, provided they are varied and harmonious. But Quintilian, following Aristotle and Cicero, has unfolded for us the most useless arts. There are four disyllabic feet, eight trisyllabic feet. What next? Quintilian makes forty species of rhythm from these. But how ridiculously and awkwardly! For in this categorization he not only uselessly listed the same rhythm in many forms but he usually contradicted himself. For if you distinguish rhythm by the last four syllables, as Quintilian sometimes also does here, and if you assume that the quantity of the final syllable does not matter—which he also agreed to—then certainly there will be several contradictions and all Quintilian's various categories will be reduced to eight.

Quintilian alleges that the rhythm in an ending where the paean precedes the spondee is at fault, as for instance in the example "Brute dubitavi." But he praises the same thing in a different species of observation. "The choreus," he says, "should allow the pyrrhic to precede it, as for instance in 'Omnes prope cives virtute, gloria, dignitate superabat.'" For in each example the last six syllables have matching rhythm, although it does not matter what the final syllable is.

"Two spondees," says Quintilian, "should usually not be connected." However, Cicero approved of this in Crassus, and Quintilian himself in three other places praised the molossus with palimbaccius as the best ending. But in this type three spondees are connected with a final indifferent syllable, as is evident also from Quintilian's own example, "Et spinis respersum." "The bacchius with the palimbaccius," says the same man, "and the spondee with the choreus make the best endings." But since he has established the final syllable as indifferent, these last two are spondees likewise. Such a great darkness has clouded the mind of this rhetorician that all too often he not only frivolously and uselessly retackles and repeats the same thing, but he says contrary, self-contradictory things. Thus he whips into these matters without dialectical syllogism and without judgment.

A very long discussion in the rest of the chapter is taken up with discussing what is the method for structure, and how judgment of it is almost completely natural; this is true. Then there is a remarkably absurd discussion about the structure of commas, cola, periods, exordium, narration, statement of facts, proof, and epilogue. Quintilian defines a comma as the expression of a thought lacking rhythmical completeness, as if indeed the rule for the comma were to depend on rhythm, so that whether a rhythm were completed or not there would either have to be or not be a comma, and as if in commas a full rhythm could not exist without commas, however, ceasing to exist. Quintilian quotes examples from Cicero, and errs along with him: "Domus tibi deerat? at habebas. Pecunia superabat? at egebas." But here I see four cola, not four commas.

Quintilian wanders off into a similar error in the theory of cola and periods, though from his treatment one could not learn anything about what they are. But I shall say, since he himself does not, that a comma is an incomplete expression of a thought; a colon is a completed expression of a thought, yet related to some other part: a period is absolutely complete and independent. For instance, a syllogism consisting of all its parts is a period; the major proposition, the minor proposition and the conclusion are cola; they in turn are commas if they cover other thoughts in one phrase, as for instance here in the following example:

> Together with the East wind, the South wind rushes, as well as the frequently stormy South West wind.

These units make three commas, and so sometimes a period will be shorter, for instance in the example,

> The wise man need answer for nothing in life apart from guilt.

And so again in these forms of speech, just as in the divisions of structure, Quintilian dreams up so many things which have not a grain of rhetorical theory but rather empty pomp and incredible sophistic ostentation. Although unskilled pupils may admire such a teacher, they will not grasp any theory from him. Now let us see how many mistakes Quintilian made in the tediously long confusion of this chapter: the introduction to the book was an artless sketch; there was no definition of this art; the partitions were ridiculous and faulty; the differences between poetic and prose rhythms were foolish; the observations on rhythm were the most confused and useless sheer trivialities, perpetuated without definite knowledge of any argument, and without any syllogistic prudence.

The tenth book displays some practice in the art which has been described. However, in that first, longest chapter Quintilian teaches that perfection in eloquence, that is, *èksis*, is acquired by reading, writing and speaking. And so the whole first chapter concerns reading, the next four writing, the remaining two speaking. In that first chapter Quintilian argues that although by conducting real cases an orator can greatly inspire the candidate for eloquence, nevertheless the reading of a written speech provides surer judgment and greater profit. For instance, although on his return from Athens Cicero listened to orators in the forum, in the senate house and on the speaker's platforms every day for ten years without break—as I have observed from his writings—in the meantime he also read various written speeches of orators. Quintilian therefore thinks that this kind of reading is more useful than listening. But I strongly disagree with him here, for I contend that he does not know the way in which this art should be practiced.

For the way in which rhetoric, just like dialectic and any other art, should be practiced is explicitly twofold—that is, analysis and genesis. For first of all we must understand the use of the art in representative examples, and then we must fashion our own like them. Just as the precepts of the art are therefore better learned by listening to a diligent, erudite teacher than by reading his book, so the practical application of the precepts is at first better achieved by listening than by reading. A new and hesitant knowledge of an art develops much more easily when someone else leads and points the way, rather than when it advances on its own. When Cicero speaks, I, as a new and inexperienced pupil, will quickly notice and admire many examples of tropes and of figures and of every style, which I could scarcely discover in his written speeches despite much observation.

On the other hand I do not prescribe that for this practice the student should hear only orators dealing with real cases, but I wish teachers pleading in the school to go ahead here with their own examples, so that not only do they reveal the art of speaking well to their pupils by means of written texts, but they make its practical use far clearer by living examples. Just a little later Quintilian teaches almost the same thing in respect to imitation. Give me a rhetorician skilled not only in teaching but also in speaking. Give me Cicero, the teacher of Caelius, Dolabella, Hircius, Pansa, Crassus, and of many others—will he not teach the pupil untrained in eloquence better by oral presentation than by his written speeches? Therefore, first of all there should be listening in the schools and then listening to all the orators everywhere else.

"But in reading, the critical faculty is more reliable," says Quintilian. I believe that the pupil's critical faculty is surely only more reliable if it has been strengthened by the instructor's critical faculty. "We are ashamed to disagree with the orator," says Quintilian. As if indeed that pupil of ours whom we must train through the studies of eloquence would approach the orator he is to hear like a judge ignorant of rhetoric, like an unskilled observer; and as if when Colotes of Teos looked at a picture of Timanthes—the one in which this painter had shown the scene prior to Iphigenia's sacrifice, when Calchas was downcast, Ulysses even sadder, Menelaus was grieving and Agamemnon's head was muffled, since that extreme grief could not be reproduced by the artist's brush—as if then, I repeat, Colotes' eyes filled with tears at such a heart-rending and sorrowful picture, and he did not instead direct his thoughts to all the rules of his art! The one person is the model of learned contemplator and wise observer, the other is the type of short-sighted listener who does not observe the art. Therefore, first of all the student of eloquence will be a hearer of fluent teachers and eloquent orators; then he will be a reader; and just as in listening, so in reading he will observe all the virtues of his art in tropes and figures. Quintilian does not recommend this. Moreover, in listing the rhetoricians whom he thinks the student of eloquence should read, he falls back to the error of the first and second book, prescribing first the poets, then the historians, and finally the orators. Thus he describes analysis for us.

Next he comes to genesis, the second part of practice, where we should write and speak by imitating or by attempting something on our very own. In the second chapter, therefore, Quintilian praises imitation; even so he does not think it sufficient, for we should attempt something beyond those whom we imitate. I gladly agree to this, except that he is seriously wrong in this case when he thinks invention cannot be imitated. Of all the parts of dialectic and rhetoric none is more easily imitated than invention, because no class of argument is not marked and described; there is not a form of any argument whose analogue could not be found in another case.

Imitation, he says, involves two things: whom we should imitate and what we should imitate. This too I admit. He clumsily mixes in a lot of things about decorum here, for up until now he has given no instructions about this, nor does it contain anything that should be treated among the rhetorical precepts of style or delivery. For if decorum is the concern of any art, it is the concern not of rhetoric but of dialectical prudence, strengthened by its great experience.

Quintilian thinks that the student should imitate many authors, not just one. I gladly accept this also since we should emulate the virtues of many rather than the faults of just one—provided, however, that you have been educated first of all by some of the best models. In the third chapter Quintilian teaches that we should write as much as possible with the greatest possible care, so that we write well rather than quickly, yet finally acquire speed by use and practice. Actually this chapter is true in part, but not in whole. For in accordance with Cicero's wish, and Quintilian's too in the fourth chapter of the second book, I wish that "luxuriance of style would show itself in an adolescent when something exists that can be trimmed. For the sap cannot last long in that which has too quickly attained maturity." Yet Quintilian himself next censures both excessive care and excessive carelessness in writing. The rest of the chapter about the room and the tablets where one writes, has, like the previous chapter about emendation, nothing at all on the level of precept.

In the fifth chapter he deals with almost the same argument, namely that we can conveniently practice writing by turning Greek into Latin speech. Such an exercise is quite unsuitable for the unskilled, beginning student of Latin eloquence who has not yet acquired an abundant vocabulary by means of which he can render Greek eloquence into Latin. Quintilian also approves of the same paraphrase from Latin texts, especially in the case of poetry, because one thing can be said in many ways. Although Quintilian rightly disagrees with Cicero here—for Cicero dismissed this exercise with the most flippant argument in the second book of *De oratore*—nevertheless this exercise can be of no benefit unless the style has already been strengthened and has matured; otherwise it will be at fault in the same way as above.

The remaining points about theses and declamations are similar, just like those contained in the whole seventh chapter, namely that skill in speaking extemporaneously is acquired by art and practice. They offer nothing new, only Quintilian's characteristic empty verbosity. And so, in the tenth book he delivers the instructions on practice in such a way that although there are instructions for parts of the art, he defines nothing clearly, he divides nothing sharply, he explains nothing practically, and above all he employs no dialectical skill or judgment.

In the eleventh book he gives instructions on decorum, memory, and delivery, devoting one chapter to each subject. Thus, the first chapter is devoted to a very long lecture on speaking fittingly, but the whole of this instruction on decorum is so vague and loose that it clearly does not fit among rhetorical precepts. For if any art can properly explain what it is fitting to see in absolutely all subjects then certainly it must be dialectic, which best reveals the general laws that are common to all things in argument, syllogism, and method; which reveals what is suitable for every subject and case; and which reveals what is truly fitting and what is not. However, although decorum is generally taught in dialectic, it is also especially and singly understood from other particular arts. From grammar, decorum in purity and elegance of speech is understood; from rhetoric, decorum in style and delivery; from arithmetic, geometry, music, and astrology, decorum in calculation of numbers, in division of great quantities, in harmonies and sounds and in the movements of the stars; from natural science, decorum in roots, plants, and animals; from moral philosophy, decorum in virtues and ethics; from architecture and agriculture, decorum in buildings and in fields; from human prudence in these matters, decorum in every word and deed and in every decision on daily affairs that lie outside any art. Finally, learning itself, as well as knowledge and practice, will demonstrate what is fitting in every subject. There will never be any separate and distinct precept concerning decorum, however, because decorum itself is that harmonious perfection which the arts by their precepts, and human reason and wisdom by themselves, reveal. Indeed, in matters lying outside any particular art, the common qualities of intelligence and nature which dialectic draws upon must be aroused and employed; likewise, usage, custom, and examples will advise us. Thus decorum covers such a wide field that it is clearly ridiculous to assign it to rhetoric as if it were its property alone.

In the second chapter Quintilian accumulates all the foolish sayings of the Greeks about places and symbols for developing the memory. He rightly laughs at these, ordering their inventors, Carneades, Metrodorus and Simonides, to hang on to their absurdities: he thinks that division and structure combined with effort and practice are simpler and better. Without hesitation I give Quintilian great praise and approval for this; and if he would only propose an art of division and order, I would give him also much greater praise and approval—for then he would explain to us the art of memory.

"The art of memory," he says, "resides completely in division and structure." If we therefore inquire into what the art of order is, and what is the art which divides and structures things, then we shall discover the art of memory. Of course my teachings have already laid out carefully this theory of order in the dialectical instructions on the syllogism and method. It is clear therefore that the art of memory is entirely the property of dialectic. Thus in this chapter Quintilian records things that are quite out of place and generally also ridiculous, even though they are closer to the truth than many of the things he has asserted up till now.

The chapter on delivery is crammed with many quite useful precepts of the same sort, but it is burdened with just as many trivialities, so that the absurdities easily outstrip the relevant teachings. Indeed his scrupulousness in the multitudinous sections concerning voice and gesture is futile, since that whole theory, gathered together in so many thousands of lines, could be put down clearly in a few words.

At the start we objected to the first assertions of the twelfth book, namely that the orator should be a good man, a philosopher, a lawyer, and a historian. Next the book takes up such questions as what cases should be dealt with first, what should be watched out for in the cases that are undertaken, learned, and waged, and even what matters you should agreeably spend your leisure on after you have retired from the forum. Not the ordinances of the unified art of rhetoric, but the business practices of the advocate (as we now call him) provide the answers to these questions.

Furthermore, the very long chapter about the classes of style contains nothing that is the property of rhetorical style. For the distinction between high, low, and middle style in speech is drawn not only from words but from the subjects themselves, so that this partition is common to invention along with style.

Therefore, if we wish to analyze everything brought together in these last five books, and if we wish to know what the outline of the theory was—even if we may not say of these books what was said before about the books on invention and arrangement (namely, that

Quintilian thoroughly mixed up art and the practice of art)—yet it can certainly be pointed out that the art of rhetoric is burdened with many useless precepts about style and delivery, and that the description of theory vaunts a far greater appearance of empty ostentation and pomp than it reveals a system of true and solid theory.

# PETRI RAMI

## VEROMANDVI

# *Rhetoricae Distinctiones in Quintilianum,*

AD

CAROLVM LOTHARINGVM,

*Cardinalem Guisianum.*

PARISIIS,

*Extypographia Matthaei Dauidis, via amygdalina, e regione collegy Rhemensis, ad Veritas insigne.*

1549.

# PETRI RAMI
## VEROMANDVI
## *Rhetoriae Distinctiones in Quintilianum,*
AD
CAROLVM LOTHARINGVM,
*Cardinalem Guisianum.*

Bene (Mecoenas optime) Graecorum illo proverbio praecipitur, Quam quisque norit artem, in hac se exerceat. Itaque tot annos, quot certe non caeterorum more gloriari placeat, sed pro tenuissimo tanti temporis fructu potius meminisse pudeat, in rhetoricis et dialecticis occupatus, an non meo quodam iure facere videar, si me in meis studiis et artibus vel eodem argumento saepius exerceam? Dialecticae atque rhetoricae artes ab Aristotele, Cicerone, Quintiliano confusae sunt, argumentum unum est, materies una: adversus Aristotelem et Ciceronem antea disputavi. Quid igitur est causae, quamobrem et Quintilianus in eandem quaestionem vocari non possit? Aristotelis logica multis et virtutibus carebat, et vitiis abundabat: multae definitiones, multae partitiones argumentorum defuerant: pro una inuentionis arte decem locis generalibus, caussis, effectis, subiectis, adiunctis, dissentaneis, comparationibus, nominibus, partibus, finitionibus, testimoniis comprehensa, infinitae tenebrae in praedicabilibus, praedicamentis, enuntiationibus, abundantia propositionum, inuentione medii, duobus analyticis posterioribus, topicis octo confundebantur: in simplicibus syllogismis non pauciores aggregabantur, de coniunctis nil praecipiebatur, de methodo omnino tacebatur, usus artis uniuersae nullus nisi in clamosa de artis ipsius tam vanis praeceptis, et sophistica altercatione tradebatur: nos arti virtutes quae deerant, addidimus, vitia tam varia deteximus, et, ut spero, excidimus: usum verum aperuimus, et rerum omnium communem demonstrauimus. Ergo dialecticum hoc certamen et artis et usus vehementer acriterque certauimus. Secundum certamen nobis adversus Ciceronem fuit. Aristotelicas enim inuentionis, dispositionisque, imo vero etiam elocutionis tenebras fere omnes ad rhetoricam transtulerat, et ex duabus artibus uuam confuderat, eamque ita confusam ad litigiosam civilium caussarum formulam traduxerat. Laudes inuentionis et dispositionis iam ante docueramus. Lucem quae elocutioni et actioni deerat, frater meus Audomarus Talaeus definitis et distributis et illustratis rerum generibus adiecit et exposuit: tenebras igitur duntaxat hic excussimus. Ecce autem Aristotelis et Ciceronis dialecticam et rhetoricam perturbationem Quintilianus sequitur, maiorem etiam ex seispo comminiscitur, omnesque omnium artium, de quibus aliquid legerat, vel audierat, scholas, grammaticas, mathematicas, philosophicas, histrionicas, palaestricas, rhetoricas, in suas institutiones amplectitur. Nos rhetoricam artem a caeteris artibus distinguimus, et de liberalibus artibus artem unam non omnium confusionem artium facimus: quae sint eius propria separamus, inertes et inutiles argutias detrahimus, quae desint indicamus, et Aristotelis tenebras sicut ante in Cicerone, sic nunc easdem propemodum in Quintiliano persequimur. Sed quoniam res eadem aduersus Aristotelem et Ciceronem ante tractata est, permulta et breuius et remissius agimus. Denique summa constantisque rationis ope nitimur, ut artium, in quibus adhuc studium operamque locauimus, vera et descriptio et exercitatio teneatur. Quot enim dies imo quot anni et aetates fallacibus harum disciplinarum commentis misere traduci arbitramur? Utinam maximo iuuentutis meae dispendio tantam miseriam expertus non essem. Utinam doctores et rhetoricae et dialecticae per nos admoniti de veritate rerum et utilitate potius aliquando cogitent, quam de iis, ad quae semel audita, nunquam iudicata, simpliciter adhaeserint, pertinaciter et obstinate decertent: fieret profecto ut succinctius artes institutae, facilius intelligerentur, et vera usus aperta via, promptius exercerentur. Veruntamen per Deum immortalem (dicet aliquis) tantumne tibi tribuis, ut vitia aut virtutes in his artibus vidisse tibi videaris, quae tantorum virorum aciem effugerint? Ego vero, Mecoenas, (te enim, tuique similes, id est candidos, nullaque peruersa opinione suffusos iudices appello) se Aristotelem in philosophia, Ciceronem et Quintilianum in eloquentia nihil esse dicam, non satis sanus esse videar. Fuerit igitur Aristoteles ingenio variis in rebus ac scientiis tam acuto, quam possit Aristoteleus quisquam cogitare: ingenii enim abundantiam quandam incredibilem in eo philosopho esse confiteor: Alexandri liberalitate fretus, ex omnium gentium inuentis et libris naturalem scientiam compilauerit, omnes philosophos non solum physicos, sed ethicos, politicos sua logica vexauerit: syllogismi in iudicando, methodi in collocando tantum interdum adhibuerit, quantum in summo philosopho requiri possit. Ciceroni dialectica ista et inueniendi, et disponendi ornamenta paria si voles, attribue, nihil detraham: imo vero non solum libenter, sed etiam vere fortasse concedam, omnium hominum qui sunt, qui fuerunt, quique postea futuri sunt, eloquentissimum fuisse: et vix tantam vel elocutionis (quanta in eius libris cernitur) et pronuntationis (quanta in historiis de eo memoratur) laudem sperari posse. De Quintiliano, faciam impudentur, si simile quicquam praedicem. Nam quamuis in eo sit ciuilis ad agendas caussas facultatis commonstrata quaedam prudentia, quanuis exempla quaedam utiliter collecta, attamen elocutionis quae summa laus eius esse possit, infinita est a Cicerone differentia. Nec enim in singulis verbis eadem est puritas, vel proprietas, vel elegantia. In coniunctis tanta est differentia, ut Cicero aureo quodam seculo, ferreo Quintilianus locutus esse videatur. Sed tamen ut temporibus illis diserti homines fuerunt, ita sane numeretur in disertis, qualis tamen fortasse nec esse possim, si velim, imo vero ne velim quidem, si possim: tales inquam, Aristoteles, Cicero, Quintilianus, tantique fuerint, an tamen qui una aut pluribus virtutibus excelluerint, protinus eos omnibus excellere est necesse? protinus omnibus in rebus necesse est non homines, sed deos existimare? De maximis aliorum generum virtutibus ubi vel Apollines, vel Ioues per me licet fuerint, hoc tempore nil quaeritur, de dialecticis et rhetoricis praeceptionibus nunc agitur, quas etiam fere omnes ab illis magna sui nominis gloria vel repertas primum, vel certe collectas ex aliis concedo. Quin adiungo, si in hisce praeceptionibus et accurate iudicandis, et ordine collocandis tot menses adhibuissent, quot annos ipse consumpsi: equidem non dubito longe veriores et distinctiores artes nobis relicturos fuisse. At res ipsa demonstrat ab his doctoribus multa quidem cumulata esse, sed non satis aestimata, hic syllogismum requiro: non satis apto ordine disposita, hic methodum desidero. Confirmo haec eadem nostris institutionibus et vere iudicata, et recte esse collocta. Quid ita? quia ad tractandum dialecticum et rhetoricum tum rationis, tum orationis usum, usum inquam vel eum qui in libris Aristotelis, Ciceronis,

Quintiliani perspicitur, dialecticae et rhetoricae artes Aristotelis, Ciceronis, Quintiliani fallaces et confusae sunt: nostrae veraces et distinctae, sicut et ars et exercitatio penitus explorata conuincit. Hoc primum, hoc medium, hoc summum contentionis meae firmamentum est. Non abutor testimoniis hominum, qui mentiri possunt, sed constantis et naturalis vsus, quem tot annos maximo quotidianae exercitationis labore persequor, usus inquam veritate et rerum experientia confirmo. Quamobrem Mecoenas, hac pulcherrima rectissimae voluntatis conscientia fretus, numquam quid sentiam de his artibus, quas profitebor, scribere erubescam, ad te praesertim non tam mecoenatem meum, quam communem bonarum literarum fautorem Galliae nostrae diuinitus oblatum. Sed in vestibulo nimium diu moramur, ad rhetoricas distinctiones accedamus.

# PETRI RAMI

## VEROMANDVI

## *Rhetoricae Distinctiones in Quintilianum,*

## AD

## CAROLVM LOTHARINGVM,

## *Cardinalem Guisianum.*

PERMAGNUM CUIPIAM fortasse videbitur ac perdifficile, quod aduersus Quintilianum mihi propono atque instituo, ut oratorias eius institutiones non legitime descriptas esse doceam: praesertim cum oratorem et praeclare definire initio, et rerum definitione comprehensarum deinde partes eleganter diuidere, et tandem singularum proprietatem partium ac naturam diligenter ad extremum et accurate persequi, omniaque singulari et consilio vidisse, et iudicio aestimasse, et methodo collocasse videatur. In hac autem disputatione Dialecticam, id est vere et constanter disserendi magistram (quantum mihi licebit) adhibebo, quo res acutius et prudentius aestimetur. Quamobrem Dialectici omnes, id est, quicunque de hac queastione vere et constanter iudicare possitis, adeste, animadvertite, vestram sapientiam excitate, repellite procul a vobis (si qui forte eiusmodi affectus animos vestros occupare parauerint) repellite, inquam, amorem, odium, praeiudicatam opinionem, leuitatem, inconstantiam, temeritatem, et quantum firma ratio conuicet, quantum conclusio certa conficiet, quantum denique veritas ipsa (qua neque refelli, neque redargui possit) obtinebit, tantum animis aequis et libentibus accipite. Ponatur igitur primum Quintiliani definitio, qua oratorem nobis suum explicauit, et ad hanc disputationum referantur omnia, quae ex omnibus Institutionum Fabianarum partibus referri conueniet. "Oratorem" (ait) "instituimus illum perfectum, qui esse nisi vir bonus non potest: ideoque non dicendi modo eximiam in eo facultatem, sed omnes animi virtutes exigimus." Hunc oratorem Quintilianus nobis instituit, quem postea libro duodecimo virum bonum bene dicendi peritum similiter definit, et illas animi virtutes exponit, iustitiam, fortitudinem, temperantiam, prudentiam, item philosophiam totam, legum scientiam, et cognitionem historiarum, et alia pleraque laudum ornamenta. Quid igitur contra istam oratoris finitionem dici potest? Ego vero talem oratoris definitionem vanam et inanem mihi videri confirmo: quamobrem? quia superuacanea et vitiosa cuiusuis artificis est definitio, quae plus complectitur, quam est artis institutis comprehensum. Artifex enim ex artium ratione definiendus, vt quantum artis veris et propriis decretis inclusum sit, tantum tribuatur artifici, nihil praeterea: definitio enim non solum est explicatio rei brevis et aperta, sed etiam rei quae definitur ita propria, ut omni solique perpetuo consentiat. Grammaticus definitur peritus recte loquendi et scribendi: non definitur peritus loquendi, scribendi et cantandi. Quid ita? quia de postremo nihil est in grammatica descriptum. Geometra non definitur peritus metiendi et medendi. Quid ita? quia nullum est in geometria praeceptum, quod docet mederi. Axioma igitur nostrum teneamus, et hoc syllogismi fundamentum ponatur:

> Artificis definitio vitiosa est, quae plus complectitur, quam est artis finibus inclusum.

tum hoc posito argumento assumamus:

> At artificis oratorii definitio nobis a Quintiliano tradita plus amplectitur, quam est artis finibus inclusum.

Rhetorica enim ars non est, quae omnes animi virtutes explicet. De virtutibus moralibus, et de virtutibus intelligentiae ac mentis proprie permulta et eleganter Ethici philosophantur: de arithmetica, geometria, mathematici: de reliquis tot tantarumque rerum scientiis, quae sunt etiam virtutes animi, docti et sapientes homines suis separatim studiis, non rhetores commentantur. Concludo igitur: Quare Fabiana ista oratoris definitio vitiosa est. At dicet Quintilianus, Philosophia moralis et illa ipsa virtutum doctrina rhetorum propria est, non philosophorum: et nunc perfectus orator informatur, qui non potest existere, nisi omnes animi virtutes assecutus. Quid si autem hoc utrunque alienum est et falsum? nonne summa complexionis et syllogismi tenebimus? Agite igitur, quaeramus quamobrem virtutum disciplina Rhetoricae pars aestimari possit. An quia et ciuitatem et ciues orator regere debeat, idcirco disciplina moralis rhetoricae propria quaedam pars erit? Sic sane Quintiliano videtur, cum ait, "Neque enim hoc concesserim, rationem recte honesteque vitae (ut quidam putauerunt) ad philosophos relegandam, cum vir ille civilis et publicarum privatarumque rerum administrationi accomodatus, qui regere consiliis urbes, fundare legibus, emendare iudiciis possit, non alius sit profecto quam orator. Quare tametsi me fateor usurum quibusdam (quae philosophorum libris continentur) tamen ea vere iureque contenderim esse operis nostri, proprieque ad artem oratoriam pertinere." Sic Quintilianus loquitur, et ita cogitat, ut oratoris nomine deum quendam mortalem omni virtute scientiaque perfectum et absolutum in republica principem appellet, non unius artis hominem cogitet. At hoc tempore de una quadam arte et virtute, non de omnium artium et virtutum absolutione praecipiendum Quintilianus sibi proposuit: et rhetoricam de liberalibus artibus unam quandam esse putat, non vero communem esse artem rhetoricam, idemque rhetoricam esse, quod artem, quod scientiam, quod virtutem existimat. Nullam enim in his oratoriis libris ciuilis facultatis scientiam, nullam vitae et officiorum disciplinam, nullam denique istarum laudum (quas oratoriae artis partes esse dicit) doctrinam in Rhetoricae partibus descripsit. Quinque Rhetoricae artis partes (de quibus postea dicam) Quintilianus esse iudicat, iuentionem, dispositionem, elucutionem, memoriam, actionem: non plures, non pauciores esse putat. Attamen in earum partium nulla philosophiam moralem (quam nunc rhetoricae tribuit) collocat. Dialectica vero huic homini vehementer defuit: a qua si didicisset in omni arte atque scientia causas rerum et veras, et proprias, et primas exquirendas esse, longe aliter oratorem definiendum censuisset: longe aliter de proprietate artium sibi philosophandum cognouisset. Duae sunt uniuersae et generales homini dotes a natura tributae, Ratio et Oratio: illius doctrina dialectica est, huius grammatica, et rhetorica. Dialectica igitur generales humanae rationis vires in cogitandis et disponendis rebus persequatur, grammatica orationis puritatem in etymologia, syntaxi, et prosodia ad recte loquendum, in orthographia etiam ad recte scribendum interpretetur. Rhetorica orationis ornatum tum in topicis et figuris, tum in actionis dignitate demonstret: ab his deinde generalibus et uniuersis velut instrumentis aliae artes sunt effectae: arithmetica in numeris, geometria in lineamentis, aliaeque in rebus aliis: quae si distinctae propriis finibus et conclusae fuerint, certe quod grammatica suo iure docebit, rhetorica non confundet, quod utraque perspicue descipserit, dialectica non attinget: usus earum coniungeretur, ut eadem sit oratio, quae et pure et ornate et sapienter loquatur et dicat, et sentiat: praecepta tamen pure loquendi, et ornate dicendi, et sapienter sentiendi distinguentur, neque confundentur. Quare Quintilianus ex hac reru[m] dialectica distinctione rhetoricam sic definire debuit, ut ei doctrinae propositam proprie et subiectam materiam a caeteris artium materiis distinctam et separatam primo comprehenderet uniuersam, deinde per partes diductam declararet. Atque ut istam rationem concludam, syllogismos duos repetam:

> Si philosophia moralis pars esset Rhetoricae, in aliqua eius parte explicanda esset.
> At id nusquam vel a Quintiliano fit, neque fieri omnino debet.
> Non est item pars Rhetoricae.
> Item, Partes materiae (quae Rhetoricae arti subiecta est) duae tantum sunt, elocutio et actio.
> Rhetoricae autem artis partes, sunt illius materiae partes, eisque omnino respondent.

Rhetoricae igitur partes duae tantum sunt, elocutio et actio. At Quintilianus instabit, ut facit, in eodem proposito, et acrius videlicet urgebit, quod Rhetorica sit virtus (id enim est libri secundi capite secundo) quod orator esse nisi vir bonus nemo possit (quod est duodecimi libri capite primo) et idcirco, opinor, virtutis doctrinam Rhetoricae partem esse concludet. Quod utrumque tamen ad opinionem Quintiliani falsum videri necesse est. Rhetorica enim virtus est quidem, sed mentis et intelligentiae, ut omnes honestae et liberales artes, quas tamen qui habeant, possint improbissimi homines esse. Non est autem moralis virtus Rhetorica (ut putat Quintilianus) ut qui ea praeditus sit, non bonus esse non possit: quamuis id Quintiliano philosophi quidam Stoici (ut libro secundo significat) hisce consectariis acute colligere videantur. "Consonare sibi in faciendis et non faciendis virtus est, nempe prudentia. Ergo consonare sibi in dicendis et non dicendis virtus erit. Item, si virtus est, cuius initium a natura datum est Rhetorica virtus erit: quia eius initium est a natura." Verum haec utraque tam acuta conclusio contorta et fallax est. Nam neque prudentia moralis est virtus, sed intelligentiae et mentis est virtus: nec ideo Rhetorica virtus moralis erit: et absurdum est ea virtutes morales putare, quorum initia a natura sint, quasi non magis sint initia vitiorum a natura, quam virtutum.

Quare Quintilianum philosophi isti decipiunt, et illi fraudulentum sophisma pro certo syllogismo contexunt. Pergit tamen Quintilianus, et a seipso affert, Dialectica est virtus, ergo Rhetorica. Immutet totum contra Quintilianus, et rectius concludet, Dialectica non est moralis virtus, quae virum bonum possit efficere: quare neque Rhetorica. Tum addit, Orator nihil potest in laudando, nisi honestorum ac turpium peritus, in iudiciis, si iustitiae sit ignarus, in turbulentis populi minis, si timidus. Quid tum Quintiliane? An qui nouit et honesta et iusta, honestus et iustus est? Quotusquisque heluo est et sicarius, qui quid honestum iustumque sit ignoret? Si timidus sit orator in causa Milonis, non bene dicet (ais) Quid tum postea? Non poterit sane grammaticus recte loqui si timeat, quia longas pro breuibus, aut breues pro longis timore conturbatus enuntiabit: et memoria conturbata barbarismos et solaecismos faciet. Ergo grammatica virtus moralis est? qaenam fuerit ista complexio? Aliud vero est alterum alteri esse necessarium, aliud eius esse partem et membrum. Dixeris sane virtutem moralem utilem, et ad omnium artium usus accommodatam, non inficiabor: artem ullam virtutem esse moralem nequaquam tamen concedam. Postremum etiam quisquilias ineptissimas Quintilianus colligit, quod in bestiis sit virtus, et in latronibus fortitudo: nec mirum ideo, si sit eloquentia moralis virtus. At Quintilianus iam non videtur Dialecticae expers et ignarus esse, sed uniuersae omnino philosophiae, et eius maxime philosophiae, quae de virtute praecipit. De virtute morali loqueris Quintiliane, quae bonos et honestos et laudabiles efficiat cultores sui, neque tamen consideras quid loquare, cum bestiis eam et latronibus attribuas. Meliora verba quaeso imposterum, vel meliora potius consilia meditere. At enim non quiescit Quintilianus tamen: duodecimo libro ad istam quaestionem relabitur, et similes apinas aggregat. "Mens mala Rhetoricae vacare non potest" (ait) Item "maxima pars Rhetoricae est de bono et aequo," tum "virtutis authoritas valet ad persuadendum." Quorum duo prima perridicula et perabsurda: tertium illi simile est, timidus orator non bene orabit. Veruntamen ista pratereamus. Atque interea neque philosophiam moralem Rhetoricae partem, neque ipsam Rhetoricam omnino moralem virtutem esse teneamus, ut Quintilianus existimavit. Veniamus ad illud potius (quod ait) a se nunc oratorem perfectum informari, qui non possit esse nisi omnibus animi virtutibus instructus et ornatus: et idcirco moralis philosophia Rhetoricae pars et in oratoris definitione virtus collocanda sit: hoc enim reliquum est quo videatur error hic uniuersus posse sustineri. Enimuero si perfecti oratoris nomine iam nunc informatur politicus ille vir, qui publicas et priuatas causas ciuium suorum tractare dicendo, qui virtutis authoritate, quique orationis suauitate possit animos audientium impellere quo velit, qualem significat poeta,

> Tum pietate grauem, ac meritis si forte virum quem
> Conspexere, silent, arrectisque auribus adstant:
> Ille regit dictis animos, et pectora mulcet.

si, inquam, vir ille politicus omnibus artibus et virtutibus instructus a Quintiliano definitur: de tam multis artibus et virtutibus non una rhetorica, sed omnes artes et virtutes (quoniam ex his constat politica illa facultas) exponendae describendaeque essent Quintiliano, grammatica, rhetorica, dialectica, mathematicae artes, philosophia tota. At Quintilianus id non fecit. Quare Quintilianus perfectum illum oratorem (quem dicit) non informat, sed (ut ante dixi) unam quandam de liberalibus disciplinis disciplinam cogitat: quam ut mirabiliorem faciat hoc modo conturbat, et seipsum hac ratiocinatione decipit, non potest perfectus orator esse sine philosophia: Ergo philosophia pars est rhetoricae. Verum Quintilianum hic ego dupliciter lapsum esse arguo et reprehendo, et quod argumento falso et quod argumentatione captiosa tam imprudenter utatur. Neque enim verum est rhetoricam sine philosophia morali exerceri, et quantum liceat, perfici non posse. Potest enim nondum percepta philosophiae moralis scientia omnis elocutionis doctrina et troporum et figurarum, item omnis actionis varietas et vocis et gestus propositis primum oratorum et poetarum exemplis explicari, ut istae dicendi laudes illic aperiantur et exponantur, et imitationis genere tum scribendo, tum dicendo exprimantur, atque omnino tandem quouis exercitationis modo tractentur et exerceantur. Duae autem illae partes, elocutio et actio, rhetoricae artis partes solae veraeque sunt, ut antea demonstraui: atqui sic est docendarum artium ordo, ut prima cum sit grammatica, sine reliquis intelligi et exerceri possit: secunda rhetorica sine grammatica non possit, sine caeteris omnibus autem possit. Et ut grammaticus perfectus, id est praestans et excellens (perfectum enim omnino nihil est nec in natura nec in arte nec in usu, quibus tamen artes vere perficiuntur) sed tamen, inquam, ut grammaticus perfectus dicendus est, qui omnes artes suae perfectiones est consecutus: sic orator plane perfectus habendus est, qui oratoriae doctrinae consummatas et perfectas laudes adeptus est: alioqui si plures artes adiungas, fuerit sane hominis qui eas habeat, perfectio maior, singularum sane artium perfectio maior non erit, sed multarum perfectio artium coniuncta erit: perfectio et absolutio Arithmeticae, non est geometriae perfectio: artium enim perfectiones ex ipsis artibus aestimandae et metiendae sunt, non extrinsecus ex alienis rebus accersendae. Quamobrem qui puer in dicendo et tropis et figuris variare orationem didicerit et ornare: item et voce et gestu congruenti pronuntiare, is mihi perfectus orator erit, si quid perfectum in artibus existimandum est, quia omnes artis oratoriae perfectiones, id est, virtutes et laudes sit amplexus. Quod ipsum Quintilianum lib. 2. (sed quid agat imprudens) confirmat. Finem oratoris non esse persuadere ait, quia id in euento fortuito (quem ars praestare sua vi non possit) positum sit, sed bene dicere, vt qui bene dixerit, quanuis non vincat, tamen finem sit assecutus, quoniam id quod arte continetur, effecit. "Nam," ait, "et gubernator vult salua nave in portum peruenire: si tamen tempestate fuerit abreptus, non ideo malus erit gubernator, dicetque notum illud, dum clauum rectum teneam." Hic Quintilianus et vere et magnifice sentit finem, id est, absolutam perfectionem rhetoricae non esse in rebus alienis et externis, sed in propria artis ipsius potestate. Quare non pudeat Quintilianum, si non a nobis, a Quintiliano certe ipso de tanto errore admoneri. Dicit initio rhetoricam perfectam sine philosophia non esse, dicit contra postea rhetoricam totam in sese conuersam esse, et eius finem atque perfectionem non extrinsecus aliunde pendere, sed ipsa arte omnino penitusque contineri. Quare concludamus sine philosophia rhetoricam perfici atque absolui posse. Attamen vide quantam licentiam, iuris nostri aequitas fiduciaque nobis largiatur. Conuici tot argumentis fallaciam argumenti, quo Quintilianus inductus est: concedo tamen ac permitto ut id omne verissimum et certissimum iudicetur, si, quod vult Quintilianus, hinc effici possit. Esto igitur non possit sine reliquis artibus ac virtutibus, non possit sine philosophia rhetoricae usus perfectus et absolutus esse, an tamen consentaneum fuerit rhetoricae partem statuere quicquid ei utile commodumque fuerit? Dicatur de dialectico, de Arithmetico quod de oratore Quintilianus dicit: non potest dialecticus, non potest arithmeticus sine rerum omnium scientia perfectus esse: quoniam omnium artium (quae ad humanitatem pertinent) usus communi quodam vinculo connexus et quasi cognatione coniunctus est: quis tamen credat dialecticum et arithmeticum recte definiri, si dicatur vir bonus disserendi vel numerandi peritus, dicaturque omni scientia et virtute perfectus? Aliud est aliquid esse necessarium, aliud est esse proprium: non potest tectum domus sine fundamento, sine terrae solo, sine deo denique esse: ergo definiendo tecto omnia ista comprehendam? Nimis absurdus hic error fuerit. Quare Quintilianus in argumento et in argumentatione labitur. At populus sic oratorem appellauit (inquies) fateor, inquam, et hanc definiendi oratoris tam inscitam inscitiam ab imperitae plebeculae inscitia profecta concedo. Vocabatur ut in Graecia *rhetor* primum, sic deinde in Italia orator is, qui causas ciuium ageret, quales aduocati sunt, qui nunc vocantur, et a rhetorica rhetores, ut a grammatica grammatici dicti sunt: quia primum rhetorica praecepit de tropis, de figuris et de his rebus, quae rhetoricae propriae essent, nullius praeterea disciplinae communes. Deinde cum rhetores disciplinae suae adiungerent, quae dialecticorum essent, inuentionem, dispositionem, memoriam, multa etiam alia confunderent, rhetoris nomen retentum est, tandem etiam sub eodem nomine et leges, et philosophia, et mathematicae artes, et historia, et virtutes sunt exaggeratae, et orator is appellatus, qui haec omnia cum eloquentia iunxisset. Verum in tradendis artibus non arbitror incertum vulgi errorem, sed certam veritatis legem sequendam esse. Constet igitur vitiosam et redundantem esse definitionem, qua nobis oratorem Quintilianus informauit: constet philosophiam moralem rhetoricae partem non esse, cum ad nullam rhetoricae partem referatur: constet partem non esse quia in nulla materiae subiectae parte contineatur: constet Stoicorum rationes falsas et captiosas esse: constet denique magnificam istam oratoris definitionem vanitatis plenam, veritatis inanem esse. Sed satis de oratoris definitione, in qua tametsi Quintilianus nec satis acutus esse, nec satis accurate disserere videatur, acutior fortasse ac prudentior in partitione quae sequitur erit. Summa igitur operis Quintiliano ad exornandum oratorem propositi partitio in duodecim libros includitur: "Primus liber," ait, "ea quae sunt ante officium rhetoris continebit. Secundo prima apud rhetorem elementa, et quae de ipsa rhetoricae substantia quaeruntur, tractabimus. Quinque deinceps inuentioni: nam et huic dispositio subiungitur. Quatuor elocutioni (in cuius partem memoria ac pronuntiatio veniunt) dabuntur. Unus accedet in quo orator ipse informandus est, ut qui mores eius, quae in suscipiendis, discendis, agendis causis ratio, quod eloquentiae genus, quis agendi debeat esse finis, quae post finem studia, quantum nostra valebit infirmitas, disseramus." Haec Quintiliani partitio est, in qua diligentiam Quintiliani magnam, ut in definitione quidem video. Omnia enim quae Graeci, quae Latini de oratore tradiderunt, in unum locum collegit: iudicium autem requiro. Eius autem partitionis (exceptis pauculis quae in elocutionis et pronuntiationis doctrina traduntur) caetera partim falsa, partim inepta, omnia certe sine dialectico lumine confusa et aliena esse confirmo. Primus liber (ait) continet ea quae sunt ante officium rhetoris. Sunt igitur, inquam, ista Rhetoricae artis aliena, nec cum de Rhetorica scribitur, in praeceptis ponenda. Atque in his rebus alienis quatuor scholae formandi pueri, qui futurus sit orator, a Quintiliano describuntur. Prima schola tribus primis capitibus traditur, de prima pueri infantis educatione, quod ad nutrices, parentes, sodales, paedagogos, literas Graecas et Latinas ad discendi et tempus, et locum, et modum, et ad initia denique mox cognoscendarum artium, de literarum ordine, de scribendo, legendo, de memoria, de pronuntiatione attinet. In quibus licet res verae et notabiles sint, et ad primam puerilis institutionis scholam necessariae, cum tamen tam multi et Latini et Graeci scriptores de hac prima puerorum educatione et schola, tam multa literis prodiderint, quis unquam Rhetoricae institutionis hoc esse dixit? Quis in Rhetoricas institutiones ut proprium aliquid inclusit? An non est ista et senatoris, et iureconsulti tam propria doctrina, quam oratoris? Artes non solum veris, sed etiam propriis institutis informandae sunt: atque aliud est esse aliquid utile, et verum, et laudabile, aliud esse alicuius artis proprium. Haec igitur schola Rhetoricae artis nihil est, neque hic cogitatio perceptioque rerum, sed aestimatio Quintiliano, sed syllogismus defuit: una enim conclusio ista omnia inducere poterat,

> Quae artium praeceptis includi debent, sunt earum propria.
> Haec non sunt Rhetoricae propria:
> Ne igitur huc includantur.

Neque porro huc recurramus, non potest orator sine hac educatione puerili existere: causa ista remotior est, non potest fortasse esse medicus perfectus sine eadem disciplina, non audiam tamen in medicina de isto puerili ludo praecipientem medicum. Nouem proximis capitibus secundae scholae grammaticus ludus aperitur, de qua primum idem sentiendum, quod de superiore; sint ista praecepta vera, sint utilia, sint oratori futuro necessaria, quid tum? An idcirco in oratoriis institutionibus admiscenda? Nonne philosopho sunt eadem Grammatica studia necessaria? Quis philosophum tamen ferret in philosophia de Grammaticorum artibus balbutientem? Haec oratori quidem ignoranda non sunt: non nego: verum cognoscantur a grammaticis, et cognita adferantur ad rhetoricam. Syllogismus idem erroris huius, qui prioris iudex esto. Non est ista schola oratoris propria: ex oratoria igitur arte tollatur. Sed tamen in ista schola vehementius offendit Quintilianus, quam in prima. Nec enim res alienas et improprias hic esse tantum dico, sed falsas et in arte et in artis exercitatione. In grammatica enim par fere et idem Quintiliani error est atque in tota rhetorica. Grammaticae partes duas facit, methodicen et historicen: illi recte loquendi et scribendi scientiam, huic enarrationem poetarum subiicit: in illa priore praecipit quaedam, sed confuse, de accentu literarum et syllabarum, de etymologia partium orationis, de syntaxi, de orthographia: quae grammaticae et omnes et solae partes sunt. Ad posterioris partis necessitatem subiicit grammatico ad poetas explicandum, historias, musicam, astrologiam, philosophiam, rhetoricam ipsam denique, cuius tamen famulam quandam grammaticam esse velit. Qui error ex imperitae plebeculae (ut de oratore dictum est) errore prosecutus est. Dicebantur enim quondam grammatici vulgo, qui in literis pueros instituebant et eis poetas enarrabant, quo in munere adhibenda esset artium praeter grammaticam variarum cognitio. Nec tamen vulgus intelligebat doctorem illum, qui in poetis explicandis varias artes doceret, esse quoque et historicum et musicum, et astrologum, et philosophum, et rhetoricae peritum, non autem grammaticum tantum. Verum Quintilianus in explicandis doctrinae praeceptis acutius, quam vulgus discernere ista debuit, et intelligere historicen (quam dicit) nullam esse grammaticae partem. Nam si magister iste in declarando poeta non exerceat solum artes et aetymologiae et syntaxis, et prosodiae et orthographiae ad pure et proprie loquendum et scribendum, sed ethicam scientiam adiungat ad mores exponendum, astrologiam ad ortus et occasus syderum declarandum, et caeteras artes ad res illis subiectas artibus exprimendum, certe id faciet non grammaticae, sed illarum disciplinarum facultate. Quod idem Quintilianus lib. 2. capite 1. fere ait, sed per imprudentiam multa conturbat. Quamobrem, ut de plerisque aliis in his sex capitibus taceam, partitio ista grammaticae in methodicen et historicen falsa est, non modo ista tot capitum schola a rhetoricis institutionibus est aliena. Ab hac tam eleganti, tamque dialectica descriptione grammaticae artis transit Quintilianus ad eius exercitationem de authoribus grammatico explicandis, de doctoris officio, de scriptione pueri. Solos autem iubet poetas Homerum imprimis et Virgilium pueris praelegendos esse: in quo vehementer ab eo dissentio. Nam ut poetas ad excitandum variis affectibus tenerum adhuc ingenium, ad prosodiae (cum versuum legibus syllabarum quantitas intelligatur) rationem legendos in paruis tamen duntaxat et exiguis rebus existimo, sit ad oratoriam verborum copiam ac forensem et ciuilem elocutionis usum, ad proprietatem et elegantiam dictionis comparandum epistolas Ciceronis, quam elegias Ouidii, et fabulas Terentii, quae sermonis fere quotidiani similes sunt, quam eclogas Virgilii malim. Alia siquidem est carminis, alia orationis elocutio. Atque hac occasione tam alienae institutionis factum fortasse est, ut Quintiliani a Cicerone tam longe abesset oratio, quoniam non imitandam Ciceronis et oratorum Ciceronis similium, sed poetarum dictionem sibi proposuerit. Labitur igitur hic primum Quintilianus, quod poetas solos pueris proponat. Iubet deinde ut in docendo et explicando poeta, grammaticus praestet illa quidem minora methodices munera de pedum proprietate, de significatione verborum: "sed maiore cura," inquit, "tropos, figuras verborum et sententiarum doceat: praecipue vero illa infigat, quae in oeconomia virtus, quae in decoro rerum, quid personae cuique coueniat, quid in sensibus laudandum, quid in verbis, ubi copia probabilis, ubi modus." Haec Quintilianus de grammatici officio, ubi videmus de duabus grammaticae partibus (quas fecit) methodicen (quae sola propria eius artis tantum erat) pene contemni: historicen, quae grammaticae nihil esset, unice commendari. Verum enimuero o Quintiliane, differat hic magister, aliena ista quanuis excellentiora et rhetoricorum ac philosophicorum studiorum (quorum propria sunt) temporibus reseruet. Illa autem disciplinae suae proprie subiecta omni cura diligentiaque tractet et exerceat, hic commoretur, hic habitet, hoc munus suum omnibus modis exornet, explicet in dictionibus singulis primam et natiuam significationem, tum phrasis et elocutionis rationem exemplis illustret, sit assiduus in exigendis literarum sonis, in accentus obseruatione, in orthographia, denique hoc ad se pertinere et totum et solum arbitretur, ut puerum sibi in disciplinam traditum recte et loqui et scribere doceat: de maioribus autem illis et altioribus quae tam vehementer hic commendas, tantum duntaxat adhibeat, quantum satis erit ad hoc methodices, quod aspernaris, munus tuendum. Ubi vero puer grammaticae partes omnes et loquendo et scribendo diligenter exercuerit, tum rhetoricas meditationes in tropis et figuris, philosophicas in reliquis laudibus adhibebit. Quod idem Quintilianus ipse postea ait, sed imprudens, ut alias tam saepe, seipsum conturbat: sic enim ait huius libri capite septimo, "Hae fere sunt emendate loquendi scribendique partes, duas reliquas significanter et ornate dicendi non quidem grammaticis aufero, sed cum mihi officia rhetoris supersint, maiori operi reseruo." Et postea capite I. lib. 2. quaeritur a grammaticis occupata esse rhetorum officia. Grammatica doctrina est bene loquendi et scribendi, ait Quintilianus: attamen idem Quintilianus iubet ut grammaticus doceat potius et ornate ex tropis et figuris et sapienter ac decore ex consilio, iudicio, prudentiaque rerum, quam bene loqui et scribere. At ista grammaticae sola sunt, illa sunt rhetoricae ac philosophiae. Quare Quintilianus grammatici doctoris propria officia isto modo non describit, sed aliena et impropria valde imprudenter confundit: in superioris illius erroris laqueos rursus incidit. "Postremum est in exercitatione grammaticae artis ut puer," ait Quintilianus, "poetarum sibi propositorum versus soluat, mox mutatis verbis interpretetur, tum paraphrasi audacius vertat, breviet quaedam et exornet, sententias propositas subiectis rationibus explicet." Verum puer iste Romanus doctori grammatico commissus quomodo Homerum mutatis verbis explicabit, qui Homeri verba nisi prius a magistro sibi exposita intellecturus non fuerit? Neque enim Graeco grammatico Romanus puer instituendus traditur, ut parta orationis facultate ad res alias utatur: unde enim parta illi infanti esset? Sed ut sermonis facultatem audiendo, legendo, imitando consequatur. Et hic tertius exercitationis error par est secundo. Ut enim grammatico praeceptori in docendo, sic nunc eiusdem artis auditori in discendo non grammaticae, sed rhetoricae, sed confirmatae iam plane et artis et exercitationis munus imponit. Quamobrem Quintilianus in hac secunda schola longe grauius errat, quam in prima. Illic enim res alienas tradebat, hic etiam falsas conturbat: et in arte grammatica, cuius partem historicen facit, et in artis exercitatione, tum quod solos poetas legendos proponat, tum quod magistrum et discipulum isto modo instruat. Atque hic non dico in conquirendis et inueniendis rebus Quintiliano curam defuisse, sed iudicii prudentiam, sed syllogismi rationem vehementer in eo desidero. Reliquis primi libri tribus capitibus duae quaedam nouae scholae Fabiano oratori describuntur: in quarum altera mathematicas artes cognoscat, in altera ad vocis et actionis dignitatem comoedos, tragoedos et palaestritas magistros adhibeat. De mathematicis autem magis, quam de grammaticis mirum est in rhetoricis artibus ita praecipi, quanquam nihil admodum Quintilianus praecipit, sed tamen finge mathematicas artes singulariter a Quintiliano instrui, quis erudiendae iuuentutis hic ordo fuerit? Rhetorica in elocutionis et actionis ratione, dialectica in praeceptis et inuentionis et dispositionis omnibus mathematicis artibus generalior et communior est, et ab illis uniuersis scientiarum fontibus singulares hi mathematici tanquam fontes fluxere. Cognitionis igitur ordine et rhetorica et dialectica praecedunt: mathemata omnia sequuntur: nec contra pro Quintiliano dici potest olim sic artes ipsas pueris traditas esse. Nam mathematicae artes primae et diu artes solae fuerunt, nec aliae poterant prius explicari, quae nullas essent, Quandiu enim lingua fuit integra, grammatica nulla fere fuit, et de rhetorica nihil admodum ante Isocratem fuerat institutum. Verum cum res non doceri solum et percipi, sed facile et doceri et percipi repertis ad id artibus possint, non iam quid solitum sit aliquando fieri, sed quid tandem oporteat fieri quaerendum esse arbitror. Praecipiunt una quasi voce omnes omnium magistrorum scholae, progressiones et institutiones artium ab uniuersis ad singularia tendere. Quare grammaticam, rhetoricam, dialecticam praecedere: mathematicas artes sequi necesse est. Hoc veritatis fundamentum, non consuetudinis abusum sequor. Ad comoedos, tragoedos et palaestritas a mathematicis nos mittit Quintilianus, utiliter fortasse si Quintiliani tempore viueremus: quia tum illi homines in propria et vocis et corporis formatione studiose elaborarunt, verum artis scriptori non conuenienter. Artes enim rerum constantium et perpetuarum et immutabilium esse debent, et eas ideas tantum spectare, quas Plato gigni negat, et ait semper esse. Tempus autem nullum fuit, locus nullus fuit, nec erit, quo non possit ornate dici, quo moderatio et vocis et gestus non possit adhiberi. Tempora et loca multa fuerunt, eruntque, ubi comoedi, tragoedi, palaestritae nulli fuerunt, nec erunt: Non igitur recte facit Quintilianus, qui artem perpetuam et immutabilem tam incertis magistris subiiciat. Atque in his omnibus scholis adhuc videmus, quam non absint rerum varietas et copia, sed quam syllogismi et iudicii ratio desit. Quicquid Quintilianus credidit oratori commodum fore, huc coniecit, non considerauit an esset proprium huius institutionis. Ad dialecticam omnes istas scholas referamus, eius iudicio permittamus: prima infantiae schola rhetoricae nihil est, secunda scholae grammaticae est, et multis partibus falsa, non solum rhetorica aliena est: tertia et quarta omnino item alienae, et varia ratione confusae. Quam igitur dialecticae sententiam expectemus, nisi ut a rhetoricis institutionibus scholas omnes istas non solum improprias, sed falsas, et inepte confusas expelli atque exterminari iubeat? Atqe haec de primo libro. Secundo prima apud rhetorem elementa, et quae de ipsa rhetoricae substantia quaeruntur, tractantur, ait Quintilianus. At tria primum magna et ampla capita sunt de tempore pueri ad rhetorem deducendi, de moribus et officiis praeceptoris, An optimo praeceptore protinus sit utendum, antequam de primis rhetoricae exercitationibus dicatur. Quae ipsa fac esse certa, vera, laudabilia, utilia: propria tamen huius artis et doctrinae ad breuem et perspicuam docendi viam descripta quomodo faciemus? Quaereret Donatus in explicatione suae artis similia, quando puer a domestica disciplina ad grammaticum deducendus, quales grammatici mores esse debeant, an protinus optimo grammatico sit utendum: illa tam utiliter in grammatica et omni disciplina quaererentur, quam quaeruntur hic in rhetorica. Sed non omnia quae vere, quae utiliter quaeri possunt, possunt etiam proprie et instituto conuenienter quaeri. Optimus praeceptor viam facilem et breuem in docendo sequi debet: cur igitur tot diuerticulis, tot meandris, tam spinosa, tam tortuosa via initur? Hic diligentiam et curam maximam in accumulandis rebus agnosco, dialecticam in discernendis et aestimandis nullam prorsus agnosco. Quatuor deinde capitibus de rhetorica exercitatione admodum confuse agitur, primo ut in narratione et fabulae et argumenti et historiae, confirmandi, refellendi, laudandi et vituperandi opere, pueri exerceantur. Hoc Quintiliani praeceptum non totum, sed ex parte reprehendo, quia nec loco, nec ordine positum sit. Ars primum describatur, tum demonstretur exercendae artis ratio in scribendo primum, tum etiam in dicendo. Sed tamen totam exercitationis disciplinam hoc loco traditam videamus. Quintilianus dederat antea grammaticis exercitationibus poetam solum: nunc historicum primo, oratorem deinde rhetoricis meditationibus attribuit: ut primo poetae, deinde historici tandem oratores pueris praelegantur. De poetis antea iam dixi, et valde miror Quintiliano id in mentem venisse, ut formando oratori putaret aptiores poetas et historicos, quam oratores esse, cum poetarum et historicorum non dico res permultas licentius et mollius expressas, sed virtutes etiam plerasque vitandas oratori vel in his institutionibus Quintilianus moneat. An formabit oratorem melius Livius aut Sallustius, quam Cicero? Ego vero ut poetae formando malim Virgilium atque Homerum, caeterosque poetas egregios et insignes, quam oratorem ullum: sic instituendo oratori Ciceronem longe historicis ac poetis omnibus praetulerim. An vero maior est oratoris in historicis, quam in oratoribus similitudo? Quapropter non solum alienum hoc totum caput, sed totius capitis consilium falsum iudico. Capita duo proxima sunt de diuisione materiarum, de dicendo, utilia: esto etiam vera. At nec loco, nec ordine sicut superiora duo posita. Dixit antea Quintilianus de Grammatica arte prius, de artis exercitatione postea: et in eo recte: Prius enim descripta cognitaque sit ars, quam de artis exercitatione dicatur. Ars autem rhetorica descripta a Quintiliano nondum est: de eius igitur exercitatione importune isto loco praecipitur: et iudicium hic ut antea syllogismumque a Quintiliano requiro. Capita septem proxima quaestiones habent de edificendo, de officio discipuli, de modo docendi discipuli, de utilitate declamandi, an cognitio artis sit necessaria: quare ineruditi videantur vulgo ingeniosores, quis modus sit in arte. Omnia sane ad institutam artis Rhetoricae descriptionem magis aliena, quam illa de quibus adhuc disseruimus. Postremum de modo artis valde videtur verum, quod Rhetoricae praecepta catholica non sint, sed ad temporis; loci, personae, causae varietatem commutabilia. At si ars rhetorica suis partibus elocutione et actione comprehensa sit, falsissimum fuerit. Tam enim constans fere ars erit Rhetorica, quam arithmetica, vel geometria, et eius praecepta de elocutione et actione tam stabilia, quam theoremata Euclidis de planitie ac linea. Sed Quintilanus suas institutiones, id est, ad forensium et ciuilium causarum Romanas formulas, astrictam variarum artium confusionem, Rhetoricam artem vocat: nec mirum est de tali arte dici, praeceptis eius non esse confidendum, cum tanta fallacia, falsaque sint, non solum omnibus locis, temporibus, personis non conuenientia. Atque haec libro primo, et libri secundi capitibus tredecim Quintilianus extra rhetoricae substantiam tradit esse. Reliqua capita octo libri secundi in partitione prooemio comprehensa dicit de substantia Rhetoricae esse: et sane decimoquarto capite substantia Rhetoricae quaedam tractatur: ubi quod etymon sit Rhetoricae Quintilianus videtur explicare velle, non satis explicat tamen: non enim Rhetorices etymologiam omnino ostendit: qui dicit Latine Rhetoricam vel oratoriam vel oratricem transferri, sed qui exponit quae sit origo verbi, et unde deducta significatio. Partitur totam doctrinam sequentem tres in partes, ut dicatur de arte, artifice, opere, partitione admodum ridicula et inepta. Definita enim prima parte, pars secunda tertiaque comprehenduntur. Non definitur in grammatica grammaticus, non grammatici opus: Non definitur in arithmetica, in geometria, arithmeticus, geometra, vel arithmetici, vel geometrae opus, quia ars demonstrat qualis artifex, quale ipsum artis opus esse debeat. Dialecticas igitur partiendi leges hic a Quintiliano requiro. Caetera autem tamen omnia tam perplexa, tam prolixa de variis et controuersis rhetoricae definitionibus, quod Rhetorica utilis sit, quid sit ars, et cuiusmodi, quod ars plus quam natura conferat, an Rhetorica sit virtus, quae sit eius materia, plane sunt eius doctoris qui rudes et incipientes huius artis discipulos velit aut deterrere, aut frangere, aut fallere: quem doctorem tamen vehementer Quintilianus octaui libri initio et vere reprehendit: non eius qui via simplici et breui cupiat ad usum artis perducere, quem eodem locum commendauit. Quid autem attinet omnium hominum errores de rhetoricae definitione, utilitate, arte veluti cumulare, falsa etiam conturbare, quod consummatis oratoribus plus ars, quam natura conferat? Distinguatur enim, ut decet, in hac perfecti oratoris quaestione, natura, ars, exercitatio, sane primas (ut oratorio secundo Cicero recte sentit) naturae, secundas exercitationi, tertias et minimas arti tribuemus. Et hoc Quintiliani sophisma falsum esse demonstrabimus: qui cum ait, consummatis plus adferre doctrinam, quam naturam: uno artis nomine et naturam, et artem, et exercitationem comprehendat, cum tamen comparet in hac quaestione naturam cum arte: hic dialectici salis ne mica quidem ulla est: nihil secernere: nihil syncere ac constanter aestimare doctor iste potest: totus in dialecticis sane plumbeus est. Sunt autem valde ridicula Quintiliani argumenta in quaestione an rhetorica sit virtus, sed de his initio quia dictum est, nihil necesse est iterum dici. Postremo capite valde occupatus est Quintilianus in inuestiganda Rhetoricae materia: et varia dissidentium hac de re opinionum sententia: tandem concludit materiam Rhetorices esse, res omnes quae ei ad dicendum subiectae sunt. Quod sane parum perspicue et plane dictum est. Primum quod alia sit artis, artificis vero alia materia. Ars rhetorica sibi proponit naturalis usus in bene dicentium exemplis obseruationem, quam praeceptis explicet: artifex, id est, orator arte rhetorica instructus proponit sibi res omnes quae dicendo possunt exornari. Sic materia grammatici, res omniae quae sunt ei subiectae ad recte loquendum aut scribendum: materia dialectici, omnes res ei subiectae ad recte disserendum: materia arithmetici omnes res ei subiectae ad numerandum: materia geometrae omnes res ei subiectae ad metiendum. Sed tamen non repugno, quin *tropikos* aliquando dicatur materies artis, pro artificis materia. Hanc igitur materiae licet non satis explicatae definitionem, tamen probo, et ad verae Rhetoricae proprias institutiones accipio. Duobus enim primis oratoriarum institutionum libris ex tam multis scholis domestica, grammatica, mathematica, comoedorum, tragoedorum, palaestritarum, rhetorum tandem, haec duo sola sunt, quae in vera Rhetorica laudari et probari possunt. Rhetorica est bene dicendi scientia: materia oratoris est res quaeuis ad dicendum ei subiecta. Cetera vero tam multa, tametsi locis aliquot vera utiliaque, tamen omnia in rhetoricae artis accurata descriptione aut aliena omnino, aut certe praepostera sunt. De duobus primis Quintiliani libris adhuc est disputatum, ubi grammatica imprimis confusa est. Quinque proximis de Dialectica agitur, de inuentione quippe et dispositione. Ergo de his partibus deinceps, et de capitibus etiam singulis est disserendum. Primo itaque capite libri tertii accumulat Quintilianus unum in locum omnium huius artis magistrorum et Graecorum, et Latinorum inuenta, et magistros ipsos nominatim recenset, curiosa plane, sed inutili diligentia. Nihil enim catalogus iste tot nominum doctrinae Rhetoricae ostendit, non magis quam in grammatica, si isto vanitatis studio omnes grammaticae scriptores nominatim persequare: nihil inquam catalogus iste doctrinae ostendit. Inopia iudicii et syllogismi, copiam vanitatis huius peperit. Tale caput proximum est, quo tamen loco non satis acute Quintilianus Rhetoricae causas et principia distinguit, naturam, utilitatem, artem, exercitationem. Quid enim? an Plato et Cicero errarunt? an Quintilianus ipse libri huius capite quinto errauit, cum docet tribus rebus Rhetoricam perfici atque absolui natura, arte, exercitatione? quid utilitas habet a tribus illis causis et principiis diuersum? nihil enim est frustra et sine utilitate aliqua vel a natura propositum, vel ab arte descriptum, vel ab exercitatione tractatum. Haec dialectica partiendi elegantia est, quod tribus membris debeas explicare, uno conficto quatuor amplificare. Tertio capite diuiditur rhetorica in quinque partes, inuentionem, dispositionem, elocutionem, memoriam, et actionem. In qua partitione nihil iam miror Quintilianum dialectica tam nudum esse, qui dialecticam ipsam cum rhetorica hic confusam non potuerit agnoscere, cum dialecticae sint, inuentio, dispositio, memoria: Rhetoricae tantum elocutio et actio. Ratio vero Quintiliani quare quinque sint istae rhetoricae partes ex uno et eodem erroris fonte defluxit, unde superioris confusionis causae fluxerunt: Non potest orator (ait Quintilianus) perfectus esse sine virtute, sine grammatica, sine mathematicis artibus, sine philosophia. Oratoris igitur natura est ex omnibus his rebus definienda: Non potest (ait idem) grammaticus absolutus esse sine musica, astrologia, philosophia, rhetorica, historia. Grammaticae igitur partes duae sunt, methodice et historice: ita nunc demum Quintilianus ratiocinatur non potest rhetorica constare, nisi res primo inveniatur, deinde disponatur, tum exornetur, postremo memoriae mandetur et pronuntietur. Quinque sunt igitur hae partes rhetoricae. Causa ista sine qua (ut quidam nominant) Quintilianum saepe fefellit et induxit. At ego longe aliter de proprietate et veris artium partibus disputandum (ut iam dixi) et ratiocinandum duco. Artium materias distinguendas et separandas esse iudico. Dialectica mentis et rationis tota est, rhetorica et grammatica sermonis et orationis: Dialectica igitur inuentionis, dispositionis, memoriae (quae mentis omnino sunt et intus sine ullo linguae aut orationis auxilio exerceri possunt: ut in plerisque mutis, ut in multis populis, qui sine sermone ullo vivunt) artes proprias habebit. Grammaticae tribuetur ad bene loquendum atque scribendum, in interpretatione etymologiae, in coniunctione syntaxis, in syllabarum breuium et longarum pronuntiatione prosodia, in recta scribendi ratione orthographia. Rhetoricae igitur ex sermonis et orationis cultu partes duae solae propriae relinquentur, elocutio et actio: proprium praeterea ac suum rhetorica nihil habebit. Neque hic Quintiliani modo disputo ex causa, sine qua res esse non potest: ex caussa propria et legitima disputo,

> Tot partes in unaquaque arte sunt instituendae non plures, quot sunt in propria eius et naturali materia:
> In materia artis dialecticae, id est naturali rationis usu, vis est inueniendi, disponendi, et recordandi:
> Tot igitur partes sunt in ea explicandae.

Item,

> In materia rhetoricae subiecta vis eloquendi et pronuntiandi sola continetur:
> Tot igitur partes in ea sunt explicandae.

Item,

> Partes alterius artis non sunt in arte rhetorica permiscendae:
> Inuentio, dispositio, memoria alterius disciplinae partes sunt, nempe dialecticae:
> Non sunt igitur in rhetorica permiscendae.

Partes autem illas esse dialecticae Quintilianus suo nobis etiam testimonio locis aliis demonstrat: libri enim quinti capite postremo de dialecticis sic ait, "Namque illi homines docti et inter doctos verum quaerentes minutius ac scrupolosius scrutantur omnia, et ad liquidum confessumque perducunt, ut qui sibi inueniendi et iudicandi vendicent partes, quarum alteram *topiken*, alteram *kritiken* vocant." Hic Quintilianus dicit a dialecticis et inuentionem et iudicium (quod magnam dispositionis in singulorum argumentorum conclusionibus et syllogismis partem continet) vendicari: Et de memoria ait tandem libri undecimi capite secundo, Si quid artis habeat, id totum dispositionis et ordinis esse. Dicat igitur a dialecticis istam quoque partem posse merito vendicari: quia in dialectica vere descripta ordinis et dispositionis ex syllogismi et methodi praeceptis doctrina verissima doceatur. Refellit hoc capite Quintilianus varias opiniones de numero harum quinque partium, sed ita plerunque ut ipse multo gravius labatur, quam hi quorum lapsus reprehendit. Quidam adiiciebat iudicium tanquam ab inuentione et dispositione diuersum. Hos reprehendit Quintilianus recte: vero argumento non recto, sed valde veri iudicii ignaro atque imperito. Iudicium Quintilianus inuentioni, dispositioni, elocutioni, pronuntiationi sic commistum arbitratur, ut ab his separari doctrina et praeceptis non possit: nec omnino intelligit ullam esse iudicii doctrinam, sed (ut postea in extremo volumine sexto est) existimat non magis arte tradi posse, quam gustum vel odorem. Ita se Quintilianus dialecticae valde ignarum profitetur, qui de iudicandi parte, de tot syllogismorum et simplicium et coniunctorum modis neque quidquam vel audierit vel legerit, qui non meminerit a Cicerone de Stoicis ita dici, quod in altera dialecticae parte duntaxat elaborarint, inueniendi artes non attigerint, iudicandi vias diligenter persecuti sint. Neque vero audiendum quod existimari forsan possit, aliud esse rhetoricum, aliud dialecticum iudicium: Unum enim est hominis iudicium ad quiduis aestimandum an id vere expediat, conueniat, deceat, an tale omnino sit, quale esse videatur, quod syllogismo solo praestatur atque efficitur: nec aliud est quidquam verum vel falsum regula syllogismi perspici, quam vere an falso dicatur quodcumque in controuersiam et contentionem adducitur. Hic quid dicam iudicii doctrinam, syllogismi disciplinam Quintiliano defuisse, cum ipse neget ullam omnino esse posse? Quid pluribus argumentis iam contendam in dialecticis rudem Quintilianum esse? Non enim solum confitetur quod arguo, sed profitetur. A dialecticis ait duas artes vendicari, alteram inueniendi, alteram iudicandi: ait quidem, sed non credit, quia affirmat iudicii artem nullam esse. Pergamus igitur, et contra rhetorem hunc iudicii arte et doctrina carentem, iudicii tamen arte utamur. Sententiam eius reliquis de rebus ad dialectici iudicii normam referamus. Deinde vero mirabiliter confusa est institutio. Quarto, quinto, sexto, decimo, undecimo capitibus agitur de oratoris materia et eius diuisione. Hanc igitur primum de quaestione contentionem expediamus. Tria causarum genera a Quintiliano primum constituuntur, demonstratio, deliberatio, iudicium: eiusque partitionis Aristoteles author adhibetur, is scilicet, qui omnium in hac arte tenebrarum inuentor et author propemodum solus fuit, qui dialecticam inuentionem primus in rhetorica arte conturbauit, qui quaestiones tam inepte, tamque ridicule (quam in Aristotelicis animaduersionibus docuimus atque hic repetemus) distribuit. At partitionem hanc primum esse falsam dico: quia sint quaestiones innumerabiles, quae nulla horum generum parte contineantur, quod Quintilianus vidit, cum ait, "Verum et tum leuiter est tentatum, cum apud Graecos quosdam, tum apud Ciceronem in libris de oratore, et nunc maximo nostrorum temporum authore, prope impulsum, ut non modo plura haec genera, sed etiam pene innumerabilia videantur. Nam si laudandi ac vituperandi officium in parte tertia ponimus, in quo genere versari videbimur, cum quaerimur, consolamur, mitigamus, concitamus, terremus, confirmamus, praecipimus, obscure dicta interpretamur, narramus, deprecamur, gratias agimus, gratulamur, obiurgamus, maledicimus, describimus, mandamus, renuntiamus, optamus, opinamur, et plurima, ut mihi in illa veteri persuasione permanente velut petenda sint venia, quaerendumque quo moti priores rem tam late fusam, tam breuiter astrinxerint." Haec ille recitat ad pompam quandam, ut rem difficilem soluisse videatur: neque videtur argumenti vim (quo contra se utitur) intellexisse, sed captiosa et fallaci solutione contentus seipsum caepit et fefellit. Sic autem Quintilianus sibi videtur huic occurrere obiectioni: "Mihi cuncta rimanti" (ait) "talis quaedam ratio succurrit, quod omne oratoris officium aut in iudiciis est, aut extra iudicia." Esto: quid tum? "Eorum de quibus iudicio quaeritur" (ait) "manifestum genus est." Concedo: quid deinde? "Ea quae ad iudicem non veniunt" (ait) "aut praeteritum habent tempus, aut futurum": quamobrem, inquam? an nulla de re praesenti quaestio, nulla disputatio, nulla dicendi occasio potest existere? Cum de hac syntaxi, de hoc quadrato, de hac stella, de hoc vulnere, de rebus huiusmodi innumerabilibus quaeritur, de praeterita re aut futura quaeritur potius, quam de praesenti? falsum igitur hoc est. Sed tamen perge. "Praeterita" (inquit) "laudamus aut vituperamus, de futuris deliberamus": An non etiam de praeteritis et de futuris et quaerendi, et consolandi, et mitigandi, et concitandi, et terrendi, et alia innumerabilia agendi offerri potest occasio? Nihil hic igitur Quintilianus concludit, nihil soluit, sed seipsum confundit. At euidens approbatio altera superiori additur. "Omnia de quibus dicendum est" (ait) "aut certa sint necesse est, aut dubia." Quid tum, Quintiliane? quid hac diuisione efficies? Certa ut cuique est, animus laudat (ait) aut culpat. Atqui multa et incerta laudamus et vituperamus, ut Cicero et Caesar in Catone: et multa certa tractamus, neque laudando, neque vituperando, ut rerum artibus et liberalibus et illiberalibus comprehensarum incomprehensibilia pene negotia: Pars igitur huius partitionis est falsa. "Ex dubiis" (ait) "partim deliberatur, partim lite contenditur": Ego vero hic idem requiro, quod in membro proximo, dubiae sint ignoranti, res infinitae artibus comprehensae: an de iis hic ignarus ex rhetoriciis Quintiliani praeceptis deliberationem aut iudicium informare, non doctum et peritum hominem adhibere et interrogare debebit? O leuem et inertem confirmationem! Hac scilicet subtilitate Quintilianus argumenta sibi obiecta refutauit? hoc modo suorum temporum authori maximo restitit? Atqui non est hoc falsa argumenta veris argumentis refellere, sed falsis sophismatis vera potius confirmare. Addit Quintilianus ad extremum velut solutionem quandam aliam. Ceteras illas species in haec tria genera recidere: sed insolenter admodum et artis scriptoris indecenter. Authoritate siquidem sua nobis imperare vult, quod nulla ratione vera probare queat. Dialecticam partiendi prudentiam hic requiro: non iam dico Quintilianus tantum sine arte iudicii labi, sed sine ulla inuentionis intelligentia vagari: Partitiones quaestionum similis ac longe maioris vanitatis sequuntuir totis capitibus quinto, sexto, undecimo, contra quas non statui maiorem orationem consumere, ut doceam et ineptas et falsas esse, sed potius uniuersa quadam tot ineptiarum confutatione utendum mihi esse duxi. Dico igitur in arte rhetorica non solum vere et proprie ex elocutionis et actionis partibus comprehensa, sed in hac Quintiliani confusione ex inuentionis, dispositionis, elocutionis, memoriae, actionis partibus conturbata, totam quaestionum istarum partitionem et diuisionem plane inutilem esse. Quamobrem vero ita sentiamus, hanc argumentationem ex Aristotelicis animaduersionibus repetamus,

> Communis rerum sibi subiectarum doctrina nullam earum partitionem requirit,

Ut in grammatica non sit diuisio rerum grammaticae subiectarum, quia grammatica communis est ars de omnibus rebus scribendi et loquendi.

> Rhetorica vel quinque partibus a Quintiliano confusa, tota communis est rerum sibi subiectarum.

Una enim communis est ars memoriae, pronuntiationis, elocutionis, nec earum varie partes ad varias quaestiones accomodatae, nisi quod nescio quid de qualitate elocutionis et genere in demonstratione, deliberatione, et iudicio praecipitur, ars tamen alia non est troporum et figurarum, sed usus alius: de inuentione et iudicio idem suo loco probabo et demonstrabo. Imo vero Quintiliani iudicio potius aquiescam, a quo rhetorica definita est non de hac aut illa re, sed de omnibus rebus bene dicendi scientia.

> Rhetorica igitur nullam quaestionum partitionem requirit.

Hic non captiose aut obscure argumentor, sed causam summam et primam partiendae quaestionis interpretor. Si quaestio diuidenda esset in rhetorica, id fieret quia ad ceteras quaestiones, artes quaedam certae accomodarentur: omnes in uniuersum illarum partes omnibus quaestionibus non conuenirent. At id falsum esse contendo, primum in tribus partibus, elocutione, memoria, actione id planum et confessum obtineo: in duabus reliquis partibus, inuentione et dispositione, idem rebus necessariis ad dicendum suscipio. Summa vero totius confusionis in una inuentione est: non est iterata saepius, non pluribus modis confusa memoriae aut pronuntiationis doctrina semel exponitur, et uno tantum loco: non est repetitis iisdem generibus et confusis conturbata elocutionis in tropis et figuris disciplina: quanuis enim multis rebus non necessariis a Quintiliano pars ista onerata est, tamen una et uno octaui et noni libri loco proposita est: de disciplina dispositionis et argumentorum et quaestionum, et partium orationis multa Quintilianus variis locis loquitur: praeceptum nullum catholicum et generale (ut eius verbis utar) interpretatur. Summa inquam confusionis rhetoricae in inuentione tota versatur: cuius causam possumus ex ratione et progressione temporum percipere. Video enim artis huius doctores et magistros in cumulandis veterum decretis, et in nouis excogitandis maius studium, quam in distinguendis et alienis et suis inuentis iudicium adhibuisse. Primi rhetores ante Aristotelem non ut generalem quandam et de rebus omnibus ornate dicendi doctrinam traderent, sed tantum ut consiliis quibusdam et monitis forensium et ciuilium causarum formulas instruerent, de ratione amplificandi ex tropis et figuris: de mouendo auditore ad iram, misericordiam, inuidiam, indignationem, et eiusmodi affectus: de generibus caussarum demonstratiuarum, deliberatiuarum, iudicalium alii alia proposuerunt. Aristoteles postea cupide et curiose in unum ea omnia accumulauit, et cum primis illis artibus uniuersos dialecticae inuentionis et communes locos conturbauit: de pronuntiatione nonnulla etiam excogitauit: memoria postea rhetoricae addita est. Tot igitur modis inuentionis artes inuoluit, quot modis inuolutas habemus, cum tamen una tantum generalis doctrina in decem locos caussarum, effectorum, subiectorum, adiunctorum, dissentaneorum, collatorum, nominum, distributionum, finitionum, testimoniorum distincta ad omnes quaestiones, ad omnes orationis partes, ad res omnes denique facillime et apertissime declarandum accomodari posset. At dicet aliquis, illae minores inuentionis artes in generibus causarum, in partibus orationis nouitiis et rudibus describuntur, maiores autem et communiores quae sunt in locis uniuersis, iis scilicet qui iam aliquem progressum in illis studiis fecerint. Audio, inquam, et hoc oratorio secundo apud Ciceronem dici scio, sic enim illic Antonius de his inuentionis locis loquitur. "Ego autem si quem plane rudem institui ad dicendum velim, iis potius assiduis uno opere eandem incudem diem noctemque tundentibus, qui omnes tenuissimas particulas atque omnia minima mansa ut aiunt nutrices, infantibus pueris in os inserunt: Sin sit et doctrina liberaliter institutus, et aliquo iam imbutus usu, et satis acri ingenio esse videatur, illuc eum rapiam, ubi non seclusa aliqua aquula teneatur, sed unde uniuersum flumen erumpat: et illi sedes tanquam domicilium omnium argumentorum commonstret, et ea breviter illustret et verbis definiat." Haec illic Antonii voce Cicero. At de Cicerone hoc in uniuersum responsum esse volo, in rhetoricis praeceptis nihil fere Ciceroniani vel iudicii vel ingenii esse, sed magistrorum et rhetorum quos audierat, vel legerat, Aristotelis maxime, artes propositas esse: Ciceronem his artibus eloquentem factum non esse, nec ex his ita perturbatis artibus eloquentiam Ciceronis, sed ex artibus nostris (quas ad eius usum accommodamus) mirabilem facile posse perspici. Attamen sit contra Ciceronis authoritas, an superiorem volumus in artis disputatione hominis cuiusquam authoritatem, quam causae vertitatem esse? Pone simile aliquod in alia artis institutione documentum. Definiat grammaticus nomen et omnes adiunctas nomini circumstantias, et accidentias exponat in uniuersum: Hoc quia commune est, quia generale, est, ad omnia nomina sufficere arbitramur: minutiores artes nullas requirimus, nec ulla specialis facilior explicari posset, quam est illa generalis. At in inuentionis doctrina idem plane est. Qui magister docet omnia quae de re aliqua dici possunt, esse vel causas, vel effecta, vel subiecta, vel adiuncta, vel dissentanea, vel comparationes, vel nomina, vel tributiones, vel finitiones, vel testimonia et ea diligenter explicat, sane omnium rationum, omniumque argumentorum doctrinam explicat: nec ulla minutius secta institutio commodior esse potest: nec tot subductionibus (quibus Quintilianus in quaestionibus, in orationis partibus utitur) ulla melior aut facilior via docetur ad cogitandum et inueniendum, quod de re proposita dicatur. Quamobrem tantae perturbationis excusatio probari nullo modo potest. Sed ad ipsas inuentionis artes, quae docentur a Quintiliano, in generibus caussarum, in partibus orationis, in locis communibus veniamus: nihil nisi decem nostros locos in his confundi doceamus, melius nihil ostendi quo inuentus instrui atque adiuari possit. Confirmo enim et recipio hosce decem locos solos esse, et praeter hos in tot inuentionibus Quintiliani nihil quod ad vere doctrinae rationem referri possit institui. Caput septimum est de demonstratione, quos igitur laudis locos a nostris diuersos Quintilianus hic exponit? Nullos, sed de nostris quattuor confundit, neque tamen integros assumit, causas, effecta, adiuncta, testimonia. Demonstrationem enim petendam esse docet a parentibus et maioribus, quae procreantes causae sunt in nostris locis. Item ex inuentis, actis, dictis, factis, quae effecta sunt: item ex animi, et corporis, et fortunae commodis, quae adiuncta sunt: Item ex testimoniis diuinis: praeterea nullum argumenti genus attingit. Nihil igitur hic Quintilianus ostendit inuentionis, quod fit non modo nostris locis magis utile atque accomodatum, sed ne distinctum quidem atque separatum. De dispositione pauca admiscet, ut vel temporum gradus, vel generum distributionem sequamur. Quorum secundum in omni disputatione, qua via et ordine procedit, sequi debemus. In primo autem secundum adhibere et possumus, et nisi non plane intelligi volumus, debemus: quod Florus in laude populi Romani praestitit, ubi gradus temporum sequitur, et tamen totam summam in quattuor partes diuidit. Idem Livius in plena per decadas historia fecerat. Quare nihil hic demonstrationis proprium Quintilianus offendit, et coniungi optime possunt, quae disiuncta esse existimat. Quae enim est ars uniuersae inuentionis, eadem est etiam demonstrationi accomodata. In deliberationis capite nullus inuentionis locus a Quintiliano traditur, nulla dispositionis via declaratur, tota res meris nugis amplificatur. De iudiciali autem genere separatim Quintilianus nihil instituit, ad eius doctrinam retulit libro quarto et quinto, quae ab aliis rhetoribus communiter praecipiunt de partibus orationis. Item quae de locis communibus inuentionis et generalibus. Quare concludamus primum in generibus causarum a Quintiliano nullus inuentionis artes proprias describi, quamobrem quaestionum et caussarum genera ita diuidi oportuerit. Deinde hoc item concludamus, nullas inuentionis artes ad laudem, nullas ad consilium non dico demonstrari, sed attingi praeter causarum speciem unam, effecta, adiuncta, testimonia diuina: quae omnia diligentissime decem locis nostris explicantur. Nam si de laude et consilio quaeratur, aperientur sane nostris institutionibus omnes illi dialecticae sapientiae fontes in causarum generibus, in effectis, in subiectorum et adiunctorum, dissentaneorum tot partibus et modis, in reliquorum argumentorum tam copiosis et abundantibus locis, ut delectus rerum ac modus pene difficilis tibi sit, tanta copia praestabitur. Qualem igitur dialecticum hic agnoscemus, qui iudicii ullam doctrinam neget esse, qui cum triplicem inuentionis artem flatuat, primam hanc in generibus caussarum tam aridam, tam inopem proponat inuentionis artem? Secunda inuentions ars sequitur in partibus orationis a Quintiliano collocata. Itaque prius de partium ipsarum numero disputat, et nobis ideo nonnihil de his est dicendum. Capite itaque nono officia iudicialis causae duo Quintilianus facit, inuentionem et depulsionem: partes quinque proemium, narrationem, probationem, refutationem, perorationem: quasi non sit de facti coniectura contentio in demonstratione et deliberatione, ut aliquid illic intendatur et depellatur: quasi nequeant etiam illae orationis quinque partes in aliis quaestionibus distingui: et haec omnia seu officia, seu membra sint iudicialis quaestione propria, non omnium quaestionum communia. Sed de partibus orationis paulo plua dicenda sunt. Hac enim partitione excepta verae et artificiosae dispositionis scintilla in totis Quintiliani rhetoricis nulla est. Methodus dialectica (ut in nostris institutionibus dictum est) hoc praecipit, ut in magna rerum disputatione (quam via et ordine persequi volumus) summa quaedam primo loco ponatur, deinde tribuatur in partes et species: easque singulas et earum particulas ad extremum ita confirmando et explicando persequamur, ut uniuersa praecedant, singularia sequantur: secundum quem methodi et dispositionis ordinem rhetores quidam viderunt, ad orandum duas esse necessarias partes (etiam si quaestio simplex esset, nec haberet partes) propositionem et confirmationem, duas non necessarias aliquando tamen assumi, ut proemium et perorationem: cuius sententiae Aristoteles author est. Alii quatuor fecerant, ut exordium, narrationem, confirmationem, perorationem: quam sententiam Cicero in partitionibus sequutus est. Alii quinque, ut hic Quintilianus: alii plures, qui tamen omnes ordinis illius artificiosi rationem quandam habuerunt, ut uniuersum quoddam praecederet, cuius partes deinde tractarentur. Exordio enim summa quaedam rerum poni solet, quae plerunque sequentibus partibus diuisae tractantur. Sed tamen hoc ita praeceptis confuderunt, ut in hac ordinis descriptione locos inuentionis et elocutionis modos conturbarent. Neque mirum: cum enim dialecticae et rhetoricae distinctas nullas artes haberent, cum mille tenebris iteratas et confusas easdem res haberent, quid mirum fuit tam varias et tam dissidentes his de rebus opiniones extitisse? Quamobrem dialecticas tertii libri laudes in partiendis quaestionibus, in explicandis demonstrationis et deliberationis inuentionibus omittamus: quantus hic dialecticus, quam acer et diligens in exquirendis rerum causis, in usu doctrinae demonstrando fuerit Quintilianus, intelleximus. Videamus qualis et quantus in partium orationis inuentione declaranda philosophus fuerit, quae genera argumentorum in exordio, in narratione noua descripserit: ad alias enim reliquas orationis partes locos generales et docendi, et mouendi, et delectandi reseruauit, nullos proprios explicauit. Vereor ne plerique parum considerent attente, quod de secunda ista inuentionis arte contra Quintilianum disputo. Facit Quintilianus quinque partes eloquentiae, inuentionem, dispositionem, elocutionem, memoriam, actionem. Omnia igitur (dico) eloquentiae praecepta Quintilianus ad aliquam harum partium referat, necesse est: nihil de memoria et pronuntiatione in exordio et narratione praecipitur: perpauca de elocutione et dispositione confunduntur. Doctrina igitur reliqua inuentionis est, quod ad veram inuentionis artem referri possit, sed totum graecanicum, sophisticum, scholasticum, et plane puerile esse confirmo. Primum caussam requiramus, quamobrem ad duas orationis partes, exordium et narrationem, inuentiones peculiares describantur: tum enim vere disputabimus, cum proprias et veras causas agemus: triplicem vero exordii causam fuisse video, ut beneuolus, attentus, docilis auditor efficiatur. At id exordii proprium non est, quod attribuitur exordio proprium, et periculosius sane fuerit auditorem in media oratione, cum res serio agitur non esse beneuolum, attentum, docilem, quam in exordio. Deinde exordium istarum rerum causa duntaxat esse comparatum falsum est, et usui contrarium: nullum enim Ciceronis exordium est in tot eius orationibus ad istas duntaxat ineptias comparatum, sed in omnibus orationibus quae quidem extant, exordium statim auditorem ipsum de caussa et aperte, et breviter, et probabiliter instituit: non autem solum beneuolum, et attentum, et docilem facit. Age vero, sit sane aliqua benevolentiae, docilitatis, attentionis in exordio praecipue habenda ratio. Videamus an id melius Quintiliani confusis peculiaribus locis, quam nostris decem communibus efficiatur. Beneuolentia ducitur a personis, aut a causis, et utriusque adiunctis (ait Quintilianus) quasi vero rei qui accusatur, persona ipsa non sit pars causae, et tam multa quae sapiens iste rhetor collegit de personarum et causarum locis, personarum adiuncta non sint, ac non omnia haec perspicue doceantur a nobis in adiunctorum loco, quae hic a Quintiliano confunduntur. Rhetorica (ita me Deus amet) breuius integra et tota tradi poterat, quam est exordiorum tam magnifica doctrina a Quintiliano tradita: nulla inuentionis solida doctrina hic est, qualis in decem nostris locis explicatur. Sed locos narrationis videamus, et requiramus hic item caussam summam, quamobrem ars narrationis propria describatur. Tria dicit esse Quintilianus ad quae proprii loci narrationis describendi sint: quia narratio debeat esse brevis, aperta, probabilis. At primum Aristoteles merito derisit, et reliqua etiam duo magis in confirmatione necessaria sunt, quam in narratione. In narrando enim, si quid parum probabile est, confirmando tandem et tractando credibile efficitur. Tum vero valde ridiculum est, cum tota dialectica et inuentio et dispositio, totaque rhetorica et elocutio, et actio huc referatur, ut aperte et probabiliter dicamus, has virtutes omnium orationum communes, uni orationis parti veluti proprias attribuere: deinde perspicuitatis et probabilitatis artes etiam hic excogitare, quasi totae artes illae suis praeceptis aliud demonstrent, atque efficiant. Sed tamen qui sunt proprii inuentionis loci, quos hic Quintilianus tradit? Attingit quidem et confundit ex causis instrumenta, ex adiunctis locum et tempus, praeterea nullum omnino. Quare nulla caussa Quintiliano fuit inuentionis hic commiscendae, nec ulla est, sed mathaeotechnia fatua pro vera arte. In his tamen ineptiis unum est singulare et dialectici artificii maxime proprium: quod Quintilianus praecipit, in narratione argumenta adhibenda esse, non autem argumentandum. Itaque dialecticos omnes irrideamus, dialecticam contemnamus, unde didicimus nullam orationem, cuius aliqua afferatur ratio, sine argumento esse: omnem autem argumenti expositionem, esse argumentationem: itaque orationem fere esse nullam, quae nihil argumentetur: quinimo nulla Ciceronis narratio est, ubi non et argumenta rerum, et rationes ponantur, ubi non etiam syllogismi et argumentationes adhibeantur. Ita Quintilianus commenta graecanica nobis tradit, non praecepta ex vero usu obseruata. Cetera, quae sunt in hoc capite tam multa, si persequar, vereor ne ipse ineptus sim. Quid vero de egressione dicam? Quintilianus eam inter figuras, quamuis addubitans, tamen collocat, et hic causae partem esse negat, et tamen totum caput tertium in egressione consumit: ne ullas apinas rhetorum tricasue omisisse videatur, tam nulla se dialecticae arte instructum ostendit. Talis adhuc est quarto et quinto capitibus de propositione et partitione, cum propositio vel quaestio sit ipsa, quae proponitur, vel syllogismi et argumentationis fundamentum, et partitio sit inuentionis locus, cuius tamen doctrinam hic nullam Quintilianus explicat, quot eius genera, quotve modi sint. Sic ista secunda inuentionis doctrina in partibus orationis videlicet explicatur, ut confundatur aliquid ex causis, adiunctis, partitione: nihil omnino ad generalem et communem usum dicendi referatur. Sed per Deum immortalem, caliginem partitionis huius in quatuor aut quinque aut etiam plures partes orationis accuratius excutiamus, quaeramus causas, *apodeixin* adhibeamus, videamus quaenam operis arte constructi legitima partitio esse debeat. Dico enim partitionem hanc orationis in partes vel quatuor, vel quinque, vel plures explodendam esse. Si quis sermonis puri (quod grammaticae artis opus est) laudes et virtutes partiri velit, sane redeat ad uniuersas artis causas necesse est, non ad unam eius partem aliquam: neque dicat orationis duas esse partes, nomen et verbum, quia in ordine et syntaxi partes illae spectentur: nec ideo nobis grammaticam quondam ad illas duas partes contrahat: imo vero (si volet omnes sermonis laudes intueri) consideret sane et etymologiam in partibus singulis, et syntaxin in earum coniunctione: prosodiam si proferatur, in syllabarum accentu et quantitate: si scribatur, orthographiam in literarum et syllabarum formatione. Denique operis grammatici partes ex artis grammaticae partes exquirat necesse est. Si quis etiam disputationis quae dialecticae artis opus est, partes expendere cupiet, referat sese ad communes dialecticae artis partes, inuentionem et dispositionem, non ad particulam eius aliquam: neque statuat dispositionis tres esse partes, propositionem, assumptionem, complexionem: neque nobis inuentiones proprias et propositionis et assumptionis et complexionis, vel earum ordines quando praecedant, quando sequantur, quando intermedio loco comprehendantur, neque nobis dialecticam hic nescio quam confusionem comminiscatur. Quid ita? quia propositio, assumptio, complexio ad dispositionis artem, non ad totam dialecticam pertineant. Quomodo igitur disputatio dialectica commode diuidetur? equidem rectam et absolutam diuisionem dialectici operis fore arbitror, si quis ad inuentionis et dispositionis (quae partes dialecticae artis verae et solae sunt) partes eius referat: ut dicat disputationem duabus ex rebus constare, argumentis, quod ab inuentionis arte praestatur, item syllogismo, aliquando etiam methodo, quod dialectici ordinis dispositione continetur. Sic inquam, veri operis laudes et partes retexemus, si ad artis legitimas et veras partes referamus. Nec aliter ars ab opere quidquam differt, quam a causis effectus. Sic Aristoteles, qui tenebras istas tam multas reperit, vel certe accumulauit, docet analysin dialectici operis ab effectione (quam genesin nominat) differre. Ponatur igitur imprimis illud,

> Operis arte constructi partitio non ex parte aliqua, sed ex arte tota sumi debet.

ac deinceps assumatur,

> Oratio est opus aliquod arte constructum: nempe (ut Quintiliano placet) arte et inuentionis, et dispositionis, et elocutionis, et memoriae, et actionis.

Tandem concludamus,

> Orationis igitur partitio, non ex una parte aliqua, ut ex dispositione et ordine in exordium, narrationem, confirmationem, refutationem, perorationem, sed ex arte tota sumi debet in inuentionem, dispositionem, elocutionem, memoriam, actionem: quoniam has partes arti rhetoricae Quintilianus attribuit.

Quamobrem tollatur ista partitio, et tanta in his praeceptiunculis et exordiorum,, et narrationum confusio. Venio nunc ad tertiam Quintiliani inuentionem: de caussarum inuentione dictum est: de exordiorum et narrationum inuentione disputatum est: superest inuentio una communis et caussarum, et partium orationis et omnium omnino rerum: quam videtur tamen Quintilianus in tertia parte orationis, id est, confirmatione posuisse: quia putaret argumentis in exordio et narratione locum non esse, sed in confirmatione sola. Nam si secus existimauit, cur attribuit uni parti, quod commune putet omnium? Age igitur, huc veniamus. Confirmo autem tam negligentem atque inertem esse huius uniuersae inuentionis doctrinam, quam specialis illius antea in causis, in partibus orationis fuit. Diuidit Quintilianus, Aristotelem secutus, probationem bifariam, ut aliae sint inartificiales, aliae artificiales: Inartificiales vocat, quae extra artem sunt, et quae extrinsecus accipiuntur a litigatore, ut preiudicia, rumores, tormenta, tabulas, iusiurandum, testes. In quo cum Aristotele labitur Quintilianus, primum cum sint his de rebus et artibus innumerabiles quaestiones, quae non veniant in forum, in quibus tamen testimonia doctorum et sapientum adhibeantur, quomodo inartificiales isto modo dicentur, quomodo inartificiale denique dici potest, quod praeceptis artis sit institutum? at praecepta et artes de his argumentis traduntur. Malim vero (ut res est) inartificiales dicere has rationes, quia nihil admodum artis habeant, et ex omnibus argumentis minimam verae probationis particulam habeant, nec omnino testimoniis credatur, sed testimoniorum potius causis fides adhibeatur. Ergo falsa ratione seductus est Quintilianus. Distribuit deinde artificiales probationes admodum leviter et inepte, ut sint in re vel persona, item ex antecedentibus, consequentibus, pugnantibus, item ex praeterito, praesenti et futuro tempore, item ex maiori, pari, minori, item ut aliae sint necessariae, aliae credibiles, aliae non repugnantes, item vel quia aliquid est, aliud sit: vel quia aliquid non est, aliud sit. Quo toto partitionum genere quid potest ineptius esse? Licet enim tales sectiones omnium rerum infinitas ex circumstantiis levissimis fingere, sed quidnam utilitatis est vel ad cognoscendam naturam argumentorum, vel ad usum tractandum? Omnis igitur probatio (ait Quintilianus) artificialis constat, aut signis aut argumentis, aut exemplis: quasi et exempla et signa, argumenta non sint. O dialecticum et acutum diuisorem! differentias signorum et argumentorum videamus, quas Quintilianus proponit, ut hanc egregiam exemplorum et signorum ab argumentis differentiam videamus. "Signa," ait, "non inueniuntur ab oratore, sed ad eum cum causa deferuntur." At hoc falsum est: signa enim quae vocat, effecta vel adiuncta fere quaedam sunt sub oculos cadentia: quae quaeri et inueniri ab oratore quaerendo in omnibus quaestionibus possunt. Verum esto, non inueniantur ab oratore, sed ad eum deferantur, sunt igitur inquam inartificialia: nec itaque partes artificialium, ut tu Quintiliane efficis: atque ita in iudicii et syllogismi vitio grauiore fueris. Aliam differentiam argumenti et signi Quintilianus facit, et mirifico quodam dilemmate comprehendit. Signa, ait, siue indubitata sint, non sunt argumenta, quia ubi ea sunt, quaestio non est: sine dubia non sunt argumenta, quia ipsa argumentis egent. At signa (inquam) indubitata sunt aut dubia argumenta igitur (ut pro te concludam) non sunt. Imo vero Quintiliane, quanto clariora sunt argumenta, quanto magis quaestionem tollunt, quanto magis quaestionem arguunt, tanto magis argumenta sunt. Ac tu ipse argumentum paulo post ita definis, ut indubitatum sit: pars igitur tui dilemmatis antecedens est falsa. Hic vero locus unus declarare potest quam acri iudicio Quintilianus fuerit, qui tam aniliter argumentetur, qui tam leuiter et inconstanter concludat, tam contra dialecticam omnem rationem ratiocinetur. Hoc enim bello dilemmate concludes nullam probationem esse argumentum sic,

> Sic probatio indubitata est, non est argumentum, quia ibi quaestio non est: Si dubia, non est argumentum, quia eget argumentis:
>
> Atqui probatio est indubitata aut dubia: Nulla igitur probatio est argumentum.

Haec dialectica est Quintiliani. Sed argumenti definitionem videamus, forsitan haec manifestiorem differentiam praebebit. Argumentum (ait Quintilianus) est ratio probationem praestans, qua colligitur aliud per aliud, et quae quod est dubium, per id quod dubium non est confirmat. Atqui haec argumenti definitio et signo et exemplo conuenit, totaque ista partitio probationis artificialis in signum, exemplum, argumentum, (ubi duae species cum suo genere tamquam ab eo diuersa genera ponuntur) et falsa et fatua plane est: qualis fere tota probationum doctrina quinto libro a Quintiliano descripta. In generali autem argumentorum doctrina (quae tota locis decem nostris traditur caussis, effectis, subiectis, adiunctis, dissentaneis, comparatis, nominibus, tributione, finitione, testimoniis) confundit et miscet Quintilianus locos velut generales, illis tamen generalibus non comprehensos solum, sed partibus distinctos, confundit inquam a persona, ut sunt genus, natio, patria, sexus, aetas, educatio, habitus, fortuna, conditio, natura, animi virtus, studia ante acta dictaque et nomen. Hos enim locos tam multos institutiones nostrae comprehendunt, et distingunt duobus effectorum et adiunctorum locis. Maior deinde inertia est Quintiliani de effectis. Haec enim in locis personarum nominatim erant proposita, et hic iterum velut ab illis diuersa repetuntur. Item de tempore, loco, casu, quae ipsa adiunctorum sunt, et tamen iterum postea ponuntur adiuncta, velut ab his dissidentia. Item de facultatibus et instrumentis et modis tanquam haec causae vel adiuncta non sint. Item de finitione, genere, specie, proprio differente, quasi proprium quidquam sit ab adiunctis diuersum, aut differentia non sit dissimilitudo: de qua tamen Quintilianus postea. Item de diuisione tanquam genus et species, de quibus tamen paulo ante, quidquam sit a diuisionis loco separatum. Item de remotione, ubi Quintilianus valde pueriliter hallucinatur, qui putat ipsam partium remotionem a diuisione genus argumenti diuersum esse. Item de initio, incremento, summa, quae tria nullum uniuersum argumenti genus ostendunt, sed cum aliis omnibus commiscentur. Item de similibus, dissimilibus, contrariis, pugnantibus, adiunctis, relatis: ubi adiuncta relatis Quintilianus valde inscienter subiicit. Item de causis et euentis, quae tamen antea nominatim posita sunt. Item de coniugatis, quae Quintilianus irridet, quia, inquit, non eget probatione, quod compascuum est, compascere licere. Hoc dialecticum Quintiliani est iudicium ei simile, quo signa antea ab argumentis distinguebantur: quod animal rationale est, hominem esse, probatione non eget. Ergo definitio tuo isto iudicio non est argumentum Quintiliane: quo quid a dialectica alienius? quid illius philosophiae inanius? Item de maioribus, minoribus. Tandem vero locos tam multos, et tam varie confusos in unam summam confusionis contrahit: ut sint omnes a personis, causis, locis, tempore, facultatibus, modo, finitione, genere, specie, differentibus, propriis, remotione, diuisione, initio, incrementis, summa, similibus, dissimilibus, pugnantibus, consequentibus, efficientibus, effectis, euentis, coniugatis, comparatione. Addit his fictionem *kat'hypothesin* vocat, quae ex omnibus argumentis peti possit, quia totidem species fictae sunt, quod vere. Hic Quintilianus negligens dici non potest, qui tam multa undique conquirat: at certe dialecticae valde ignarus, et syllogismi expers videri potest, qui non videat hanc *hypothesin*, propositionem esse syllogismi connexi, cui nisi assumptio aut expressa aut intellecta coniungatur, argui inde et probari et concludi nil possit qui (inquam) non intelligat aliud inuentionem esse, quae argumenta suppeditet: aliud dispositionem, quae argumenta collocet. At *hypothesis* illa pars est syllogismi connexi: quae argumentum disponit cum quaestione, et quae omne genus argumenti capere potest, quod syllogismus potest. Syllogismus tamen non est argumentum, neque sane propositio syllogismi argumentum est. Atque haec commenta cum tam inscite et confuse Quintilianus generalibus et uniuersis locis commisceat, attamen affirmat multo etiam plures inuentionis locos tradi posse: in quo fallitur: extra enim decem locos, causas, effecta, subiecta, adiuncta, dissentanea, comparata, nomina, tributiones, finitiones, testimonia, argumenti genus nullum est. Omnia hic comprehensa et eorum generibus ac partibus clarissime in nostris institutionibus sunt distincta. De exemplis confusio similis est. "Omnia" (ait Quintilianus) "necesse aut similia, aut dissimilia, aut contraria esse": paulo post tamen seipsum scilicet condemnans, etiam maiora et minora et authoritates adiungit: et quae contraria exempla putat esse, ut Marcellus ornamenta hostibus Syracusanis restituit: Verres eadem sociis abstulit. Haec dissimilia sunt, non contraria. De usu argumentorum pleraque dicit partim falsa, partim vera. Admiscet etiam quaedam de dispositione, quae dispositionis tamen artificiosae cuiusmodi est, in syllogismo et methodo nihil habent. Iubet autem Quintilianus ne a potentissimis, ad leuissima decrescat oratio: et tamen postea libri septimi capite primo dicet contra, ubi docebit reo firmissimum quodque primum refellendum, et ad infirmissima deinceps veniendum. In capite de refutatione similes nugae sunt, sine ullo tamen inuentionis praecepto. Ad extremum multa de enthymemate et epicheremate colligit Quintilianus, quibus probat se eundem esse, quem tot antea locis probauit, in dialectica nempe valde plumbeum: et quae de syllogismo dicit, magis ea se vel audita, vel ex aliquo authore lecta describere. Aristotelem sui erroris authorem Quintilianus hic habet. Dialecticos ab oratoribus, non vero rerum usu, sed captiosis Aristotelis commentis distinguit: ut illi syllogismis utantur, hi fusa liberius oratione. Non intelligit hic homo ut grammaticae, sic dialecticae ex omnibus inuentionis et dispositionis partibus usum in omni oratione communem esse: dialogos, sermones, contentiones, poemata, orationes denique (cuiuscunque generis sint) omnes magis dialecticas, quam oratorias esse. Nulla fere est oratio sine ratione et argumento, sine rationis et argumenti collocatione, quod dialecticae est. At Quintilianus Aristotelis somnia secutus (qui dialecticos scholasticis altercationibus, rhetores forensibus et ciuilibus contentionibus fatue distinxit) putat syllogismo oratores, quam dialecticos rarius uti. Quasi vero non sit similis et dialecticae et rhetoricae ratio in dialogis Platonis, et in forensibus Ciceronis actionibus, non tam frequentes, animaduertantur syllogismi, quam vel in Aristotelis spinosissimis sophismatis. Si Quintilianus distinctas inuentionis et dispositionis artés cognouisset, et ad earum normam Ciceronis orationes expendisset, reperisset in Ciceronis orationibus syllogismos frequentiores, quam possent in ullis philosophorum scriptis notari. Hic Aristotelis error Quintilianum fefellit, qui simpliciter Aristotelis illud commentum sequutus est, nunquam attendit, an hoc vere diceretur. Nam si obseruasset, errorem illorum manifestissime deprehendisset, cum videret dialecticam tam esse in poetarum et oratorum, quam in philosophorum libris usurpatam et tractatam. Atque haec de argumentorum inuentione tertio, quarto, quinto libris. Totus sextus liber qui sequitur, in monendi et delectandi artibus consumitur: ubi nihil dialecticae, nihil rhetoricae proprium est. Generales ut sunt, ita generaliter exponantur rhetorica in elocutione et actione, dialectica in inuentione et dispositione: multi ex his uniuersis rerum fontibus riuuli oriuntur, qui tamen non sunt harum artium praeceptis permiscendi. Artes inuentionis tres docentur a Cicerone et Quintiliano: ad docendum loci describuntur in generibus caussarum, in partibus orationis, et tandem communes omnium quaestionum. Secundo ad mouendum quaedam etiam praecepta ponuntur: postremo ad ridendum. At in inuentione loci ad docendum soli sunt explicandi, motus et delectatio proprias artes nullas habent: petuntur autem communiter ex locis illis inuentionis: item ex elocutione et actione: maxime vero ex morali disciplina, ubi agnoscas quid virtus, quid vitium, quibus rebus boni viri gaudeant, quibus improbi exultent, quibus utrique item offendantur: quod Cicero saepe testatur, qui in oratoriis affirmat ex omnibus philosophiae partibus illam partem esse idcirco oratori maxime necessariam: et Aristoteles, qui tantam dialecticae et rhetoricae confusionem peperit, affirmat rhetoricam ratione motuum et affectionum partem quandam esse moralis philosophiae: et ad illam philosophiam moralem, mouendi totam artem refert: et Quintilianus ipse ideo philosophiam moralem primo libro rhetoricae partem dixit esse. In extremo sexto libro de differentia consilii et iudicii disserit Quintilianus, et iudicium putat, ut dixi antea, non magis arte tradi posse, quam gustum, quam odorem. Hic in cumulando diligentiam Quintiliani non requiro, in iudicando prudentiam desidero. Dixit antea duas esse dialecticae partes, inuentionem et iudicium: nunc quasi dialectica ars nulla sit, et quod de iudicio in syllogismis praecipiat, inartificiosum sit, ait iudicium arte tradi non posse. Atqui tamen haec iudicii doctrina tanta est, tam mirabilis, tam diuina, ut qui vel ceteras artes norit, hanc ex praeceptis vel obseruatione aliqua non norit, nihil vere percepisse, nihil firme cognouisse videatur. Atque haec de inuentione a Quintiliano confusa sunt. Dispositionis doctrinam libro proximo septimo videtur Quintilianus explicare velle: quod si fecisset, syllogismi modos omnes, et methodi vias et doctrinae et prudentiae docuisset, quemadmodum in nostris institutionibus est explicatum. At in principio Quintilianus indicat nullam dispositionis artem in omnes materias certam tradi posse, in quo vehementer errat. Nam syllogismi et methodi artificiosae certa doctrina est, et omnium rerum, quae via et ratione tractandae sunt, communis. Quare quid plura iam contra hunc hominem de arte dispositionis dicenda sunt, qui eam non solum ignorat, sed arbitratur nullam esse posse. Quae vero Quintilianus nomine dispositionis tam multa toto hoc libro scribit, ea sunt de formulis caussarum ciuilium, et de consuetudine quadam litigandi in Romano foro, quae fuit illo seculo. Attamen omnia eiusmodi, ut nullum omnino solidum ac perpetuum, vel ad illas ipsas Romani fori formulas praeceptum praebeant. Reuocat autem huc tota illa sophismata tertii libri de generibus statuum et quaestionum coniectura, finitione, qualitate, actione, scripto et voluntate, contrariis legibus, syllogismo, amphibologia, in quibus singulis nullum dispositionis praeceptum generale est. Confunduntur etiam quaedam inuentionis praecepta in coniectura et finitione, de caussis, factis, consiliis, ut verissime confirmari possit, quinque libris tertio, quarto, quinto, sexto, septimo, a Quintiliano non informari inuentionis et dispositionis artem: sed utriusque partis doctrinam multis rebus falsis, alienis, inutilibus obrui. Quamobrem iam licet istam et inuentionis et dispositionis contentionem totam concludamus, et nostras institutiones cum Quintiliani institutionibus, usum nostrum cum usu Quintiliani coniungamus, ut intelligi possit uberius ad extremum quid hac de re statui possit. Nos artes inuentionis et dispositionis dialecticae arti, cuius partes propriae sunt, vere attribuimus. Quintilianus dialecticae doctrinam rhetoricae falso subiicit. Nos quaestionem definimus, et de partibus admonemus, quod ad usum inuentionis et dispositionis attineat. Quintilianus quaestionem non definit, nullum quaestionis usum ostendit, sed omnium generum sophismatis hanc doctrinae partem confundit. Nos inuentionem definimus, genera partimur, generum species singulas et partes exponimus, et insignibus exemplis illustramus. Quintilianus nec inuentionem, nec inuentionis genera, nec generum species, nec omnino partes ullo verae definitionis aut partitionis lumine exornauit, sed pro una illustri et communi rerum omnium inuentione, tres obscurissimas et turbatissimas artes aggregauit, primam in generibus causarum, secundam in partibus orationis, tertiam in generalibus et omnium tum caussarum, tum partium orationis locis communibus. Nos syllogismi et methodi, id est, uniuersae dispositionis laudes omnes persecuti sumus: Quintilianus nullum omnino certum et perpetuum praeceptum hic intellexit: Nos clarissimo ordine et ad intelligendum aptissimo, generales praeceptiones primo, speciales deinde collocauimus: Quintilianus autem qua via, quo ordine, qua dialecticae methodi ratione totam confusionem tot artium composuit? Comparat orationem via et ratione distinctam Plato perfectae animalis excellentis figurae, cuius caput sursum erigatur, pedes deorsum deprimantur, pectus, venter, ac reliqui artus intermediis locis ordine collocentur: ita orationem dialectice collocatam iudicat summo ac primo loco res uniuersas, infimo singulares, intermedio tum uniuersis inferiores, tum singularibus superiores amplecti: ut a capite disputatio per partes ad extremas particulas deducatur. Verumenimuero quodnam esse animalis monstrum putaremus, cuius pedes essent susum erecti, deorsum caput affligeretur, ipsumque caput una cum ventre in pedis unius, tanquam vertice aliquo absorberetur? Talis sane triplicis apud Quintilianum inuentionis est collocatio: pedes enim sunt singulares caussarum artes, quae primo et summo loco sunt: venter partes orationis, quae sunt magis communes, quam artes demonstratiuae: et deliberatiuae caussae, minus communes quam loci generales: caput communes omnium quaestionum loci: quae tamen et orationis, et communium locorum doctrina in uno iudiciali caussae genere, id est, in uno pede confunditur. Itaque tota artis explicatione non modo in rebus ipsis permulta absurde peccauit Quintilianus, sed in ordine et dispositione videmus, quam confusus sit et perturbatus. Quid vero futurum putamus, si tam inertis, tamque inanis confusionis usum requiramus? Exercenda est et inuentionis et dispositionis doctrina, sicuti quaeuis alia disciplina, modis duobus, primo, ut per eam in alienis exemplis cognoscamus, et consilium ex argumento, et iudicium ex conclusionis modo, et totam omnino prudentiam ex collocationis et ordinis methodo: secundo ut per eandem artem similia ipsi et dicendo et scribendo exempla confingamus. Enimuero ponatur aliqua Ciceronis oratio, inuentio et dispositio ex artibus Quintiliani disquiratur, quid primum ad hanc exercitationis rationem tota illam tam accurata de statibus doctrina, an rationalis quaestio sit, an legalis, utrum quaeratur an est, quid est, quale est, an status sit ambigui, an syllogismi, an legum contrariarum, an scripti et sententiae, an translationis: quid inquam, ista mihi proderunt ad rationem inuentionis? Nihil. Iam vero quas artes Quintiliani ad explicandum quid hic Cicero voluerit, quo genere argumenti, quam solido usus sit, quas, inquam, inuentionis artes hic adhibebo? An genera caussarum repetam, et partium orationis tot institutiones excutiam, et locorum communium rationem totam huc referam? Curnam, Deus bone, confusio tanta, et quamobrem miscenda est, cum res tota clarissima et facillima sit? Nosse vis, et expendere consilium in Ciceronis oratione tibi proposita? Refer ad partem quaestionis utranuis eius argumenta, considera quid eius sint, caussane an effectus, subiectum an adiunctum, dissentaneum, comparatio, nominis ratio, tributio, definitio, testimonium, tum hoc assequere compendiaria et facili via, quod Quintiliani tam molestis salebris assequi vix, ac ne vix quidem possis. Postremo faciamus idem in Quintiliani de dispositione artibus periculum, quomodo iudicium Ciceronis, quomodo methodum cognoscam. At tantum abest ut Quintilianus ullam iudicii doctrinam doceat, ut affirmet omnino nullam tradi posse: tam caecus in omni dispositionis arte, ut profiteatur in omnes materias communem esse nullam posse. Aristotelis et Quintiliani error fatuitate par fere est: ille negat in Topicis communem inuentionem tradi posse, quam tamen tot tenebris inuoluit, quam multas in eius libris demonstrauimus. Hic vero iudicium dialecticae partem esse dicit, et tamen idem nescio quo modo somnians ait iudicii doctrinam nullam esse, nullam artificiosae dispositionis communem esse doctrinam. Quare quid iam requiram hoc loco, quomodo possit secunda exercitationis ratio ex hisce Quintiliani artibus tractari? Non potest ex his consilium, non potest iudicium, non potest methodus in propositis authoribus intelligi: quomodo igitur his artibus easdem virtutes assequi scribendo et dicendo poterimus? Quamobrem cum sit ars inuentionis et dispositionis a Quintiliano tam negligenter, tam insipienter exposita, cum nihil perfecte vel definitum, vel partitum, vel aestimatum, vel collocatum sit, cum verus earum partium usus illinc elici nullo modo possit, statuite dialectici, quos initio contentionis meae iudices appellaui, statuite, inquam, qualem dialecticum rhetorem hunc a vobis deceat aestimari.

De dialectica et inuentionis, et dispositionis doctrina contra Quintilianum adhuc dialectice quidem egimus. Sequitur de elocutione institutio Quintiliani tam prolixa fere, tamque confusa, quam quinque proximis libris fuit de inuentione atque dispositione. Summas rerum, ut adhuc feci, duntaxat attingam, institutum persequar: dialecticam prudentiam hic item ab hoc magistro requiram, quomodo definierit, quomodo diuiserit, quomodo declarauerit, quod doctoris consilium, quae ratio, quod iudicium, quae sapientia fuerit, qualem denique se dialecticum praebuerit. Elocutio rhetorica praeceptis his definienda et explicanda fuerat, quibus grammaticum nihil, nihil dialecticum admisceretur: ut cum puritas orationis grammaticis decretis, rationis subtilitas et prudentia dialecticis informata esset, tum quid ad ornandum ex tropis et figuris, ex vocis et actionis gratia et dignitate reliquum pertineret, hic definitionibus, partitionibus, et exemplis exponeretur. At Quintilianus sui similis est, miscet et conturbat in rhetoricae elocutionis praeceptis et grammatica et dialectica. Elocutio (ait primo capite octaui libri) spectatur in singulis et coniunctis verbis: quid tum? In singulis intuendum ut sint latina, perspicua, ornata, apta. In coniunctis, ut emendata, ut collocata, ut figurata. Haec partitio Quintiliani est, in qua consideremus quaenam dialectica teneatur. Primum enim Latini emendati sermonis elegantia rhetoricae nihil est, grammaticae tota est: ut enim nullus barbarismus, nullus solaecismus insit, grammaticae virtus est. Itaque haec tam multa in hac partitione redundant, et dialecticam nullam hic esse demonstrant: quia cum de rhetorica elocutione disputes, non erit profecto verum grammaticas res admiscere. Quod Quintilianus nescio quo modo confitetur cum ait, Sed ea quae de ratione latine atque emendate loquendi fuerint dicenda, in libro primo, cum de grammatica loqueremur, exequuti sumus. Verum hic Quintilianus idem est hic qui adhuc fuit, sine dialectico consilio, sine syllogismo, sine iudicio. Verum (ait) illic tantum ne vitiosa essent praecepimus, hic non alienum est admonere, ut sint quamminime peregrina et externa. At Quintiliane, non eadem solum libro primo tradidisti, cum de grammatica diceres, quae hoc libro repetis, sed etiam longe quam hic plura: et te valde tamen in tanta cumulandi diligentia demonstras obliuiosum et immemorem, atque, quod arguo, dialecticae expertem. De perspicuitate rerum et decoro idem sentiendum est: Rhetoricae enim (quae in verborum elocutione et actione tota posita est) fere nihil habent. Secundo capite perspicuitas informatur ex verbis propriis: proprietas autem admodum ridicule diuiditur in modos octo. Omnis significatio verbi propria est, aut mutata aliquo genere tropi per metonymiam, ironiam, metaphoram, synedochen, ut postea declarabo. Itaque si vere statuere volumus, unica proprietatis in verbo est ratio, unicus est modus. At Quintilianus ait primo dici propria, quorum prima haec intelligentia et significatio fuerit: quod est verum. Secundo modo dicitur proprium, ait, inter plura quae sint eiusdem nominis, id unde caetera ducta sint. At Quintiliane, hic secundus modus a primo diuerso non est. Omnis dictio proprie aliquid significat: significatio tamen haec saepe ad aliam rem significandum aliquo tropo mutatur. Id vero unde caetera ducta sunt proprium solum est, caetera *tropikos* usurpata. Ergo dialectica luce adhibita vides secundum istum proprietatis modum a primo non differre. Tertius est modus, cum res communis pluribus in uno aliquo habet nomen eximium. At Quintiliane, synecdoche est hic modus proprietatis: quoties enim ex genere species significatur, synecdoche postea a te definitur. Cur igitur tropus isto loco turbatur, ac non potius in troporum doctrina docetur modificatas significationes, si id opus esset, etiam proprias esse? Quartus modus est, cum quod commune est aliis nomen, alicui rei peculiariter tribuitur. Hic error non similis est proximo, sed idem cum eo plane. Quintus modus est, quo nihil est significantius. At id aliquando proprium nomen est, ut a primo modo nihil differat, aliquando modificatum, et hic nihil docet. Sextus modus proprietatis in his quae bene translata sunt. At cur hic de metaphora potius ista conturbantur, quam proprio et legitimo troporum loco docentur? Septimus modus est in his quae sunt in quoque praecipua: at id interim proprium verbum est, ut hic modus cum primo consentiat, interim modificatus est. Octauus modus, cum verba plus significant quam eloquuntur: emphasin tamen mauult Quintilianus appellare. Atque haec genera proprietatis facta sunt octo, quae in rhetorica bene tradita nulla omnino essent. Grammatica propriorum verborum rationem habet, rhetorica modificatorum: sic a modificatis propria distinguenda sunt. Quintilianus autem ex duobus significationum generibus,, propriarum et modificatarum, fecit genera propriorum octo, tam subtiliter et acute, ut secundum genus nihil differret a primo, octauum a Quintiliano ipso reiiciatur, tertium, quartum, sextum sint tropi synecdoche et metaphora, quintum et septimum primo genere, aut tropo aliquo contineantur. Et hic curam et solicitudinem in congerendis rebus video, dialecticum iudicium, dialecticum syllogismum nullum video. Praetermitto permulta falsa, permulta inepta, quia sit infinitum singula persequi. Opponit Quintilianus obscuritatem perspicuitati, et eius modos alios in singulis, alios in coniunctis verbis exponit. At Quintiliane, quam obliuiosus es, quam valde es immemor tui? Partitus es elocutionem ex verbis singulis et coniunctis: in singulis perspicua collocasti. At nunc etiam in coniunctis eorum doctrinam permisces, et te ipsum valde in definiendis artibus et distinguendis perturbatum esse doces. Similis est inconstantia et confusio tertio capite de ornatu, ubi prooemium est sua longitudine ineptissimum. Ornatus doctrina tandem sequitur in singulis et coniunctis verbis, cum tamen in prima partitione in singulis tantum verbis ornatus a Quintiliano positus sit: et istam constantiam dialecticam primum deprehendo: Ornatus, ait antea, totus in singulis verbis. Deinde, ornatus duo genera, alterum in singulis, alterum in coniunctis. Singula trifariam partitur ut propria sint, aut ficta, aut translata. At Quintilianus antea subiecit verborum proprietati translationem, nunc eandem tanquam distinctam a proprietate separat: de nouitate verborum repetit quaedam libro primo confusa: de translatis hic nullum verbum facit. Ita Quintiliani doctrina de verborum singulorum ornatu concluditur ut magnifica nobis promittantur, promissa ipsa nulla fiant. Coniunctorum verborum ornatus pari, vel multo etiam maiore confusione turbatur. Diuiditur primum bifariam, quam concipiamus elocutionem, quam efferamus. Illic considerandum esse dicit quid augere, quid minuere velimus, ubi tota dialectica rhetoricaque comprehenditur, ne nihil agere doctorem tantum iudicemus: hic vero quibus tropis, figuris, sententiis, numeris utamur: ubi tota dialectica rursum in sententiis, et elocutio ex tropis et figuris et numeris miscetur: tam egregie Quintilianus partitur hanc doctrinam, ut quicquid illi venerit in bucca, id effuderit, dialectici salis ne micam quidem adhibuerit. Atque quod multo absurdius est, neutram propositarum partium exequitur, sed vitiorum nescio quas sordes a grammaticis undique corradit, et in cultu (quem a duabus illis partibus diuersum facit) reliquam tanti capitis loquacitatem consumit, ubi statuit illustrationem: quam tamen figuram nono libro facit, nec intelligit hanc illustrationem separati praecepti nihil habere, sed ex omnibus et inuentionis et dispositionis et elocutionis partibus fieri posse: et omnia illustrationis exempla, quae hic adhibet Quintilianus, sunt ex effectis, adiunctis, comparatis, in quibus tam caecus est, tam a dialecticis inops et destitutus, ut artem exemplorum, quibus utitur, non intelligat, quinetiam aliud genus pro alio proponat, ut pro Archia, ubi collatio minorum est, similitudinem esse putat, hoc loco, Saxa et solitudines voci respondent, bestiae saepe immanes cantu flectuntur atque consistunt, nos instituti rebus optimis non poetarum voce moueamur? Subiicit illustrationi *brachylogian*, cuius hoc exemplum quod ponit (Mithridates corpore ingenti perinde armatus) non intelligit similitudinem esse, quam tamen illustrationi proximo modo subiecerat: Subiecit illustrationi rursus Emphasin, cuius partem admodum ridicule figuram, reticentiam, facit. Postremo quicquid potest huc undique adgregat *apheleian*, *deinosin*, *phantasian*, *exergasian*, *epexergasian*, *energeian*, non modo sine arte, sed omnino sine ulla artis specie: cuiusmodi capita duo proxima sunt de amplificatione et de sententiarum generibus, quorum capitum artem nullam omnino Quintilianus intelligit. Praecipit hoc libro de elocutione, At ista genera amplificationum et sententiarum non elocutione verborum, sed rerum inuentione fiunt: et amplificationum genera, quae diuersa Quintilianus putat, eadem fere sunt. Primum enim et secundum ex uno loco comparationis oriuntur. Incrementum siquidem, cum ex minoribus ascendis ad maiora, comparatio est, cuius tamen artem Quintilianus ab incrementi arte diuersam putat. Ratiocinatio et congeries artis certae nihil habent: possunt ex omnibus argumentorum generibus accipi. Sententiarum autem genera, quae Quintilianus recenset, sunt ex contrariis, comparatis, aut figura aliqua, at sine arte ulla, imo vero contra omnem artis rationem confusa. O philosophi, o dialectici, et veri rerum iudices, considerate quae sunt, et cuiusmodi quae dico, quae propono: pudet enim me, pudet tam putidam, tam insulsam loquacitatem, qualis est, talem dicere ac demonstrare, admonere satis esse existimo. Boni iudicis est ex legum et iuris scientia nosse quibus meritis unaquaeque res digna sit: factum propono, de qualitate vos statuite. Atque de tribus totius octaui libri partibus duae integrae, quinque capitibus adhuc conturbatae sunt ex grammaticis, dialecticis, et rhetoricis quibusdam, ita tamen ut vel grammaticae, vel rhetoricae, vel dialecticae artis forma nulla sit. De rhetorica elocutione pollicetur Quintilianus praecepta se traditurum, at de troporum et figurarum (quibus tota ars elocutionis bene descripta continetur) arte nihil est institutum. Reliquo libro octauo troporum doctrinam nobis Quintilianus pollicetur. Namque tropum definit initio et partitur et dialecticae methodi viam scilicet aliquando sequitur. Verum si recte iudicare volumus, nihil accurate definit, nihil acute partitur, nihil via et ordine disponit. Tropus (ait) est mutatio verbi vel sermonis a propria significatione in aliam cum virtute. At tropus in singulis verbis totus est, in sermone coniunctum nihil habet. Nam cum formae orationis mutantur, figurae sunt, non tropi: et quas sermonis mutationes Quintilianus putat tropos esse, docebo suo loco tropos non esse. Quare falsa est primum ista definitio. Quintilianus troporum genera duodecim facit, metaphoram, synecdochen, metonymiam, antonomasiam, onomatopoeiam, catachresin, metalepsin, epitheton, allegoriam, periphrasim, hyperbaton, hyperbolem. At quatuor tantum sunt, metonymia, ironia, metaphora, synecdoche, ut planum faciam cum de generibus singulis dixero: falsa item est Quintiliani hac in parte doctrina, tam excellentem in definiendo, in partiendo dialecticum videmus. Disserit primo loco Quintilianus de metaphora, quam non definit: partitur autem sic, ut praestiterit non partiri. Itaque inanes eius et ridiculas partitiones omittamus, quod aut necessitatis, aut significtionis, aut decoris gratia adhibetur: quasi non haec inter se misceantur, et aliqua sit metaphora necessitatis causa adhibita, non etiam significationis. Addit tamen tribus generibus quartum modum ad vitandam obscuritatem, ait: quasi et hic modus decoris gratia non fiat. Omittamus et aliam inertiae similis partitionem, quod metaphora sit ab animali ad animal, ab inanimo ad inanimum, ab animalibus ad inanima, ab inanimis ad animalia: liceat enim partitiones innumerabiles tales confingere, quae artis utilitatem nullam prorsus habeant: et cum metaphora similitudinis pars sit (metaphora enim tropus est ex simili simile significans) cum inquam similitudinis pars sit, quae non ex hoc vel illo rerum genere, sed ex tota rerum natura sumi possit, tam vanum et inutile est inertes species hic velle consectari, quam si quis docere conaretur unde genus, unde species, unde contraria, unde denique primi illi dialectici rerum fontes orirentur. Hoc primum tropi genus retineo: tot nugas et ineptias, quot hoc loco Quintilianus collegit, reiicio. Secundum genus Quintilianus synecdochen facit, et eius multa genera recenset, cum numerus pro numero, totum pro parte, genus pro specie, antecedentia pro consequentibus, et contra sumuntur: quorum ultimum elocutionis nihil est, ut hic,

> Aspice, aratra boues referunt suspensa iuuenci:

argumentum est ex adiunctis, unde meridies et nox appropinquare intelligitur, et Quintilianus haec intelligit, et sciens turbat: reliqua non intelligit Quintilianus uno diuisionis genere contineri, ut recte synecdoche definiatur, cum ex parte totum contraue significatur. Nam et species pars est generis: et genus totum speciei, et pluralis numerus singulari comparatus totum aliquid est parti collatum. Tertium tropi genus est Quintiliano, metonymia, et definitur nominis pro nomine positio, sed admodum vitiose. In omni enim tropo est nominis alieni pro proprio nomine positio: cuius vis est (ait Quintilianus) pro eo quod dicitur, causam propter quam dicitur ponere: at id perpetuum non est. Saepe enim tropus hic etiam ex effectis causas, non solum ex causis effecta, item ex subiectis adiuncta, contraue significat. Atque ut intelligi possit quam sit ista iners et confusa troporum ars, exempla Quintiliani ad hoc quatuor locos referam. Ex causis effecta significantur, cum dicitur, Ceres et Bacchus pro frugibus et vino: nam dii illi earum rerum inuentores et authores finguntur. Contra ex effectis causae significantur, ut Pallida mors, tristis Senectus: ideo enim et pallida et tristis, non quia sit, sed quia faciat: ex subiectis adiuncta, ut bene moratas urbes, pro ciuibus: et homines deuorari, cum eorum patrimonium consumitur: denique quoties continens pro contento, possessor pro re possessa, dominos pro subditis dicimus. Contra vero ex adiunctis subiecta, ut sacrilegium pro sacrilego, audaciam pro audaci. Quare omnis huius tropi confusio tollitur una ista vera definitione, Metonymia, est tropus ex causis effecta, subiectis adiuncta contraue significans. Quaerit autem Quintilianus similitudinem quandam inter synecdochen et metonymiam, sed fallitur. Itaque in hoc genere veram doctrinam retineo, et artificiose compono, tenebras tollo. Quartum genus tropi Quintilianus antonomasiam facit et definit, quae aliquid pro nomine ponit, definitione, tropi proximi definitioni simillima. Conuenit enim tropis omnibus pro nomine proprio aliquid ponere. Hae Quintiliani definitiones sunt eiusmodi, ut nihil definiant: sed fallitur etiam grauius Quintilianus. Antonomasia enim (quam fingit) aut synecdoche est, ut Pelides, Tytides pro Achille et Diomede. Generalia enim nomina sunt pro specialibus, aut argumentum quoddam, ut definitio Iouis in hoc exemplo,

—diuum pater atque hominum rex.

Item definitio Scipionis in hoc exemplo, Euersor Carthaginis et Numantiae. Itaque tollatur e tropis hoc genus, quod a ceteris nihil habet diuersum, aut tropus omnino non est. Onomatopoeia quintum tropi genus, est Quintiliano, ut mugire, sibilare, et similia. At mutatio significationis hic nulla est: nihil enim aliud significarunt unquam haec nomina, et haec prima est eorum significatio: non est igitur illic tropus. Catachresin sextum tropi genus facit Quintilianus et definit, quae non habentibus nomen suum accomodat quod in proximo est. Verum haec definitio tropis omnibus conuenit, et Catachresis inter tropos ponitur errore eodem quo Antonomasia. Hic tropus incidit in alios, aut omnino tropus non est,

—equum diuina Palladis arte
Aedificant,

metaphora est ex simili simile significans: dura, esto: at concessa tamen: sic enim dicimus et aedificare naues, et orationem exaedificare, et similia. At dicatur si placet haec durior metaphora, Catachresis, non recuso: sed intelligatur a metaphora genere ipso nihil differre. Leo pariet, metaphora est satis dura, qualis est parens pro patre, quia parere foeminae est, tamen hoc posterius valde usitatum est: parricida pro interfectore, pixis pro pixide, cuiuis materiae, synecdoche est: specie quippe pro genere: dicatur etiam si lubet haec synecdoche *katachresike*. Conatur tamen Quintilianus metaphoram a Catachresi separare, quod abusio sit ubi nomen defuit, translatio ubi aliud fuit, at utrunque falsum est. Metaphora enim necessitatis caussa aliquando adhibetur, ut ipse Quintilianus antea dixi, et Catachresis est aliquando, ubi nomen fuit, ut parricida pro interfectore, parens pro patre. Tollatur igitur genus hoc, aut metaphorae et synecdochae, aut omnino alicui tropo subiiciatur, separata tropi species nulla dicatur. Atque etiam si vere loqui volumus, omnis tropus Catachresis est: non enim sua significatione et propriam rem exprimit, sed abutitur aliena. Septimum genus est tropi metalepsis, et definitur quae ex alio in aliud viam praestat: quae definitio omnis argumenti communis est: vitiosa igitur. Atque hic tropi nullum omnino genus est, et Quintilianus nullum eius usum admodum esse putat. Tollatur igitur, primum quia nulla significationis mutatio est, nec ideo tropus: deinde quia usum nullum habet. Octauum tropi genus est epitheton, maiore errore huc obtrusum, quam superiora. Quid enim est tam frequens in epithetis, quam propria significatio? calidus ignis, bruta terra, humida aqua. Aliquando autem mutatur significatio, et metaphora est, ut cupiditas effrenata, neque ideo tamen nouae doctrinae hic quidquam desideratur: neque quia epitheton est, ideo tropus est, sed quia metaphora, synecdoche, metonymia, aut ironia est. Tollatur igitur ex hac doctrina epitheton. Nonum tropi genus allegoria est Quintiliano, ac definitur inuersio, aliud verbis, aliud sensus ostendens, ac etiam interim ironiae propria est. Allegoria autem si fiat ex continuis metaphoris, non est nonum tropi genus, non magis quam si frequens metonymia aut synecdoche continuaretur. Neque enim hic diuersa troporum genera dicerentur, sed multae metonymiae, multae synecdochae: ita illic multae metaphorae sunto, diuersum genus ne esto. Si tamen lubet allegoriam dicere, continuatis in oratione metaphoris, non recuso: sed ne imperite in arte describenda pro genera ponatur quod genus non sit,

> O nauis referent in mare te noui
> Fluctus. O quid agis? Fortiter occupa
> Portum.

Hic metaphorae multae sunt: nauis pro republica, fluctus maris pro belli ciuilibus, portus pro pace. Atque omnes istas metaphoras allegoriam nominemus, genere a metaphora non separemus. Hoc aliquando obscurum est, aenigma dicitur: nomine quidem recte. Aenigma autem Quintilianus allegoriae speciem esse putat, et falso putat: cum omnis allegoria ex tropis sit, aenigmata multa sint sine tropis, ut haec, quae falso inter tropos recenset Quintilianus,

> Dic quibus in terris, et eris mihi magnus Apollo,
> Treis pateat caeli spatium non amplius ulnas.

Omnia enim propriis verbis nullis modificatis in hoc aenigmate explicantur. Et ex omnibus artibus licet ignaris et imperitis artium tales obscuras sententias proponere, ubi tropi nihil omnino sit. Allegoriam credit etiam Quintilianus aliquando sine tropis esse, ut apud Virgilium,

> Certe equidem audieram, qua se subducere colles
> Incipiunt, mollique iugo demittere cliuo,
> Usque ad aquam, et veteris iam fracta cacumina fagi,
> Omnia carminibus vestrum seruasse Menalcam.

Quod si verum esset, certe tropus nullus esset, quia non esset mutatio verbi a propria significatione. At metaphora est in verbo (Menalcas) quo pro pastore significatur Virgilius: allegoria autem nulla hic est. Subiicit Quintilianus allegoriae ironiam in quo labitur. Ironia enim ipsa tropi genus est separatum. In omni allegoria significatur ex simili simile: in ironia significatur ex contrario contrarium. Subiicit errore multo maiore, *sarkasmon, asteismon, antiphrasin, paroimian, myktirismon.* Neque enim tropi hic quidquam est, cum verbis propriis haec omnia decidi possint. Decimum tropi genus periphrasin Quintilianus facit. At periphrasis omnibus propriis verbis effici potest: nec idcirco tropus ullus est omnino, sed argumenti genus ex dialectico definitionis loco. Undecimum genus hyperbaton facit Quintilianus, in quo cum significationis nulla mutatio sit, nullus etiam tropus erit: et si quid in rhetorica elocutione de hyperbato dici potest, in compositione commodissime dicetur, cuius gratia verba alia differenda, alia praeponenda sunt. Duodecimum genus et postremum hyperbolen facit Quintilianus, quae si in verbo est, metaphora quidem est significans ex simili simile: saepe etiam metonymia: sed in quo etiam maius inclusum est, si res amplificatur, ut volitare gloriae cupiditate, ut scelus pro scelerato: aut minus si extenuatur, ut veri ac fortis tribuni plebis stridorem perferre non possit. Hyperbole autem si in verbo non est, ex omnibus argumentis accipi potest, et ideo tropus non est. Quamobrem ex duodecim generibus a Quintiliano in hac doctrina confusis, antonomasia, onomatopoeia, metalepsis, epitheton, allegoriae tot species (ironia excepta), periphrasis, hyperbaton, et extra singula verba hyperbolen tropi non sunt. Neque hic Quintiliani diligentiam desidero, qui pro paucis generibus troporum, tot nugarum genera cumularit, sed iudicium et prudentiam desidero: qui si hunc unum syllogismum conficere potuisset, numquam tam multa confudisset:

> Tropus omnis est mutatio significationis:
>
> > Antonomasia, onomatopoeia, metalepsis, epitheton, tot allegoriae praeter ironiam, species, periphrasis, hyperbaton, hyperbole extra singula verba, significationis mutatio nulla est:
>
> Quare tropus non est.

Si inquam, Quintilianus ex definitione sua conclusionem hanc efficere potuisset, numquam in istam ignauiam, atque inertiam incidisset. At dialectica (quam suis scriptis tantopere confudit) vehementer illi defuit. Atque etiam ut intelligi certius possit, quatuor esse tantum troporum genera, metonymiam, ironiam, metaphoram, synecdochen, causam planius et apertius ex locis dialecticae inuentionis explicabo.

> Omnis mutatio propriae significationis ex causis ad effecta, subiectis ad adiuncta, dissentaneis ad dissentanea, comparatis ad comparata, toto ad partem, contraue, est metonymia, ironia, metaphora, synecdoche.

Metonymia enim est mutatio significationis ex causis ad effecta, ex subiectis ad adiuncta, contraue: Ironia ex dissentaneis ad dissentanea: metaphora ex comparatis ad comparata: synecdoche ex toto ad partem, contraue.

> Omnis autem tropus est mutatio propriae significationis in verbo ex causis ad effecta, subiectis ad adiuncta, dissentaneis ad dissentanea, comparatis ad comparata, toto ad partem, contraue.

Nam reliqua rerum (quae videntur significari posse dictione simplici) genera nihil habent ab illis distinctum. Nam coniugata et notatio circunstantiae sunt nominis, non rei significatae. Definitio et testimonium simplici dictione non significantur.

> Omnis itaque tropus est metonymia, ironia, metaphora, synecdoche.

Veruntamen fallor fortasse, et inconsiderato inuestigandae veritatis studio inductus longius progredior, quam fines dialectici syncerique iudicii postulent. Troporum genera Quintilianus duodecim fecit: ego duntaxat quatuor instituo, antonomasiam, metalepsin, epitheton, allegoriae tot (excepta ironia) species, hyperbaton, in coniunctis verbis, hyperbolen tropos esse non puto: quia in his a significatione propria dictio nulla necessario mutetur. At Quintilianus tropum distinguit initio noni libri a figura, idque tam sapienter, ut omnes troporum propositae species retineantur. Tropus est dictio ab eo loco in quo propria est, translata in eum in quo propria non est (ait) figura est conformatio quaedam orationis remota a communi, et primum se offerente ratione. Haec tropi et figurae differentia est a Quintiliano posita: vera, certa, necessaria, fateor. Ornatus enim elocutionis, est mutatio dicendi a proprio et vulgari modo ad elegantiorem quendam et praestantiorem: isque duplex est in uno verbo tropus, in oratione figura dicitur: hoc verissimum discrimen est. Verum Quintilianus in hac tam vera sententia constanter permanere non poterit. Istum discriminis syllogismum, illud tam firmum iudicium captione nescio qua mox inducit. Syllogismus enim discriminis ita est,

> Tropus est mutatio dictionis:
> Figura non est mutatio dictionis, quia est orationis mutatio:
> Figura igitur non est tropus.

Verius, inquam, hoc syllogismo et constantius nihil esse poterat. Quid igitur Quintilianus? Hunc syllogismum captiose paulo secus repetit, et plurali numero sophisma instituit. Definit paulo ante tropum dictionem translatam a proprio loco: vidit igitur antonomasiam, allegoriam, hyperbolen plerunque, periphrasim in dictioni singulari non esse. Aliter igitur loqui instituit, et ita ratiocinatur,

> In tropis ponuntur verba alia pro aliis:
> In figuris non ponuntur verba alia pro aliis: nam propriis verbis figura fieri potest:
> Figurae igitur tropi non sunt.

Propositionem inductione conficit:

> In tropis ponuntur verba alia pro aliis.

Ut in metaphora, metonymia, antonomasia. At Quintiliane, quid agis? Haec antonomasia non est dictio translata a proprio loco, ut eloquentiae Romanae parens pro Cicerone,

> —diuum pater atque hominum rex,

pro Ioue: oratio enim non est dictio. Tropus igitur non est. Tum vero Quintiliani captioso isto et posteriore syllogismo Quintilianum conuincam: assumit enim in figuris non poni verba alia pro aliis, quia omnia propria possint esse. At in illa Quintiliani antonomasiam e troporum genere secernam. Sed reliquam istam inductionem videamus, quemadmodum in tropis ponantur verba alia tonomasiam e troporum genere secernam. Sed reliquam istam indutionem videamus, quemadmodum in tropis ponantur verba alia pro aliis. Metalepsis si verbum pro verbo ponat, metonymia, ironia, metaphora, aut synecdoche est. De catachresi et allegoria satis dixim, quomodo tropi subiicerentur. Onomatopoeia pro alio ponitur (ait Quintilianus) quo usuri fueramus, si illud non fingeremus. At quibus verbis, o Quintiliane, uteremur in affectionibus animalium propriis exponendis, si ista non fingeremus? ridere, ululare, boare.

Cuiusmodi igitur ista est ratio, et quam a dialectico iudicio inops et aliena? Periphrasis utitur pluribus pro uno (ait Quintilianus) ergo tropus est. Quid est? Quomodo hic Quintiliane, iudicas? Quam longe a definitione tua discrepas? At longe aliter concludo et iudico, longe alium syllogismum conficio,

Omnis tropus est dictio a significatione mutata:
Periphrasis non est dictio a significatione mutata:
Non est igitur tropus.

Considera Quintiliane, quam illa tua fallax, quam sit ista constans et firma conclusio. Epitheton (ais) coniunctione Antonomasiae sit tropus. At nec Antonomasia, nec Epitheton tropus est. Utere tuo adversus te iudicio, utere tuo syllogismo.

Tropus est dictio mutata a significatione:
Epitheton saepe proprium est, nec mutatam habet significationem:
Epitheton igitur tropus non est.

Atque hoc syllogismo omnes falsas troporum species a Quintiliano in hac doctrina confusas tollo et abiicio. Laborat tamen Quintilianus in hoc primo noni libri capite vehementer: quaestiones sibi obiicit, quas dissoluere non potest: vult rhetorum graecorum et latinorum opiniones retinere: videt tamen definitionibus exempla non congruere: tandem Gordium hunc nodum, quem soluere non potest, quasi frangit. Figurae, inquit, et tropi nomine saepe eadem sunt, et habent valde scrupulosam disputationem, sed ea nihil pertinent ad praesens institutum: imo vero o Quintiliane, nomine et definitione et genere omnino distinguuntur tropus et figura: et si verum sequi potuisses, nunquam tam ambitiose diligens videri voluisses: non est ista scrupulosa tua disputatio. Significationes figurae et definitiones varias Quintilianus colligit. At unica vera et propria et perspicua definitio pro tot nugis satis esset. Figurarum genera duo facit: reprehendit eos qui pauciora, et qui plura genera facerent. Utinam graecanica ista vanitas tibi paulo remissius Quintiliane placuisset: Artes constare debent utilium et constantium institutionum traditionen, non omnes hominum errores et vitia colligere. Quaeris deinde qui numerus cuique subiiciatur: Duos ad verbum Ciceronis magnos locos recitas inter se etiam dissidentes. Oratorio enim tertio quadraginta tres verborum figurae a Cicerone afficiuntur: in oratore tamen tantum ab eodem septemdecim ponuntur. Figurae sententiarum illic quadraginta octo, hic quadraginta quinque. Verum quid citatus hic Cicero doctrinae nobis adfert, inconstans praesertim et a se ipso dissentiens? Excusandus credo tibi Cicero fuit, quia tu ab eo dissensurus esses. At Quintiliane, quomodo seipsum Cicero in oratore excusauit, cum a se oratorio tertio dissentiret? Quam vero non decet Quintiliane in arte describenda errorem cuiusquam et falsam opinionem defendere, ut veritatem interim deferas et prodas? Ut discipulos (quos instituendos suscipis) fallas et decipias? Reprehendis rhetoras quosdam, qui figuras affectus esse dicerent: hoc item dicit Cicero, cum figuras facit, iracundiam, execrationem, conciliationem. Cicero tamen peccasse nihil videtur: vetat enim tanti hominis, opinor, authoritas id libere profiteri. O iudicem verecundum et humanum! At mallem dialecticum, mallem constantem, mallem verum. Secundo capite sententiarum figurae tractantur a Quintiliano: figura non tamen sententiae quid sit, non definitur. Est autem in absoluta sententia totius orationis conformatio, et ideo mutatis verbis etiam manet: eius genera certa quidem nulla adhuc noui: communiones tamen quaedam ipsarum inter se figurarum notari possunt. In interrogatione enim et responsione sunt permultae (Interrogationem illam dico, qua petitur aliquid et quaeritur) in interrogatione igitur solum, qua petitur aliquid, est optatio, deprecatio, addubitatio, communicatio. In responsione permissio, concessio continetur: in utroque genere prolepsis et subiectio: in fictione prosopopoeia et apophasis: in abruptione digressio, auersio, reticentia, correctio: in amplificatione exclamatio, sustentatio, licentia. Ita species artis adumbrata quaedam in hac doctrina diceretur. At Quintilianus non definit figuram sententiae, non partitur: sed suo more, ut superiora, ita sequentia haec permiscet et confundit. Numerat in figuris interrogationem et responsionem, et affectibus distinguit: cum tamen nec interrogatio, nec responsio, nec affectus ipse figura ex sese sit, quanuis in his figurae quaedam notentur. Possunt enim haec omnia esse *aschemata*, id est recta et sine figura. Subiectionem Quintilianus vocat, cum nobis ipsis respondemus, a qua putat prolepsim genere diuersam esse: at fallitur, quia in omni prolepsi est interrogatio quaedam et interrogationis responsio, quae subiectio est. Non persequar fictos a Quintiliano prolepsis modos, quales licet innumerabiles in omnibus figuris fingere, sed sine doctrina, sine usu. Miscet hic etiam correctionem: ut, Quanquam illa non poena, sed prohibitio sceleris fuit. At correctionis alia ratio est, et a prolepsi distincta: similis est error in addubitatione, communicatione, permissione, concessione: Illae enim duae primae figurae in interrogatione, duae secundae in responsione perpetuo sunt. Addubitando enim et communicando quaerimus utique aliquid, et rogamus: in permissione et concessione quasi quaesitum aliquid sit et rogatum, ita respondendo permittimus et concedimus. Sunt item in quaerendi quodam et rogandi genere optatio et deprecatio, de quibus nullum verbum Quintilianus facit. Sustentatio sicut et exclamatio et licentia, figurae in amplificatione semper occupatae sunt. At duas postremas tollit Quintilianus e figurarum genere et numero. At quia formae sunt dicendi a communi et vulgari consuetudine remotae, figurae sane erunt. Huc aggregat sine nomine figuras augendis affectibus accomodatas. At nec affectus, nec simulatio figura est: Ironia enim tropus est, non figura. Est enim mutatio significationis a dissentaneo ad dissentaneum, vel in his exemplis quae recenset in his figuris Quintilianus. A quo repudiatus, ad sodalem tuum virum optimum M.Marcellum demigrasti. Ironia est in solo verbo (optimum) non in tota oratione. Quinetiam in aliis exemplis idem est. Ut pro Sylla, Nisi paucos fuisse arbitramini, qui conari aut sperare possent se tantum imperium posse delere. Ironia enim est in verbo (paucos) possunt autem ironiae multae coniungi: Ut in Clodium, Integritas tua te purgauit, mihi crede, pudor eripuit, vita anteacta seruauit: et tamen tropi multi sunt, ut in allegoria, non figura una. In abruptione figurae sunt, digressio, auersio, reticentia, correctio. At correctionis separatim (ut dixi) mentionem nullam Quintilianus facit. Illustrationem figuram putat, initio tamen capitis huius in Cicerone figura non putauerat, cum Ciceroniana illa lumina numeraret, quae ipse figuras non censeret. Figura vero non est, sed potest ex omnibus et argumentis et figuris fieri. Concessionem, confessionem, consensionem tres figuras Quintilianus genere distinctas arbitratur: ego genus unum, duo summum puto, et confessioni valde finitimam esse concessionem video. Contra *ethopoiian* separat a prosopopoeia Quintilianus. At separari nullo modo potest. Corrolarium vero tanti capitis (quo de figuris sententiarum dicitur) in Emphasi oratione longissima consumptum est, quae est, cum ex aliquo dicto latens aliquid eruitur. At hoc Quintiliani ratiocinationis cuiusdam et conclusionis est, figurae nihil. Neque enim est noua orationis forma, sed vis quaedam cogitationis solers et acuta. Atque hoc genus, ut ex Quintiliani verbis constat, in scholis rhetorum tum maxime ferebatur. Tandem vero ne negligens videretur Quintilianus fuisse, aut non omnes ineptias hominum in has institutiones contulisse, praeter figuras probatas, et praeter Ciceronis figuras tam memoratas colligit tres et quadraginta nouas figuras. Quamobrem?

Ne ut iudicium et prudentiam locis omnibus a Quintiliano, sic diligentiam requirere possemus. Laborauit, inuestigauit, legit, animaduertit, cumulauit denique quamplurima: at bona, utilia, vera, propria iudicare et secernere non potuit: initio libri huius tropum a figura separare non potuit: imo vero non potest hic figuram definire, non potest figuras a non figuris seiungere. Instrumento uno Quintilianus caruit ad artis institutionem, maxime tamen necessario: syllogismus, syllogismus, inquam, imo vero etiam methodus ei valde vehementerque defuit. Versatus sit in foro tot annos, in ludo iuuentutem exercuerit: at docendi artem non tenuit: aut certe in his libris non adhibuit. Veruntamen figurae verborum reliquae sunt, et magis etiam confusae, quam sententiarum figurae fuerunt: ad eas igitur accedamus. In his vero tantam confusionem non apud Quintilianum solum, sed omnes rhetoras video, ut maior nulla adhuc fuerit. Nihil est arte tractatum, non definita in uniuersum verborum figura, non generum distributio facta, multae pro figuris non figurae sunt admistae: exemplis species eadem, tanquam tamen diuersae sunt distinctae: denique, quod caput confusionis est, non modicum, figurae nominibus inter se apud artis huius authores tam confusae sunt, ut aliae aliarum nominibus plerumque sint appellatae. Sed nunc de Quintiliano, qui tertii capitis initio dicit figuras saepe mutari, quod verum esto: tum vero quale est, quod Quintilianus ait ad hanc probationem: "Veteres," ait, "et praecipue Cicero, dicebant inuidere hanc rem: non huic rei." At Quintiliane, non solum isto modo Cicero non loquitur, sed male etiam Latine ab Actio carmen illud conuersum profitetur in Tusculanis, Florem liberum quisnam inuidit meum? Atque hic locus admonere nos potest, quam negligenter in Ciceronis lectione sit hic homo versatus, qui non modo Ciceronis dictionem et phrasim imitandam sibi nullam proposuit, sed nec obseruauit quidem, aut animaduertit qualis esset. Duo genera figurarum in verbis Quintilianus deinde facit, grammaticum et rhetoricum: nec usquam meminit eius quaestionis, quam explicandam suscepit. Rhetoricas institutiones suas appellat ac debuit appellare grammadialectoricas, quia in his grammatica, dialectica, rhetorica confunduntur. Doceat enim grammaticus grammaticas, rhetor rhetoricas figuras: non misceantur in rhetoricis grammaticae: et aliquando tollatur bella ista defensio, Necessarius est usus harum figurarum oratori, propterea hic traduntur: potest enim orator etiam his uti, cum a grammaticis didicerit: sed tamen quae sunt hae grammaticorum figurae, quas hic sibi confundendas

Quintilianus existimauit? In his enim tam malum grammaticum Quintilianum fuisse conuincam, quam malum rhetorem esse adhuc docui. Metaplasmi fere vocantur a grammaticis, quando in oratione genus generi, numerus numero non respondet: partes aliae pro aliis ponuntur. In quo denuo Quintilianus indicat non modo Ciceronis, sed nullius hominis phrasim sibi propositam fuisse. "Facere contumeliam a Cicerone reprehendi notum est" (ait) "affici enim contumelia dicebant." Verum Quintiliane, Plautus et Terentius facere contumeliam ante Ciceronem dixerunt: Tu contumeliam alteri facias, tibi non dicatur, (ait ille), Hic autem, Tu nouo modo ei faceres contumelias: et quanuis usitatius esset, contumelia afficere, quam contumeliam facere: attamen etiam latine dicebatur, contumeliam facere: et in reprehendendo Antonio cupiditas paulo longius Ciceronem produxit. Ergo Quintilianus in elocutionis et phrasis genere rursum labitur. Similes deinde lapsus sunt ut vetustatis obsoletae exempla notat in Virgilio, Vel cum se pauidum contra mea iurgia iactat. Progeniem sedenim Troiano a sanguine duci. Quasi vero non similiter etiam utroque Cicero, venuste scilicet et usitate sit usus, vel quod est in eodem decreto scriptum (ait pro Flacco) Sedenim hoc non solum ingenii, sed etiam naturae atque virtutis (ait pro Archia.) Immiscet deinde Quintilianus inter figuras grammaticas de figuris sententiarum Apostrophen, quae tamen antea tradita suo loco inter figuras sententiarum fuerat. Atque totus hic de grammaticis figuris tam confusus locus Quintiliani dialecticam ualde demonstrat. Redit deinde a figuris grammaticis ad rhetoricas figuras. Primum earum genus fecit per adiectionem, et figuras enumerat repetitionis sine nominibus *epizeuxin*, *epanalepsin*, *anadiplosin*, *epanodion*, *anaphoran*, *epistrophen*, *symploken*: confundit inter eas *polyptoton*, et gradationem, quae duae commutationem habent: non adiectionem et asyndeton, quae detrectationem habent, non adiectionem: conturbat etiam multa de congerie, qua *metabolen* vocat, et de dissipatione, de synonymia verborum et sententiarum quae figurae speciem per se nullam obtinent. Secundum deinde genus sequitur, quod detractione fieri Quintilianus dicit: in quo species quinque enumerat, *elleipsin*, quae metaplasmus est in poetis magis aliquando permissus, quam unquam ulla in oratione laudatus, tantum abest ut figura sit. Asyndeton et *synezeugmenon* grammaticae magis, quam rhetoricae figurae adduntur. Tum *synoikeiosis*, et *paradiastole*, quarum illa res contrarias coniungit, haec similes discernit: quod elocutionis nihil est omnino, nec ideo figurae quicquam. Tertium genus triplex additur ex similibus, paribus, contrariis. At tota ratio contrariorum argumenti est, elocutionis nihil est, ideoque figura esse non potest. In primo similium genere, *prosonomasian* figuram facit ex eo schemate quod antea *polyptoton* appellauit: ut mulier rerum omnium imperita, in omnibus rebus infoelix. Haec enim casuum varietas polyptoton est. Paronomasiam pro correctione item hic confundit: ut quae lex priuatis hominibus lex esse non videatur. Miscet etiam *antanaklasin*, ut filius ad patrem, non expecto pater mortem tuam. Et pater contra filio, Imo rogo expectes: ubi figura nulla est, sed sarcasmum ex ambigua verbi significatione. Illic enim expectare significat desiderare, hic vero praestolari. Atque his duobus nominibus *tes prosonomasias kai paronomasias*, cum nihil significetur, nisi figura ea in qua verbum paululum immutatum atque deflexum varas significatione usurpetur: ut, non emissus. sed immissus, non orator, sed arator, quae breuiter et perspicue posset explicari, cum, inquam, nihil aliud significetur, hic tamen longissima oratio et ineptissima confunditur, ut nihil tamen noui doceatur. Quatuor deinde similium genera a Quintiliano proponuntur, *parison, homoioteleuton, homoioptoton, isokolon,*, cum primum et quartum idem sit, et utrumque fiat e paribus membris, nec quicquam differant. *homoioteleuton* etiam falso putat Quintilianus esse in his exemplis, Vicit pudorem libido, timorem audacia, rationem amentia. Postremam e figuris verborum facit *antitheton*, in eoque fallitur: argumentum enim figura non est, *antitheton* autem ex dissimilibus argumentum est: non igitur figura. Colligit Quintilianus ad extremum omnes rhetorum ineptias et nugas, ne credo parte aliqua institutionis rhetoricae diligentiam Quintiliani potius, quam prudentiam requireremus. Separat tandem Quintilianus a figuris compositionem, sed ineleganter admodum et inconsiderate. Quid enim est figura, Quintiliane? Conformatio (ait) elocutionis remota a vulgari consuetudine: At, inquam, compositio et numerus est elocutionis conformatio remota a vulgari consuetudine: est igitur figura. Hanc autem syllogismi conclusionisque regulam si didicisses, si adhibuisses describendae artis et componendae doctrinae legem, Quintiliane, ista tam inconsiderate numquam effudisses. Mirabile vero rhetoris huius ingenium est: praecepturus enim de compositione Quintilianus non definit initio, deinde non diuidit, sed longissimo exordio utitur et verbosissimo, ubi ratio doctrinae nulla est, quemadmodum antea fecit in capite de ornatu. Exordio tandem concluso sequitur compositionis doctrina, in qua tres primum diuisiones ineptissimae collocantur: prima est orationis in victam et solutam. Quid enim, Quintiliane? Recipis te de virtutibus elocutionis praecepta positurum, et hic tamen ex compositione virtutis et vitii elocutionem distribuis, ut alia composita sit, quod est laudis et virtutis: alia incomposita, quod est vituperii atque vitii. Corrigis tamen te, et ais in sermone et epistola numeros laxiores potius esse, quam nullos, ut oratio cuiuscunque generis sit, composita esse debeat: quod sane tam verum est, quam de reliquo orationis ornatu. Tropi quidem sunt et figurae in omni oratione, sed pro rerum, quae tractantur, et personarum, quae docentur, ratione ornatus augetur, aut minuitur. Secunda diuisio est in *kommata, kola, periodon,* quae diuisio compositionis non est. Potest enim oratio his omnibus partibus esse distincta, et tamen ineptissime composita. Atque tota illa consideratio grammaticae est, cum in grammatica docendum sit, quomodo puer orationem interpunctis diuidere, et quibus modis debeat distinguere. Tertia partitio omnium stultissima est, qua tribuitur compositionis ratio trifariam in ordinem, iuncturam, numerum. Primum compositio ipsa et numerus idem plane est: siquidem oratio numerosa et composita eadem est, nec ulla est composita, non numerosa, siue contra: etsi quicquam de reliquis partibus ad compositionem necessarium dicitur, idipsum commodissime in numero diceretur. Ordo vero de quo praecipitur, hic a Quintiliano falsus est: neque crescere debet perpetuo oratio, ut ait Quintilianus, sed cum minuendi gradus pares sint amplificandi gradibus, quoties extenuanda res erit, toties decrescat oportet oratio. Est et alius naturalis ordo (ait Quintilianus) ut viros et foeminas, diem et noctem, ortum et occasum dicas potius, quam retrorsum. Veruntamen si quid ordinis ista dignitas ut plerunque obseruanda est, certe de rebus ipsis, non de verborum ordine obseruanda est. At plerunque tempus quod sequimur, contra est: Fratres gemini dicendum (ait Quintilianus) non gemini fratres. At Liuius (cuius lacteum candorem tantopere hic ipse magister admiratur) primo libro ait geminos fratres, et tergeminos fratres. Tam prolixa vero de ordine partium orationis altercatio valde ridicula et inepta est, qualis est in iunctura de hiatu vocalium et asperitate consonantium: ubi valde miranda est Quintiliani negligentiane dicam an ignorantia nescio. De vitiis disserit quae de vocalibus et consonantibus in compositione possunt accidere: de virtutibus, quae sunt huic necessario exprimendae, verbum nullum facit. Ex literarum enim naturali bonitate magis, quam ex temporum in syllabis dimensione omnis singularum dictionum et grauitas, et iucunditas, et splendor, et obscuritas, et magnificentia, et subtilitas, atque omnino omnis numeri virtus oritur. Nec satis est monere, qui pedes numerum suauiter instituant, qui concludant. Multum enim interest quae sint in pedibus longae aut breves vocales: longae fuerint prima et tertia vocales, an nihil interesse inter utriusque sonos arbitramur? An nihil accessionis fieri ad vocalium sonos ex consonantium coniunctione iudicamus? Imo vero potest numerus alius alio vel gratior, vel ingratior esse, nec ista per syllabas distinctio temporum, sed vocalitas, sed *euphonia* numerum efficiet. De tertio tandem compositionis membro, quod tradit Quintilianus, quomodo rhythmum diuidit? Rhythmus (ait) par est ut dactylus, at sexcuplex, ut paean: aut duplex, ut iambus. O partitionem et ineptam, et insulsam! Primum quid utilitatis habet ista partitio, etiam si vera sit? Quae pars deinde compositionis, quae ratio doctrinae refertur ad istam parium, sexquiplicium, duplicium comparationem? nulla omnino. Deinde vero quam est ridiculum et insipidum sic partitionem informari, ut plures partes relinquas, quam complectare? At maiorum rerum cum minoribus collatio quinque differentias habet *pollaplasion*, unde duplex est ratio: *epimorion*, unde sexquiplex. *epimere, pollaplasiepimorion, pollaplasiepimere*: de quibus tribus postremis generibus nihil hic attingit Quintilianus, et primi generis unam tantum attingit, cum sit eiusdem generis amphibrachys e breui, longa, breui: habet enim rationem multiplicem triplam, et dochimus, cuius postea Quintilianus meminit e breui, duabus longis, breui, longa, si medio spatio diuidatur, rationem efficiet *epimere*. Quare tota ista partitio explodenda plane est, et ad Aristotelis (a quo videtur Ciceroni et Quintiliano reperta) sophisticas argutias referenda. Verum perge: singulares sunt deinde metri et rhythmi differentiae, quas Quintilianus instituit. "Metrum," inquit, "constat ordine, rhythmus spatio temporum: ideoque hic qualitatis est, illud quantitatis: quasi vero nullus sit ordo in prosa oratione, et non intersit plurimum longaene, an breues sequantur. Secunda differentia primae sapientia par est, in rhythmo indifferens est" (ait Quintilianus) "dactylusne ille priores habeat breues, an sequentes: in versu pro dactylo poni non poterit anapaestus aut spondaeus." Quid ergo, Quintiliane? Si nullus est in oratione ordo syllabarum longarum et breuium, nec refert an tres syllabae (quarum una longa sit, duae breues sint) faciant anapaestum, an dactylum, quid est quod postea tam multa de ordine longarum et breuium in pedum coniunctionibus commentaris? Quorsum tot obseruationes tuae, si nihil interest, praecedant breues an longae? Aliae duabus his differentiis sequuntur similes differentiae, quod metrum sit in verbis, rhythmus in corporis motu: quasi vero versus ille,

Sic fatur lachrymans, classique immittit habenas,

potius in singulis verbis, quam in uniuerso sex pedum numero concludatur. O doctorem doctrinae, quam profiteris, expertem! Verum tot ineptias omittamus, et caetera consideremus. Vitaueris in soluta oratione carmen perfectum, et initio orationis initium carminis, et in fine, finem: ex omnibus et omnium generum syllabis, sed variatis et moderatis orationem componere licebit. At Quintilianus Aristotelem et Ciceronem sequutus, vanissimas artes nobis explicauit. Pedes dissyllabi sunt quatuor, trissyllabi sunt octo. Quid tum? Ex his obseruationes numerorum quadraginta Quintilianus efficit. Verum quam ridicule atque inepte! Nam in hac obseruatione non solum eundem numerum modis pluribus inutiliter obseruauit, sed sibiipsi plerunque repugnauit. Nam si per quatuor extremas syllabas, quod Quintilianus etiam hic interdum facit, numerum distinxeris, et ultimam pro indifferenti (quod eidem etiam placuit) sumpseris, certe omnes Quintiliani obseruationes, tam variae ad octo redibunt, atque aliis aliae repugnabunt. Affirmat Quintilianus numerum ex paeane primo et spondaeo vitiosum esse in clausula, ut, Brute dubitaui. At eundem mutata obseruationis specie laudat. Accipiet (ait) ante se choreus et pyrrichium, ut, Omnes prope ciues virtute, gloria, dignitate superabat. Sex enim postremae syllabae in utroque exemplo parem numerum habent, cum sit ultima indifferens. Duo spondaei (ait Quintilianus) non fere coniungi patiuntur, quod tamen Cicero in Crasso probauit, et Quintilianus ipse in tribus aliis obseruationibus laudauit, molossus et palimbacchius optime claudunt. At ultima indifferenti tres spondaei hic coniunguntur, ut patet etiam Quintiliani exemplo, Et spinis respersum. Optime claudit (ait idem) bacchius et palimbacchius, spondaeus et choreus. At ultima indifferenti posita, spondaei item duo postremi sunt. Tanta caligo rhetoris huius menti offusa est, ut non modo nugatorie saepius idem repetat inutiliter, iteretque, sed sibiipsi contraria repugnantiaque dicat: ita sine dialectico syllogismo, sine iudicio his in rebus versatur. Longissima reliquo capite oratio consumitur, quis modus compositionis sit, quomodo eius iudicium pene naturale totum sit, quod verum est: tum de incisorum, membrorum, periodorum, historiae, exordii, narrationis, confirmationis, epilogi compositione, quod est sane perridiculum. Definitur a Quintiliano incisum, sensus non expleto numero conclusus, quasi vero incisi ratio pendeat ex numero, ut si numerus expleatur, aut non expleatur, idcirco incisum esse aut non esse necesse sit, et in incisis non possit non plenus esse numerus, nec tamen incisa esse desinant. Citat Quintilianus a Cicerone exempla, et cum eo errat, Domus tibi deerat? At habebas. Pecunia superabat? At egebas. Verum ego hic membra quatuor video, non incisa quatuor. Simili errore in membrorum et periodorum doctrina vagatur Quintilianus, nec ex eius oratione sciri potest, quid horum quicquam sit. Dicam vero, quoniam ipse non dicit, incisum, est imperfecta sententia: membrum, perfecta quidem, sed alio tamen relata sententia: periodus omnino perfecta atque absoluta, ut syllogismus omnibus ex partibus constans periodus est: propositio, assumptio, complexio membra, quae si uno verbo sententias complectantur alias, incisa sunt: ut hic,

Una Eurusque, Notusque ruunt, creberque procellis Africus,

Incisa tria sunt: periodus itaque aliquando breuior erit, ut

Nihil sapienti praeter culpam in vita praestandum est.

Atque in his orationis formis, sicut in compositionis partibus tam multa quae fabulatur Quintilianus, nullam doctrinae rhetoricae micam habent, sed inanem pompam et sophisticam ostentationem nescio quam: ut imperiti discipuli magistrum talem admirentur, ab eo doctrinam nullam consequantur. Quambobrem videmus in capitis huius tam prolixa confusione quam multa Quintilianus peccauerit: exordium libri instar sine arte, definitio huius artificii nulla, partitiones ridiculae et vitiosae: numeri poetici et oratorii ineptae differentiae, numerorum obseruationes confusissimae et inertissimae sine certa argumenti ullius scientia, sine ulla syllogismi prudentia merae fere ac perpetuae nugae. Decimus liber descriptae artis exercitationem quandam demonstrat. Primo autem capite longissimo illo quidem, eloquentiae habitum, id est *hexin* parari legendo, scribendo, dicendo praecipit Quintilianus. De legendo itaque totum primum caput est, de scribendo quatuor proxima, de dicendo reliqua duo. Atque primo illo capite disputat Quintilianus, tametsi orator veras causas agendo eloquentiae candidatum excitare multum potest, scriptae tamen orationis lectionem certioris esse iudicii et maioris fructus. Quemadmodum Cicero cum reuersus Athenis, decem annos perpetuos (ut ex scriptis eius obseruaui) quotidie in foro, in curia, in rostris oratores audiuit, legit etiam interim scriptas oratorum varias orationes. Quintilianus igitur existimat lectionem eiusmodi, quam auditionem utiliorem esse. At vehementer hic ab eo dissentio, et exercendae artis huius cum rationem ignorare contendo. Rhetoricae enim sicut et dialecticae et cuiusuis exercendae artis ratio duplex omnino est, *analysis* et *genesis*. Primum enim est ut artis usum in propositis exemplis cernamus, deinde similia his effingamus. Ut igitur praecepta artis melius cognoscuntur audiendo diligenti et erudito doctore, quam eius legendo libro, sic usus praeceptorum primum melius audiendo, quam legendo exercetur. Recens est et infirma artis cognitio, quaefacilius multo alio ducente, et viam indicante sequitur, quam per se progreditur: multa et troporum et figurarum et omnis elocutionis exempla rudis et nouitius discipulus dicente Cicerone perspiciam subito et admirabor, quae in scriptis eius orationibus vix multa obseruatione tandem deprehenderem. Neque tamen in veris causis duntaxat oratores ad hanc exercitationem audiri iubeo, sed magistros orantes in schola suis exemplis hic praeire volo, ut non solum discipulis bene dicendi artem ex pictis praeceptis ostendant, sed multo magis usum viuis exemplis aperiant: quod idem fere paulo post in imitatione Quintilianus docet. Da mihi rhetorem non solum docendi, sed etiam dicendi peritum. Da Ciceronem qui Caelio, qui Dolabellae, qui Hircio, qui Pansae, qui Crasso, qui multis aliis fuit, an non rudem eloquentiae discipulum melius audientem docebit, quam eius orationes docerent? Haec igitur scholastica auditio prima sit, deinde omnibus locis oratores omnes audiantur. At in lectione firmius iudicium est (ait Quintilianus) credo scilicet discipuli iudicium esse solum, quam si iudicio praeceptoris confirmatum fuerit. Pudet dissentire (ait Quintilianus) quasi vero discipulus iste noster in eloquentiae studiis exercendus ad oratorem audiendum iudex rhetoricae ignarus non peritus obseruator accesserit, et Colotes Teius cum Thimantis tabulam spectaret (qua pictor hic viderat cum immolanda Iphigenia, tristis Chalcas esse, maestior Ulysses, moereret Menelaus, obuoluendum caput Agamemnonis esse, quoniam summum illum luctum penicillo non posset imitari) tum, inquam, in hac tam miserabili et lamentabili pictura Colotes lachrymis oculos complerit, non in omnes artificii rationes animum potius intenderit. Alia docti contemplatoris et sapientis obseruatoris persona est, alia improuidi, nec artem animaduertentis auditoris. Quamobrem primum fuerit eloquentiae discipulus, auditor et disertorum magistrorum et eloquentium oratorum: deinde lector et ut in audiendo, sic in legendo obseruabit omnes artis suae laudes in tropis et figuris. Hoc Quintilianus non monet. In commemorandis autem rhetoribus quos eloquentiae discipulo legendos putat, relabitur ad errorem primi et secundi libri, poetas primum, deinde historicos, oratores tandem proponit, atque ita nobis analysin describit. Deinceps accedit ad genesin, secundam exercitationis partem, ut imitando vel per nos ipsos aliquid conando scribamus et dicamus. Secundo igitur capite laudat Quintilianus imitationem, nec tamen satis esse putat: sed conandum aliquid supra eos, quos imitamur: in quo libenter assentior, nisi quod non imitabilem inuentionem existimat, in hoc enim grauiter erat. Ex omnibus enim dialecticae et rhetoricae partibus nullam facilius est imitari, quam inuentionem, quia nullum est argumenti genus non notatum et descriptum: nullius forma est argumenti, cuius simile nullum possit in alia causa reperiri. Duo (ait) imitationi esse proposita, quos imitemur, quid imitemur: hoc etiam concedo. Multa miscet hic de decoro inepte: de hoc enim nihil adhuc praecipit, nec in rhetoricis elocutionis vel actionis praeceptis quicquam est tradendum. Hoc enim si cuiusquam artis est, dialecticae prudentiae est magno usu rerum confirmatae, non rhetoricae. Plures imitandos, non unum Quintilianus existimat, id etiam libenter accipio, ut potius multorum virtutes, quam vel unius etiam vitia consectemur, modo tamen in optimis quibusque confirmatus prius fueris. Tertio capite praecipit Quintilianus quamdiligentissime, et quamplurimum scribendum esse, ut bene potius quam cito scribatur, tandem vero celeritas usu et consuetudine comparetur. Quod ex parte quidem, non totum verum est. Volo enim, ut Cicero, ut Quintilianus etiam libri secundi capite quarto vult, "se efferat in adolescente foecunditas, ut sit quod amputari possit. Non enim potest in eo succus esse diuturnus, quod nimis celeriter maturitatem est assecutum." Quanquam reprehendit Quintilianus ipse deinde in scribendo nimiam et diligentiam et negligentiam. Reliquum caput de loco, de caeris, ubi scribatur, sicuti caput proximum de emendatione nihil admodum praecepto ullo dignum habet. Quinto capite tractatur fere idem argumentum, quod scriptio conuertendis in sermonem Latinum Graecis commode adhibeatur. Quae sane exercitatio rudi et nouitio eloquentiae Latinae discipulo non conuenit, qui verborum copiam nondum pararit, ut ea Graecam eloquentiam latine reddat. Probat etiam Quintilianus eandem ex latinis conuersionem, praesertim de carminibus, quia res una dici pluribus modis possit. In quo etsi merito a Cicerone dissentit Quintilianus (Cicero enim hanc exercitationem in secundo oratore argumento leuissimo tollit) attamen haec exercitatio non nisi confirmato iam et corroborato stylo prodesse poterit, et in eodem vitio cum superiore fuerit. Reliqua de thesi et declamationibus similia sunt, qualia sunt toto capite septimo, quod extemporalis dicendi facultas paretur arte, exercitatione, nihil habent noui praecepti, sed inanem loquacitatem propriam Quintiliani. Quamobrem de exercitatione libro decimo ita praecipitur, ut de artis ipsius partibus est praeceptum, nihil perspicue definitum, nihil acute partitum, nihil ad verum usum congruenter expositum est, nullum denique dialecticum vel consilium vel iudicium est adhibitum.

Undecimo libro de decoro, memoria, pronuntiatione praecipitur, et in singulis rebus capita singula consumuntur. Primo itaque capite longissimus sermo de apte dicendo consumitur, sed hoc totum decori tam prolixum praeceptum valde in rhetoricis praeceptis est indecorum. Videre enim quid deceat omnino omnibus in rebus, si qua possit ars proprie explicare, dialectica certe fuerit, quae leges omnium rerum communes, et maxime generales ostendit in argumento, syllogismo, methodo, quid conueniat in omni re atque causa, quid vere deceat, quid non deceat. Attamen quanuis id generatim in dialectica praecipitur, id etiam priuatim et singulatim ex aliis artibus singulis intelligitur. Decorum in sermonis puritate et elegantia ex grammatica, in elocutione et actione ex rhetorica, in numerorum supputatione et magnitudinum diuisione in concentibus et sonis, in astrorum motibus ex arithmetica, geometria, musica, astrologia: in stirpibus et plantis atque animalibus ex physica: in virtutibus et moribus ex ethica philosophia: in aedificiis, in agris ex architectura et agricultura: in omnibus et dictis et factis, in omnibus rerum quotidianarum et nulla arte comprehensarum consiliis ex humana earum rerum prudentia: denique in omnibus rebus quod decorum sit, cognitio ipsa atque scientia et usus declarabit. Nec tamen separatum de decoro et distinctum ullum praeceptum erit, quia decorum ipsum conueniens ea perfectio est, quam artes suis praeceptis, quam ipsa humanitatis ratio et sapientia demonstrat. In rebus vero nulla arte singulari comprehensis, communes ingenii et naturae dotes, quas dialectica interpretatur, excitandae et adhibendae erunt: usus item mores, exempla admonebunt. Quare quod tam late pateat, ridiculum sane est rhetoricae veluti proprium subiicere.

Secundo capite Quintilianus accumulat Graecorum omnes ineptias de locis et imaginibus ad memoriam conformandum: quas ipsas merito deridet, et suas nugas Carneadem, Metrodorum, Simonidem, earum inuentores habere iubet, simpliciora et meliora putat esse diuisionem et compositionem cum labore et exercitatione coniuncta: quod sane maxime in Quintiliano laudo et probo: ac si diuisionis artem et ordinis proponeret, multo magis etiam laudarem et probarem: tum enim memoriae artem nobis explicaret. Ars memoriae (ait) tota posita est in diuisione et compositione. Quaeramus igitur quae sit ars ordinis, quae sit ars, quae res diuidat et componat, tum memoriae artem inueniemus. Est autem in dialecticis syllogismi et methodi praeceptis tota haec ordinis doctrina diligenter in nostris institutionibus exposita. Vera igitur illic memoriae ars et dialecticae propria omnino est. Itaque Quintilianus in isto capite res alienas quidem, et plerunque etiam ridiculas tradit, sed tamen vero propiores, quam adhuc permultas tradidit. Cuiusmodi caput de pronuntiatione multis quidem praeceptis utilibus refertum, sed totidem nugis oneratum, ut ineptiae facile necessarias institutiones superent. Vana siquidem curiositas et in tam multis et vocis et gestus sectionibus, cum tota illa tot versuum millibus accumulata doctrina paucis verbis perspicue tradi posset. Duodecimi libri prima illa initio a nobis disputata sunt, quod orator sit vir bonus, quod philosophus iureconsultus, historicus: proxima autem quae primum sint agendae causae, et quid in his suscipiendis, et discendis, et agendis sit obseruandum, itemque postquam a foro discesseris, quibus rerum otium sit obiectandum, non unius artis rhetoricae decreta, sed eius aduocati (quem nunc vulgo dicimus) studia quaedam demonstrant. Et longissimum caput de generibus dicendi, rhetoricae elocutionis proprium nil habet, nec enim distinctio grauitatis, humilitatis, mediocritatis in oratione sumitur ex verbis tantum, sed ex rebus ipsis, ut haec partitio sit communis inuentionis cum elocutione. Quamobrem si lubet quinque postremorum librorum subductis rebus considerare, quae descriptio doctrinae fuerit, ut non liceat idem dicere, quod de superioribus inuentionis libri ante dictum est, et artem et artis usum penitus a Quintiliano conturbari: certe vere confirmari poterit multis et inanibus praeceptis artem rhetoricam in elocutione et actione onerari, et longe maiorem inanis ostentationis et pompae speciem iactari, quam verae et solidae doctrinae rationem demonstrari.

# INDEX TO INTRODUCTION

LANDMARKS IN RHETORIC AND PUBLIC ADDRESS

Also in this series

*Chironomia; or, A Treatise on Rhetorical Delivery.* By Gilbert Austin. Edited by Mary Margaret Robb and Lester Thonssen

*Lectures on Rhetoric and Belles Lettres.* By Hugh Blair. Edited with an introduction by Linda Ferreira-Buckley and S. Michael Halloran

*Chirologia: or the Natural Language of the Hand, and Chironomia: or the Art of Manual Rhetoric.* By John Bulwer

*The Philosophy of Rhetoric.* By George Campbell. Edited and with a new introduction by Lloyd F. Bitzer

*Lectures Read to the Seniors in Harvard College.* By Edward T. Channing. Edited by Dorothy I. Anderson and Waldo W. Braden

*Cicero on Oratory and Orators.* Translated and edited by J. S. Watson

*Selected Essays on Rhetoric.* By Thomas De Quincey. Edited by Frederick Burwick

*The Rhetoric of Blair, Campbell, and Whately.* By James L. Golden and Edward P. J. Corbett

*Essays from Select British Eloquence.* By Chauncey Allen Goodrich. Edited by A. Craig Baird

*The Rhetorics of Thomas Hobbes and Bernard Lamy.* Edited with an introduction and critical apparatus by John T. Harwood

*Lectures Concerning Oratory.* By John Lawson. Edited and with an introduction by E. Neal Claussen and Karl R. Wallace

*The Colonial Idiom.* Edited by David Potter and Gordon L. Thomas

*A Course of Lectures on Oratory and Criticism.* By Joseph Priestly. Edited by Vincent Bevilacqua and Richard Murphy

*Quintilian on the Teaching of Speaking and Writing: Translations from Books One, Two, and Ten of the Institutio Oratoria.* Edited by James J. Murphy

*Lectures on Rhetoric and Belles Lettres.* By Adam Smith. Edited and with an introduction and notes by John M. Lothian

*Elements of Rhetoric.* By Richard Whateley

*Puritan Rhetoric: The Issue of Emotion in Religion.* By Eugene E. White

*The Selected Writings of John Witherspoon.* Edited by Thomas Miller